Melancthon Williams Jacobus

Notes, Critical and Explanatory, on the Book of Exodus

From Egypt to Sinai

Melancthon Williams Jacobus

Notes, Critical and Explanatory, on the Book of Exodus
From Egypt to Sinai

ISBN/EAN: 9783337240158

Printed in Europe, USA, Canada, Australia, Japan

Cover: Foto ©Andreas Hilbeck / pixelio.de

More available books at **www.hansebooks.com**

CRITICAL AND EXPLANATORY,

ON THE BOOK OF

EXODUS.

FROM EGYPT TO SINAI.

BY

MELANCTHON W. JACOBUS,

PROFESSOR OF BIBLICAL LITERATURE AND EXEGESIS IN THE THEOLOGICAL SEMINARY AT ALLEGHENY, PA.

NEW YORK:
ROBERT CARTER & BROTHERS,
530 BROADWAY.

1874.

Entered according to Act of Congress, in the year 1873, by
MELANCTHON W. JACOBUS,
in the Office of the Librarian of Congress at Washington.

INTRODUCTION.

THE BOOK OF EXODUS.

AFTER the Genesis comes the Exodus. After the Book of the Creation comes the Book of the Redemption. Glancing back at the heads of history, we have the Creation and the Fall of man followed by the Deluge, in which there was the saved remnant, and this succeeded by the Dispersion and Population of the Globe, with the national differences at length limited by the Divine plan to bring forward a chosen nation for God Himself.

Abraham, called from among the Chaldees, enters Canaan as a strange land, and is led by the Divine Providence to Egypt, where his household, at first honored, becomes enslaved, but grows under the special favor of God into a nation, and is miraculously redeemed from the bondage, as His own chosen people.

The kingdom of God on earth is thus brought into strong contrast with the kingdom of Satan, and the issue is fairly joined. The powers of darkness are always found rallying against the powers of light. God interposes, and achieves the victory for His Church over His foes and theirs.

In all this, the principles of the Divine administration for all the ages are plainly set forth. And this signal Deliverance becomes a pledge for all the future, a historico-prophetical transaction, referred to by the prophets, and the Psalmists, as the impressive type of the greater Deliverance to come in the last time by Jesus Christ.

The Church, in bondage to the world-kingdom of successive ages, is to be led forth in the future as it has been led forth in the past, and by a series of splendid interpositions of Divine power and grace, opening the sea for her, overwhelming her enemies, leading her through the wilderness by the Angel of His Presence, giving her water out of the Rock, spreading her table with manna, and with meat, and vanquishing the foe. Step by step, the Jordan is finally to be crossed, and the Land of Promise is to be entered.

The christian reader finds also his own religious history shadowed forth by the same wonderful narrative, involving the same great principles of the Divine administration. So that " these things, which were written aforetime, were written for our learning, that we through patience, and comfort of the Scriptures might have hope." This, therefore, is history pregnant with religious truth. Some will read these wondrous chapters of the Pentateuch as a parable, because they are so redolent of instruction for all time. But it is history, gleaming all over with pictorial teaching for all men, and for all the ages.

This Book sets forth God's Redemptive dealing on the lower plane of temporal events, according to the Divine plan of working out in the lower department His illustrations of the higher, and thus, as with Jesus in His miracles, through the avenues of the bodily transaction reaching to the affairs of the soul.

But for the very reason that this Book of Redemption stands so at the gateway of inspired History in reference to the Salvation of men, it has been most persistently assaulted as most absurdly incorrect in detail, and unhistorical. This is done mainly by begging the whole question. It is first assumed by such that a miracle is impossible, and then the record is pronounced upon in the light of a mere natural development and is denied. But the supernatural is not impossible if once it be admitted that there is a God. For God is supernatural. And then at once it is plain that the supernatural act is only natural to a supernatural Being. On the other hand, to work out reconciliations of science with Scripture, by finding the miracle to be only some exaggeration of the natural working, or the natural forces only extraordinarily operated, in a way to tone down the miracle and to bring it within the scope of the natural law, is most absurd, because if once the possibility of miracle be admitted, we may safely follow the narrative, and not be treating the miracle as "*too hard* for the Lord." Nay, if the probability of miracle in God's dealings with men be admitted, as we must admit as surely as there is a God, then we have only to receive these glimpses of the Infinite as God's own methods of revealing Himself and the higher world to men. It would seem as if precisely to confront such scepticism as that of our day, which finds no God in the world, and puts the laws of nature so called, in the place of God, that these Egyptian miracles were wrought in such close connection with natural law, God here will show Himself to the unbelievers to be the God of nature—working in the domain of nature so as to manifestly control the forces of nature and to sway them at His bidding—ordering the natural phenomena in a way to show a supernatural personal power behind the phenomena, and directing the laws of nature so as to show the lawgiver in them all. This close and convincing relation of the miracle to the natural phenomenon, has encouraged those who strive to find in the operation only an exaggerated account of the common physical order of things. But if this could be accepted as only a poetic account of common events, how then can we account for the history as to momentous results brought about by these events? It was the effect of these miracles upon Pharaoh which led to the Deliverance of the Israelites from his oppressive bondage. And it would be idle to say that after all, there was nothing in these mighty operations in nature, beyond the working of natural law. Even *De Wette* has admitted the impossibility of thus explaining away these miracles as they are related in the narrative. The only alternative must be to deny the history, because it is the history of miracle. Though faith must be founded on testimony, yet here would be an arbitrary limitation of testimony and of history, so as to dictate and choose the things to be believed however amply attested. Jehovah was here showing Himself to be the Personal power in Egypt and in all its affairs, and thus He was propounding His supreme claims as against their idol deities. It was the *Personal* will displayed throughout—forewarning and executing accordingly—bidding the natural forces to come and go at His pleasure—and discriminating in the results between the Israelites and the Egyptians—this proved the Personal God. The magicians were put to shame. "They *did so with their enchantments*"—They wrought some resemblances to the miracles, "they *did so*"—*thus*—after the same fashion—*imitating* as to the appearance—"*with their enchantments*"—by their jugglery and tricks of magic—and only so far as to embolden those who would not believe in God, but would believe in imposture. Pharaoh is a representative unbeliever—lured on by shams and deceits of magicians and their experiments, until overwhelmed by the great miracle of the Judgment Day. As *Professor Henry* has well said, *The more Law, the more Law-giver.* The more proof we find of Law, the more proof we have of a Law-giver. And these magicians of Moses' time are referred to by name as types of their successors in every age, and in our day, " ever learning and never able to come to the knowledge of the truth. Now as Jannes and Jambres withstood Moses, so do these also resist the truth. Men of corrupt minds, reprobate concerning the faith. But they shall proceed no further, for their folly shall be manifest unto all men *as theirs also was.*"—2 Tim. 3: 8.

To what shameless puerility are men of learning left who maintain that the most we can legitimately gather from these records is " the *not ourselves which makes for righteousness* "—and that this abstraction is the explanation of the name *Jehovah.* And *Strauss* at length declares that " the *choice only lies between the Miracle—the Divine Artificer—and Darwin.*" It has been well said, that in proof of the possibility of miracle, the christian man may put forward the miracle of his own regeneration. This is a convincing proof to himself and may become so to others also. This is in the domain of *"the greater works,"* than these of the physical phenomena. If "the Christian is the world's Bible and the only Bible that it reads," let not that be unhistorical, as the written revelation is not. But the denial of miracles has led Strauss and his school to the denial of Immortality and of a PERSONAL GOD. The standing miracle of the ages and most essentially *historical*, is the Jewish nation itself. A chaplain of Frederic William I. of Prussia was ordered to give the briefest possible proof of the truth of Christianity, and he replied—"*The Jews,* your Majesty."

TITLE.

The name of the book, "Exodus," means *Departure—going out—* and refers to the leading fact recorded—the Departure of the children of Israel out of Egypt. It forms an important chapter in the National Annals of the Hebrew people which are also Ecclesiastical records in the history of God's ancient Church.

AUTHOR.

The arguments for the Mosaic authorship of Genesis are valid for this Book also—(*See Notes on Genesis—Introduction*). The New Testament is explicit to this effect. Our Lord calls it "the Book of Moses," Mark 12: 26. "Now that the dead are raised, even Moses showed at the bush," Luke 20: 37, etc.

HISTORICAL CREDIBILITY.

The history itself is amply attested by the use of it in the National songs—reciting the leading particulars. As in Psalm 66. "Come and see the works of Jehovah. He is terrible in His doing toward the children of men. He turned the sea into dry land. They went through the flood on foot. There did we rejoice in Him." So in Ps. 68, most expressly in sublime passages referring to the Exodus. Also in Ps. 74. "Thou didst divide the Sea by thy strength," etc. In Ps. 77. "Thou leddest thy people like a flock by the hand of Moses and Aaron." And then the leading events are recited in detail in Ps. 78. And how could this Psalm have been composed, or how could it have been sung by generations of the people as a National song if there had been no such history? Ps. 81 mentions the proving at Meribah. So Ps. 86, Ps. 89: 10, Ps. 103. "He made known His ways unto Moses," etc. The history is sung in course, in Psalms 105 and 106.

The Prophets also refer to the history of the Exodus in a way to show that this stupendous Deliverance was at the basis of Israel's religious history, and the pledge of the more glorious deliverance that was yet to come. "Art thou not it (He) that hath cut Rahab (Egypt) and wounded the Dragon? Art thou not it that hath dried the sea, the waters of the great deep, that hath made the depths of the sea a way for the ransomed to pass over?" (Isa. 51: 10.) "Where is He that brought them up out of the Sea with the Shepherd of His flock? that led them by the right hand of Moses with His glorious arm, dividing the water before them to make Himself an everlasting name, that *led them through* the deep as a horse through the wilderness that they should not stumble?" (Isa. 63 : 13 ; Isa. 43 : 9.) So in Jeremiah "Neither said they where is the Lord that brought us up out of the land of Egypt," etc. (Jer. 2 : 6 ; 16 : 14 ; 23 : 7.) See Introduction to "*Notes on Genesis*," pp. xi., etc.

MOSES.

As surely as the Jewish people exists, so surely does its peculiar history point back to Moses at the Exodus. Great as were the Pharaohs, Moses was greater than they. And the occupation of Judea by this people came to pass only in consequence of their deliverance from the bondage of Pharaoh and the destruction of the haughty and godless oppressor. All history must be denied, and its foundations subverted, if we attempt to demolish these records upon which the Jewish history stands. How then did Moses, impotent as he was by himself, and unaided by any world-power, accomplish this wonderful deliverance in the face of the world's proudest and most powerful kingdom? Without battle or blood, and without human intervention, what was the secret of his success, if we do not find it here written in the wonder-working power of God? It would be far more difficult to believe in the Exodus itself, apart from the Divine interposition, than it would be to credit that interposition as here narrated. The history is natural in the midst of the supernatural. All occurring in strict conformity with the known peculiarities of the respective people, and with the usages and physical features of Egypt itself, so as to furnish the ample internal evidence of veracity on the part of the narrator, who must also have been an eye-witness of the events. And at this day it would be as idle to deny the existence of the Jewish people, in their strong peculiarities of race and usage, as to deny these early chapters in their national annals, on which their history is founded, or to deny the facts of Moses' Leadership as their Champion under God before Pharaoh. "*Moses in whom ye trust*," said the Saviour to the Jews of His day (John 5 : 45). "Not all that came out of Egypt by Moses," said Paul to the Hebrews (Heb. 3 : 16). "All were baptized to Moses in the cloud and in the sea" (1 Cor. 10 : 2). "Jannes and Jambres withstood Moses" (2 Tim. 3 : 8). And the history, including all that is supernatural about it, must be received as surely as we believe that there is to-day this Jewish people upon earth who sing of this Exodus as a leading chapter in their national annals. There is no accounting for their history, nor even for their existence, if these events of the Exodus be denied. It is only a strange infatuated zeal to get rid of the idea of a Personal God that brands the record as unhistorical, when the history is as much the history of the supernatural as it is of the natural, and you cannot dissever the two without destroying the history.

THE PASSOVER.

And how can this religious festival of the Jewish Church be accounted for, celebrated by a whole nation during three thousand years, unless these records of the Exodus be true? It has not more real connection with the harvest "first fruits," than it has with these "first fruits" of Israel's Redemption. Can we suppose that the sacred and devout worship of the Jewish Church, and of the Christian Church as grafted upon it, could have proceeded during three thousand years upon a sheer fiction, or on a mere mythology? That grand Redemptive act in history, as typical and foreshadowy of the Redemption by Christ Jesus, was planned by the Divine mind, and the fact was given to be celebrated as revealing God's purposes of grace for His Church and people in all the ages. Just as the Messianic idea is the golden thread upon which all the events of history are strung. As well could we think of a "*Fourth of July*" being celebrated by our own nation during nearly one hundred years, and yet disbelieve and deny any such event as the Declaration of our National Independence.

THE DECALOGUE.

The Mosaic code of Ten Commandments has impressed itself upon the history of the civilized world. And whence could it have originated if not as recorded in this Book of Exodus? As the acknowledged standard of morality, and as the true basis of moral legislation, whence was it derived if not from God, and where was it given if not at Sinai? Is it not grossly absurd to account for it only "as the product of a necessity in human society, gradually taught by experience, and finding in this fact the reason of its unalterable obligation?" Will *Strauss*, as the prince of disbelievers, accept the Sabbath law as thus originated, and will his followers so agree to admit its unalterable obligation? But that law refers to the fact of Creation, and bases itself upon the resting of God from His works at the end of the creative week. And then if this Moral Code grew only gradually out of the public necessity, who tabulated it in its present form of ten commands? Why ten and no more? But is it not more easy to credit the record for any intelligible origin of such a code, and for its necessary sanction of Divine authority? True indeed, it had its roots in the public necessity, and has proved itself in utmost accord with it through all the ages. But it originated not with that people in the wilderness, recent from the degradation of Egyptian bondage. It had its origin in God, who in connection with the Redemptive act, there grouped the fundamental principles of morality into a Code for all nations and for all ages, and of universal application. But wherever the Decalogue is read, there is read the Preface to the Commandments in those significant words which assert the historical verity of the Exodus records—" I am Jehovah thy God, which have brought thee out of the land of Egypt, out of the house of bondage." The Law of Ten Commands stands thus distinctly prefaced by the history of this Deliverance from Egypt; and you can as well deny the Decalogue and its Divine obligation as deny the Exodus itself as here recorded.

CHRONOLOGY.

The Chronology cannot be positively determined, but may be regarded as an open question.

The Period of the Patriarchs from the Covenant to the Exodus is computed at 430 years (*A. M.* 2086–2516), though some high authorities reckon 400 years as belonging to the sojourn in Egypt. Gen. 15 : 13, Exod. 12 : 40, and Acts 7 : 6, with Galat. 3 : 17, are the passages which need to be compared. In Galatians the period from the Promise to the Exodus is stated as being 430 years. And the other passages do not necessarily conflict with this. For Palestine is noted in several passages as being to them a strange land, and so answering to the description in Gen. 15 : 13. And their sojourn there is to be reckoned with the dwelling in Egypt as part of the entire time. So the *Sept.* and the *Samar Pent* add the words " And in the land of Canaan," to define the sojourn. So counted, the half of the whole period would fall to each locality. We may be tempted to concede the entire time for Egypt because of a seeming relief in working out the large increase of the people during their abode there. But *see Notes* Ch. 12 . 40, where the passage reads " Now the sojourning of the children of Israel, who dwelt in Egypt, was four hundred and thirty years." The entire *sojourning* (not in Egypt, but) *of the people who dwelt in Egypt*, is given in the same terms as we find in Galatians, more explicitly set for the period from the promise to the law—" The law, which was four hundred and thirty years after " the promise. This exactly defines the time, and puts it within most express limits, and must therefore be followed. See also *Ellicott* on Galat. 3 : 17, Notes.

ANALYSIS.

The History divides itself into five special topics.
I. Moses' commission to Israel in Egypt.—(Six chapters) chs. 1–6.
II. The ten plagues and the Passover—(Six chapters) chs. 7–12.
III. The Exodus and onward to Sinai—(Six chapters) chs. 13–18.
IV. The Law given—(Six chapters) chs. 19–24.
V. The Tabernacle—(Sixteen chapters) chs. 25–40.

SYNOPSIS OF THE HISTORY.

BOOK I.

ISRAEL IN PREPARATION FOR GOD'S SALVATION.

Chaps. I to XI.

§ 1.	Israel in Egypt.—Jacob's Family.	Ch. 1: 1–6.
§ 2.	*House of Bondage.*	Ch. 1: 7–14.
§ 3.	The male children doomed to death.	Ch. 1: 15–22.
§ 4.	*The Birth of Moses.*	Ch. 2: 1–10.
§ 5.	Moses' Patriotism and his flight.	Ch. 2: 11–25.
§ 6.	*Call of Moses.*	Ch. 3: 1–10.
§ 7.	Moses' objections and God's answer.	Ch. 3: 11–22.
§ 8.	*Doubts removed.*	Ch. 4: 1–9.
§ 9.	Moses' further objection, etc.	Ch. 4: 10–31.
§ 10.	Moses and Aaron before Pharaoh.	Ch. 5: 1–23.
§ 11.	*Jehovah's promise.*	Ch. 6: 1–8.
§ 12.	Moses' discouragement, God's order.	Ch. 6: 9–30.
§ 13.	Miracles according their mission.	Ch. 7: 1–13.
§ 14.	*The First Plague* (Blood).	Ch. 7: 14–25.
§ 15.	The Second Plague (Frogs).	Ch. 8: 1–15.
§ 16.	The Third Plague (Lice).	Ch. 8: 16–19.
§ 17.	The Fourth Plague (Flies).	Ch. 8: 20–32.
§ 18.	The Fifth Plague (Rinderpest).	Ch. 9: 1–7.
§ 19.	The Sixth Plague (Boils, etc).	Ch. 9: 8–12.

SYNOPSIS OF THE HISTORY.   xix

§ 20.	The Seventh Plague (Hail).	Ch. 9: 13-35.
§ 21.	The Eighth Plague (Locusts).	Ch. 10: 1-20.
§ 22.	The Ninth Plague (Darkness).	Ch. 10: 21-29.
§ 23.	The Tenth Plague (threatened death of the 1st born)	Ch. 11: 1-10.

BOOK II.

THE COVENANT CONSECRATION AND SEAL.—EXODUS TO SINAI.

Chaps. XII to XVIII.

§ 24.	Institution of the Passover.	Ch. 12: 1-14.
	And of Feast of Unleavened Bread.	Ch. 12: 15-20.
§ 25.	*Jehovah's Passover.*	Ch. 12: 21-28.
§ 26.	The Tenth Plague executed.	Ch. 12: 29-36.
§ 27.	*The Exodus (begun).*	Ch. 12: 37-42.
§ 28.	Ordinances of the Passover.	Ch. 12: 43-51.
§ 29.	Sanctification of First Born, etc.	Ch. 13: 1-16.
§ 30.	*The Exodus (continued).*	Ch. 13: 17-22.
§ 31.	God's marching orders and the pursuit.	Ch. 14: 1-18.
§ 32.	*The Red Sea crossed.*	Ch. 14: 19-31.
§ 33.	*Review.* Triumphal song.	Ch. 15: 1-21.
§ 34.	*The Bitter Waters sweetened.*	Ch. 15: 22-27.
§ 35.	*The Bread from Heaven.*	Ch. 16: 1-35.
§ 36.	Murmuring for lack of water. Horeb.	Ch. 17: 1-7.
§ 37.	*Defeat of Amalek.*	Ch. 17: 8-16.
§ 38.	Jethro's visit to Moses.	Ch. 18: 1-27.

BOOK III.

SINAI.—THE LAW GIVEN.

§ 39.	The Moral Law introduced.	Ch. 19.
§ 40.	*The Ten Commandments.*	Ch. 20: 1-17.
§ 41.	The Civil Law.	Chs. 21-23.

BOOK IV.

GOD'S PUBLIC WORSHIP PROVIDED FOR.—THE TABERNACLE.

Chaps. XXIV to XL.

§ 42.	Divine directions for the building and arrangement of Jehovah's Dwelling-place.	Chs. 24-31.

§ 43. *The Golden Calf.* . . . . . . Ch. 32.
§ 44. *The People forgiven.* . . . . Ch. 33: 1–20. Ch. 34.
§ 45. The Preparation of the Tabernacle and furniture. Chs. 35–39.
§ 46. *The Tabernacle set up.* . . . . Ch. 40: 1–38.

There are many and strong reasons for supposing that the Book of Job was written during Moses' sojourn in the wilderness with Jethro and was brought with him to Egypt for the instruction and consolation of the people in their bondage, and to work in them a spirit of patience and confidence under the Divine dealing. It would sufficiently set forth the justice of God in men's afflictions, and the impossibility of self-justification while it would impress upon them the need of a mediator with God, and would exhibit in very striking passages the great leading truths of Salvation by a Redeemer, Job 19: 25–27; 33: 23–28. This was possibly the first and only written revelation as yet existing. But now there was to be given a new and more complete revelation for the training of the covenant people in the fundamental ideas of sin and of expiation. There was now to be announced a law and a system of ordinances, as the basis of religious living: and herein also the church was to receive a well defined and Divinely appointed polity for its own visible establishment and for the conservation of the truth, in preparation for the Advent of the Messiah. At the same time the Covenant Angel—the *Jehovah* revealed to Moses in Midian as the glorious Personage in the Burning Bush presiding over the interests of His suffering church and securing her Deliverance was to appear as the living Head and guide of His people through the wilderness.

The *Passover* was given to be the top and crown of the ordinances, the first idea being that of RELEASE. And so Pilate, at the trial of the Messiah, found the custom grown up, along with the Paschal celebration, to *release a prisoner* at the feast (John 18: 30). So that all through the Scripture, the Messianic idea is the fine gold-thread that glistens in the whole fabric of revelation, and is at length wrought into the glowing portrait of Jesus Christ—" That it might be fulfilled which was spoken by the Prophet, *Out of Egypt have I called* MY SON."

A SUMMARY VIEW OF THE TRANSACTIONS ATTESTED BY EGYPTIAN MONUMENTS, AND OF THEIR CONNECTION WITH HEBREW HISTORY.

DYNASTIES.	TRANSACTIONS KNOWN FROM CONTEMPORARY MONUMENTS.	CONNECTION WITH SCRIPTURAL HISTORY.	
		According to Speakers Com. and others.	According to Brugsch and others, as here adopted.
XIIth Dynasty: seven Pharaohs. from Amenemha I. to Amenemha IV., and a queen regnant.	A period of great prosperity; foreigners, especially from Western Asia, received and promoted under the early kings; and under the later kings works of extraordinary magnitude executed to secure the irrigation of Egypt, and to guard against the recurrence of famine.	Abraham received and favored. Joseph saves Egypt from famine; the Pharaoh master of the resources of Egypt.	
XIIIth to XVIIth Dynasty:	The early Pharaohs still masters of Egypt. Invasion of the Hyksos. Salatis master of Avaris, i. e., Tanis, or Zoan. Egypt divided; the worship of Set, Sutech, or Baal, established by the Hyksos in the north; wars between the Theban dynasty and Apepi, or Apophis, the last king of the Hyksos.	The Israelites in Goshen rapidly increasing and occupying the whole district, but in a condition of dependence, or partial servitude.	Abraham in Egypt under the Hyksos. Joseph minister of Apophis.
XVIIIth Dynasty: Aahmes I. (Amosis).	Aahmes I., or Amosis, captures Avaris and expels the Hyksos. Buildings of great extent undertaken or completed with the aid of forced laborers or mercenaries. The worship of the Theban deities re-established.	Beginning of a systematic persecution of the Israelites, who are employed as forced laborers in restoring or building forts and magazines in their own district.	The Israelites are supposed to remain during the whole period of the 18th dynasty in undisturbed possession of the district of Goshen.
Nefertari.	The Egyptian Queen, a Nubian by birth, possessed of great influence, both before and after the death of Aahmes.	Moses saved and adopted by an Egyptian princess.	
Amenotep I., or Amenophis.	Expeditions into Ethiopia: the Queen-sister in power; succeeding as Regent.	Flight of Moses into Midian.	

xxii SUMMARY VIEW OF TRANSACTIONS

Dynasties.	Transactions known from Contemporary Monuments.	Connection with Scriptural History.	
		According to Speakers Com. and others.	According to Brugsch and others, as here adopted.
Thotmes I.	Expeditions into Nubia and Mesopotamia; immense increase of the Egyptian power.		
Thotmes II. and Hatasou.	First part of the reign prosperous; no indication of foreign or intestine war; latter part of the reign a blank, followed by a general revolt of the confederates in Syria. Hatasou, queen regnant, and retaining power for seventeen or twenty-two years.	Return of Moses; the Exodus; destruction of Pharaoh and his army.	
Thotmes III.	First attempt to recover the ascendancy in Syria in the 22d year. Wars: repeated incursions into Palestine, Phœnicia, Syria, and Mesopotamia, terminating in the fortieth year of this reign.	The Israelites in the wilderness; entrance into Palestine of Joshua in the fortieth year after the Exodus.	
Amenotep (Amenophis) II.	Expedition into Syria by sea; overthrow of the confederated nations to the north of Palestine.	Progress of the Israelites in Palestine.	
Thotmes IV.	A reign without notable occurrences.		
Amenotep III.	A prosperous reign; supremacy maintained in Syria and Mesopotamia; no intimations of warfare in Palestine; the Queen Tei, of foreign origin, favors a new and purer form of religion.		
Amenotep IV. or Khu-en-Aten. Princes not considered legitimate.	The religious revolution completed: followed by a period of disturbance and exhaustion.	Cushan Rishathaim in Palestine.	
Horemheb.	End of eighteenth dynasty.		
XIXth Dynasty: Rameses I.	No considerable events; notices of war with the Cheta, who from this time are dominant in Syria.	The interval between Cushan Rishathaim, and Jabin, extends to the later reigns in this dynasty. Palestine remains, to a great extent, in the possession of the Amorites and other people of Canaan; sometimes overrun by neighboring people, and towards the close of the period subject to the Philistines in the south, and the Cheta, or Hittites, in the north.	

ATTESTED BY EGYPTIAN MONUMENTS. xxiii

Dynasties.	Transactions known from Contemporary Monuments.	Connection with Scriptural History.	
		According to Speakers Com. and others.	According to Brugsch and others, as here adopted.
Seti I.	The Shasous or Nomads from Egypt to Syria, and the Cheta and nations of Mesopotamia, broken and subdued by a series of invasions. The empire reaches its highest point of civilization and power.		
Rameses II.	During many years Rameses II. is co-regent with his father with royal dignity. On his accession as sole monarch, he invades Syria, defeats the Cheta, with whose king, however, he afterwards contracts an alliance on equal terms, marrying his daughter. Captives are employed in great numbers in building, restoring, or enlarging fortresses, cities, and temples; among them Aperu at Pa-Rameses and Memphis. The reign lasts sixty-seven years, but the date of its commencement, whether from his father's death, or his admission to royalty, is uncertain.		First beginning of the persecution of the Israelites; the birth, early life, and exile of Moses.
Merneptah.	Beginning of reign signalized by victory over Libyan and Mediterranean invaders: no expeditions into Asia: general state of amity with the Cheta: eastern frontier of Egypt carefully guarded: indications of unbroken peace and prosperity in the district about Pa-Rameses.		The plagues of Egypt, followed by the Exodus.
Seti II., Siptah; is close of the XIXth Dynasty.	A period not distinguished by foreign wars: letters, however, flourish, and the nation appears to be peaceful and contented.	Palestine in a state of depression, Philistines in the south, Jabin in the north; revolt against Jabin, overthrow of Sisera; war against Jabin continued for some years.	The Israelites in the wilderness.
XXth Dynasty: Rameses III.	A long series of successful wars in Africa and Asia: Palestine traversed, Syria invaded, and the Cheta overthrown. The reign lasts at least twenty-seven years. Aperu employed on the royal domains.	Israelites recover possession of Palestine after the overthrow of Jabin.	The conquest of Palestine begun under Joshua.

Dynasties.	Transactions known from Contemporary Monuments.	Connection with Scriptural History.	
		According to Speakers Com. and others.	According to Brugsch and others, as here adopted.
Rameses IV.	A peaceful reign, occupied chiefly in great buildings. Aperu, captives of war, employed in the quarries.	The events recorded in the book of Judges after the time of Deborah and Barak.	The entire series of events from the passage over the Jordan to the close of the book of Judges.
Rameses V. to XI.	A period of uncertain duration, the reigns generally short and undistinguished.		
Rameses XII.	In this reign the Egyptians retain an acknowledged pre-eminence in Syria and Mesopotamia.		
Rameses XIII.	Close of the twentieth dynasty.		

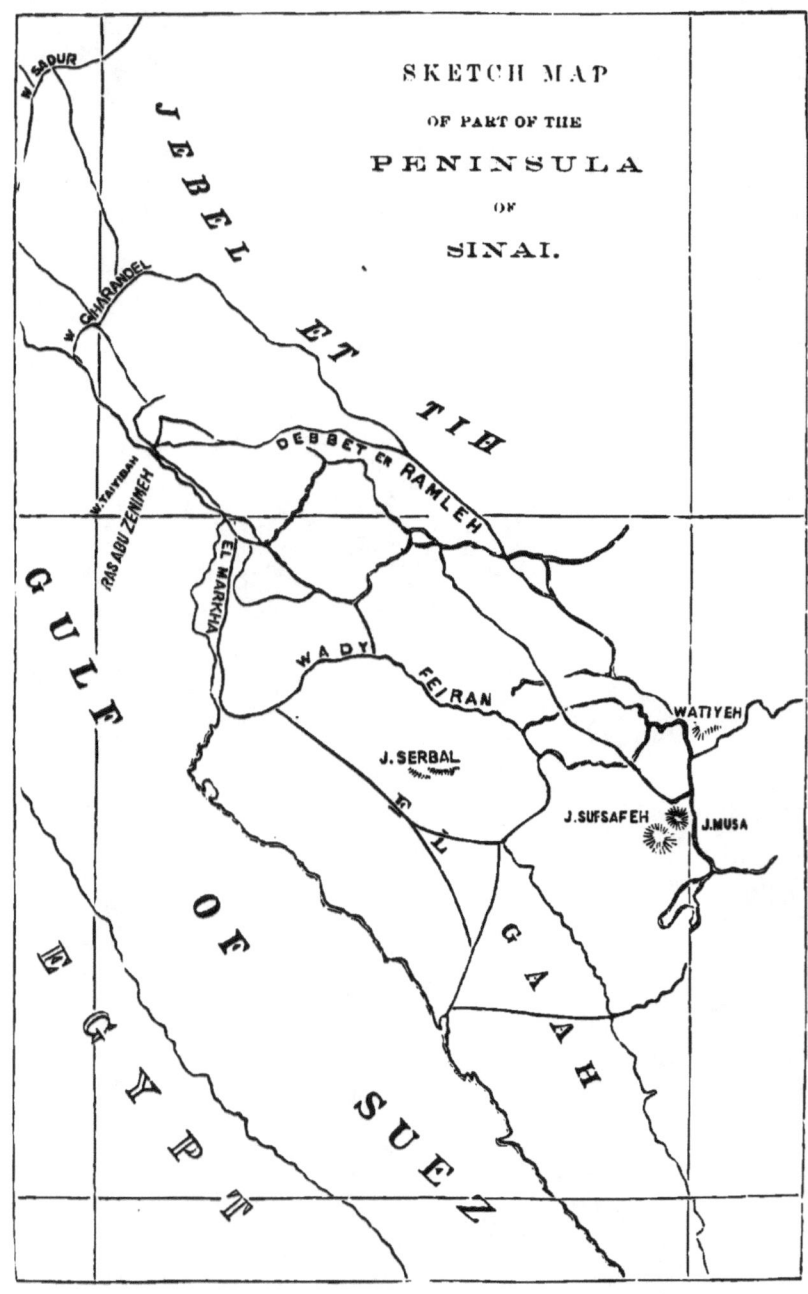

THE BOOK OF EXODUS.

CHAPTER I.

NOW these *are* the names of the children of Israel, which came into ᵃEgypt; every man and his household came with Jacob.

---
a Ge. 46: 8.

BOOK I.

ISRAEL IN PREPARATION FOR GOD'S SALVATION. Chs. I–XI.

CHAPTER I.

§ 1. ISRAEL IN EGYPT. JACOB'S FAMILY. Ch. 1: 1–6.

The family of Jacob are now to become the people of Israel. They were led by God to a Gentile land to have their development into a nation, under the oppressions of a heathen power. For already the covenant God of Israel makes it apparent that He does not confine His manifestations to the Holy Land. (Acts, ch 7.) From a family the children of Jacob (Israel) are (1) to be enlarged into national dimensions under the signal Providence of God. They are (2) to attain their independence by the agency of Moses. They are (3) to receive a Divine Law and Constitution, by a solemn act of consecration as a holy people—and (4) they are to be introduced to their own land, where they shall be placed in training as the covenant people of God. And thus God's promises to Abraham are here to be traced to their signal fulfilments. (Gen. 15: 5, 13, 15, 16, and 46: 3, 4).

1–5. *Now these are the names.* Literally—*And these*—showing the connection of the narrative. The sacred historian begins, here, the narrative of Israel in Egypt. He reverts to the entrance of Jacob and his family into the land, in order to relate the Exodus of the people from the bondage of Pharaoh. It will be shown how the *family* developed into a *nation*, by the wonderful Providence of God,—and how they were prepared, by such amazing increase and enlargement to go forth, in God's time, as an independent people. The fact is to be noted that it was the entire family of Jacob, but small at utmost, which came down into Egypt first or last, for this is the covenant fact. They are therefore called—*the children of Israel*—the names are given for exactness—*Israel* being the new

EXODUS.

2 Reuben, Simeon, Levi, and Judah,
3 Issachar, Zebulun, and Benjamin,
4 Dan, and Naphtali, Gad, and Asher.
5 And all these souls that came out of the loins of Jacob were seventy ᵇ souls: for Joseph was in Egypt *already*.
6 And Joseph died,ᶜ and all his brethren, and all that generation.

---

b De. 10; 22.   c Gen. 50: 26.

---

name and the covenant name, reminding of God's promise, which is here traced to its fulfilment. (1) As to the increase (Gen. 15: 5,) and (2) as to the oppression (Gen. 15: 13,) and (3) as to the Deliverance (Gen. 15: 14). *Which came into Egypt.* (See on Gen. 46: 27.) The catalogue here is different. Eleven sons of Jacob are named, and Joseph is added with explanations. These were the recognized heads of houses at the time—and it is said—*Every man and his household came with Jacob*—that is, these sons with their families—their wives and children. The entire family is now reckoned, *who came out of the loins of Jacob,* (66) as *seventy souls.* This would exclude the sons' wives. But as *Joseph was in Egypt already,* it is proper to include him and his two sons, and besides these Jacob himself is counted, for the object is to make up the entire family, in order to show the increase. This reckoning yields the number *seventy.* There was an intended significance in this. (See Deut. 32: 8.) It had a reference to the nations of mankind, whose number was seventy as given in the ethnological table. (Gen. ch. 10.) So there were seventy elders of Israel. (Exod. 24: 1, etc.) Seventy members of the Sanhedrim,—and seventy disciples sent out to the missionary work—all along looking to a special relation of Israel to the nations of the earth. So says the Jewish book *Zohar,* (see Lightfoot, Luke 3: 36,) "Seventy souls went down with Jacob into Egypt that they might restore the seventy families dispersed by the confusion of tongues." Stephen (Acts 7: 14) cites from the Septuagint the number *seventy-five,* which was made by including more of Joseph's descendants. But as speaking to those who used the Septuagint, he quoted from their Bible, the different enumerations. "*Jacob* was included because the natural head (says Murphy) is essential to the unity and integrity of the family." (See on Gen. 46: 27, *my notes.*) But the figures in Acts 7, may be explained by noticing that there were probably two sons' wives dead—Judah's (Gen. 38: 12) and Simeon's (Gen. 46: 10; Comp. Gen. 28: 1) leaving only *nine.* Adding these nine to sixty-six, there would be *seventy-five.* And these were reckoned by Stephen in "*all his* (Jacob's) *kindred,*" as being Joseph's kindred—by blood, probably of Keturah, Ishmael and Esau. (See *Hale's Chronol.*) Besides Jacob's own family, it is probable that many migrated with him who were not of his loins. A few are referred to by Joseph where he distinguishes his brethren from *his father's house,* or *servants.* (Gen. 46: 31; Comp. Gen. 30: 43; 32: 5, 7, 16; see Gen. 12: 16).

6. *Joseph died.* It was after the death of Joseph and his house—himself the secular strength of the family in Egypt, the source of their early prosperity there—that God so wonderfully increased them. *All that generation*—the entire migrating company had passed away. Some refer the term *generation* here, to the ordinary sense of thirty-three years, or a third of a century,

7 And the children of Israel were fruitful, and increased abundantly, ᵈ and multiplied, and waxed exceeding mighty; and the land was filled with them.

8 Now there arose up a new king over Egypt, which knew ᵉ not Joseph.

---

d Ge. 46: 3.   e Ec. 2: 19.

—average life—others to a *century*. Joseph lived 110 years. He died about 70 years after the migration, and he lived to see the fourth generation. (Gen. 50 : 23. See notes.)

§ 2. HOUSE OF BONDAGE. Ch. 1 : 7–14.

7. The great fact is here recorded of the large increase of the covenant people—*the children of Israel*—and there is a heaping up of terms to express it—*were fruitful* —brought forth young, as animals, or fruit, as plants, *and increased abundantly*, swarmed like fish *and multiplied*, became numerous *and waxed exceeding mighty*, from a verb based on a noun meaning *a bone* qualified by the duplicated adverb *exceedingly*, with the preposition *in*, or *with*, to denote the manner—in *exceedingly exceeding* measure. *And the land was filled with them*. Goshen, in particular where they were located, though they were also scattered in Lower Egypt, through the Delta, as we afterwards see. The land was favorable to their large and rapid increase, and the circumstances also at first were highly favorable, kept mainly distinct and living on the fat of the land. (Gen. 47 : 11.) Besides all this, the Divine promise had a signal fulfilment to this effect. No miracle needs to be supposed. Egypt was a land extraordinarily fruitful in people and cattle. *Aristotle, Hist. Animal* and *Rosenmuller Morgenland* 1. p. 252.)

8. *Now there arose up*. To show that the growth of the people is not to be explained by continued favor of the government, nor by continued power of Joseph, but that it came to pass in spite of opposition and oppression, it is here stated that *another king* came into power, a new king, of new policy—probably of a new dynasty. See 1 Kings 3 : 12. 2 Kings 23 : 23. *Who knew not Joseph*—who had no regard for Joseph, and ignored his claims. This is the scriptural sense of the term. Joseph had been 40 years dead, and it had been 100 years since he was prime minister, and no wonder that a new king should forget or disregard his services long past. Acts 7 : 18. The Egyptian chronology leaves us in some uncertainty as to the dynasty which now reigned. If the Shepherd kings were they in whose time Joseph and Jacob had come to Egypt, and they were now expelled and supplanted by the ancient Theban kings, then we can see how Jacob's descendants, as a shepherd race, would be held in suspicion. But the chronology is much disputed, as is all the Egyptian chronology. *Bunsen* makes the king under whom Joseph was ignored to have been Thothmes, of the 18th dynasty. *Lepsius* contends, and so do most Egyptologists, for Rameses II., (Sesostris) 19th dynasty. A recent authority says : "The calm judgment of history confirms the stigma placed upon him by the Bible (Exodus) as the oppressor of the Hebrews." *Lenormant and Chevalier* p. 257. Others think that this change of dynasty was earlier and an invasion of the shepherd rule under which Joseph flourished, and that it was an Assyrian conqueror, now come to power. (Smith's Dict. *Pharaoh*.) There were probably different kings at this time at differ-

ent capitals of what is now known as Egypt; especially at Thebes and Memphis; and the shepherd kings may have been located at Bubastis or On, near Memphis and near to Goshen. According to *Osburn* it would seem that the era of Osortasen I., (12th dynasty) was next after the era of the Pyramids. He is called "the sun of the world (making) offerings." His successors held their court at Abydos, in Upper Egypt, while another race of monarchs had their seat at Memphis, in Lower Egypt. The names of two of these have been discovered in tombs in the burial place of Ancient Memphis. The tombs indicate a high advance of art. The Pharaoh to whom Joseph was prime minister was according to Manetho named Aphophis. The next era was that of Amosis called "Avenging Lord of Upper and Lower Egypt." And between his accession and that of Osortasen, a period of 150 years or thereabouts, six kings reigned. This Amosis expelled the shepherd kings and gained the throne of all Egypt. It was the golden age of Egyptian history. This was after the death of Joseph and his generation. Goshen, as it lay between Egypt and Canaan, was open to alliances of the neighboring nations from among whom the Israelites had come. The prosperity of this immigrant people excited the jealousy of the native kings even after they had subjected them. Hence this policy of bondage to reduce them and crush them out. This Amosis or one of his immediate successors was the new king who knew not Joseph, which would make the epoch that of the 18th dynasty, or nearly so. *Osburn*, p. 9. So Speaker's Commentary.—*Osburn* says: There were 16 kings in the 18th dynasty who reigned for about 348 years And under the last of these the Exodus took place, and Egypt never recovered from the blow which this event inflicted on her prosperity. *Osburn*, p. 10. See also the histories of Manetho preserved by Josephus. See Essay in Speak. Commentary, vol. i, p. 443. But it is doubtful whether there were foreign kings reigning in Egypt during the Israelitish sojourn, and Manetho's accounts are very legendary. This Egyptian historian Manetho has referred to the Exodus, but in a distorted narrative. The Hebrews are represented as leprous and impious Egyptians, who were under the headship of a priest of Heliopolis, named Osarsiph (Joseph), or Moses, and who rebelled on account of oppression and occupied a city called Avaris (Hebrew), and by the aid of the people of Jerusalem, they subdued Egypt and held it for 13 years, but were at last defeated by the Egyptian king and driven to the borders of Syria. Moses is here miscalled a priest of Heliopolis, and then confounded with Joseph, marrying a daughter of Potipherah, priest of On. "Avaris" is a disguise of the term "Hebrew." Osarsiph is a corruption of Joseph, and in this way of indistinct reference, we have as much as we might expect from the Egyptian historian in recording such a shameful chapter of their history. This city Avaris which was assigned by the king to these leprous persons is said by Manetho to have been abandoned by the shepherds. It was after these offcasts had been sent to the mines for a long time. They took an oath to obey their leader, Moses, in all things, and not to worship the gods. The narrative confirms the leading facts. (See Appendix A, p. 168). *Osburn* seems to understand this of the Era of Decline, and a second invasion of the shepherds, whereby the infant son of the Exodus Pharaoh was driven into Ethiopia.

9. The crafty policy of the new king is here detailed. It was his aim to crush them out by oppression, or at least to control them. The people of Israel are represented

CHAPTER I. 29

9 And he said unto his people, Behold, the people of the children of Israel *are* more and mightier than we:

10 Come on, let us deal wisely ᶠ with them; lest they multiply, and it come to pass, that, when there falleth out any war, they join also unto our enemies, and fight against us, and *so* get them up *out* of the land.

11 Therefore they did set over them task-masters, to afflict them ᵍ with their burdens. And they built for Pharaoh treasure-cities, Pithom and ʰ Raamses.

---

f Ps. 83: 3, 4.   g ch. 37.   h Ge. 47: 11.

---

as *more and mightier* than the Egyptians, though they had been only a little more than a century in the land. If this king was Rameses II., (Sesostris) of the 19th dynasty, it is held that the kingdom of Lower Egypt had become greatly reduced by the internal disorders of immigrating tribes from Canaan, Moabites and Israelites, and that this king sought to reduce the whole land under one rule, and having succeeded at length, he sought to crush the prosperous Israelites by forced labors on the public works. Their domain was the narrow Delta of the Nile, and they were *more and mightier* not than the whole people of Egypt, but than the people of this king at this time, or than the native population in that district, or more in proportion to the space occupied, or it is an exaggerated statement of this king as a pretext for the oppression.

10. *Let us deal wisely.* Heb. *Deal adroitly with him*—the people Israel. The word means to deal with deep device of worldly wisdom, political craft, diplomacy. It is plain that the monarch was in circumstances to dread an *outbreak of war* from one or other quarter. He was probably subject to annoyance from surrounding enemies, and from such as made him fear especially, that this people of Israel would form alliance with them, and thus would make common cause against the monarch, and would then quit the land for Canaan. The term "go up" here used, is the term for *going up* to Canaan. Gen. 13: 1. He seems thus to have known of the land whence they came. He was fearful that they would achieve their independence.

11. The policy adopted to meet such case was to *set over them task-masters—(lit) masters of burdens*—bailiffs over the serfs—(Delitzsch) chiefs of tributes, Sp. Com. (Gr.) *masters of works*, or labors—*overseers-in-chief*. These were common in Eastern lands—overseers, armed with a whip or stick, to bastinado the lazy workmen who were driven in gangs of tens and hundreds. Thus the Hebrews were made to be serfs, and degraded to the lowest, most menial condition, so as to break their spirit by the bondage, and check their increase and thrift. Captives were employed on the public works of Egypt, and on some of the monuments are inscriptions that no free citizen had been employed upon the building. To *afflict them*, lit., to *bend them down—wear out their strength—by hard feudal labor*, according to the policy of oppressors. ¶ *And they built.* And so (Israel) built—was compelled to build—*for Pharaoh, treasure cities*—storage cities, *supply cities*, for storing up the harvests for the demands of trade and for time of war. The Gr. has *fortified cities*, and it is probable that they were such. The context implies that it would be in the immediate vicinity

12 But the more they afflicted them, the more they multiplied and grew. And they were grieved because of the children of Israel.

13 And the Egyptians made the children of Israel to serve with rigour:

14 And they made their lives ⁱ bitter with hard bondage, in mortar, and in brick, ᵏ and in all manner of service in the field: all their service, wherein they made them serve, *was* with rigour. ˡ

---

i ch. 2: 23.   k Na. 3: 14.   l Lev. 25: 43; Is. 58: 6; Je. 50: 33.

---

of Goshen, where they abode, and the fact that Goshen lay along the eastern frontier, where warlike operations were constantly required by the aggressions of the Canaanites strengthens the conclusion. *Osburn*. ¶ *Pithom*. This is held by Wilkinson to be *Thoum*, on the E. bank of the Nile, about 12 Roman miles from Heliopolis. *Osburn* finds the Hieroglyph of *Damietta* to be the same with Pithom, and thinks the locality favors the supposition. But it is probably too far to the north. *Raamses* answers to an inscription found on such a city, a compound word of Hebrew meaning, "*the stronghold, the fortified city of Raamses*." (*Migdol-raamses*.) It may be that they were compelled to name it in Hebrew as a memorial of their degradation. *Migdol* is referred to in ch. 14 : 2, "between Migdol and the Sea"—the Red Sea, or Gulf of Suez. *Osburn* thinks it probable that this *Migdol* is the same with *Raamses*, and then *Pithom* (if *Damietta*) would be at the northern extremity of the eastern frontier of Egypt, and Raamses at the southern extremity. They were built for the supply and defence of Egypt against the invasions of the Canaanites. Hengstenberg thinks that Raamses was not near Heliopolis, but that it is on the site of Aboo-Keisheid, which is on the Canal about 13 French leagues from the Red Sea. (Egypt and Moses). And this is the more probable opinion, and that Pithom is the same as the Patumos of Herodotus near Bubastis on the Canal connecting the Nile with the Red Sea. The scholars who accompanied the French Expedition placed Pithom on the site of the present village of Abasseh, at the entrance of the Wady Sumilat, where there was at all times a strong military post. "Raamses then lay N. W. of the Bitter Lakes, and Pithom a few miles farther west, both in the land of Goshen, or of Raamses." So Speakers' Com. says, "Both cities were on the Canal which had been dug or enlarged long before under Osortasen of the 12th dynasty. *Pithom* means 'House, or Temple of Thum (or Tum) the Sun-God of Heliopolis." p. 251.

12. *But*—The signal failure of this scheme is here noted. Lit.—*As they afflicted them, so they multiplied*. In very proportion to the oppression was their multiplication. This seemed only to advance those whom they sought to check and control. This was vexatious to the Egyptian authorities. *And they were grieved*—*dismayed*—alarmed, because of the children of Israel. There was something in all this, which gave evidence of a higher power working in their behalf.

13, 14. Instead of ceasing their oppressions, they were goaded on by a relentless passion to press these measures to the full. And they made the children of Israel to serve with *rigor*—lit.—*with crushing severity*—*And they embittered their lives with hard servitude.* Their very chagrin at ill-success made them more severe. And this was only the means by which the people were to be driven to revolt. ¶ *In mortar, in brick,* etc. The remains of brick structures in Egypt have silenced the cavil against this record; and they who have alleged that brick-making was not practised in Egypt have been met by the ample proof of this history. In 1851, I visited the Pyramids at Sakhara, which are of brick. And specimens of pottery (of mortar—potter's clay) I saw and handled—especially the earthen jars in which the *Ibis*—the sacred bird of the Egyptians—is sealed up and deposited in the tombs. Piles of these by the thousand unbroken — and heaps of the broken jars lie at the entrance of these tombs — show, at least, how extensively this earthen ware was manufactured, as is here indicated. In a painting found in the tomb of Roschere at Thebes, foreigners are represented engaged at this servile work in mortar and brick; some busy upon the clay and some upon the finished brick. *Roselini* says of the figures: " Some laborers are employed in transporting the clay, and some in intermingling it with straw—others in taking the bricks out of the form and placing them in rows. Still others with a piece of wood upon their backs, and ropes on each side, carrying away the bricks already burned or dried." Native overseers (taskmasters) are standing beside them with sticks uplifted in hand. Professor Onger, of Vienna, has examined the bricks of the pyramid at *Dashour,* and he has found chopped straw in the texture of the bricks. *Herodotus* also mentions such a mode of brick-making with straw. *Wilkinson* says: " Brick-making was followed by only the meanest in the community, who had not even the satisfaction of working for themselves, for it was a government monopoly, and the pay for a tale of them was a small remuneration for this laborious drudgery in mud. They had the recommendation of cheapness, and also of durability, in that dry climate; and those made 3,000 years ago, whether with or without straw, are even now as firm and fit for use as in the reigns of the Amunophs and Thotmes, whose names they bear. When made of the Nile mud, or of alluvial deposit, they required straw to prevent their cracking. Slaves and captives were set at this work. The Jews were employed in erecting granaries, treasure cities, and many public monuments for the Egyptian monarch. To meet with Hebrews in the sculptures cannot reasonably be expected (he says), since the remains of that part of Egypt where they lived have not been preserved. But it is curious to observe other foreign captives occupied in like manner, and overseen by similar taskmasters, and performing the same labors, as the Israelites described in the Bible; and no one can look at the paintings of Thebes, representing brickmakers, without feelings of the highest interest." Vol. II., Chap. viii., pp. 195-6-7. " There is no intimation that the Israelites were employed in building pyramids, which were erected by kings of Lower Egypt, with few exceptions, long before this period." *Sp. Com.* Their features mark them as Hebrews. Such historians as *Heeren* admit the striking confirmation of this history here found, " proving the great antiquity of the Mosaic writings, and especially of this Book of Exodus."

14. *Service in the field.*—This was especially in irrigation — digging canals in all directions, and drawing and carrying the water, besides planting, ploughing, etc. We have seen this work extensively going on there. *Hengstenberg* remarks: "There is scarcely a country in which the cultivation of the land requires so much peculiarly *servile* labor as in Egypt. Irrigation especially is there very laborious."—*Egypt, etc., p.* 86.

15 And the king of Egypt spake to the Hebrew midwives; of which the name of the one *was* Shiphrah, and the name of the other Puah;

16 And he said, When ye do the office of a midwife to the Hebrew women, and see *them* upon the stools, if it *be* a son, then ye shall kill him: but if it *be* a daughter, then she shall live.

17 But the midwives feared ᵐ God, and did not as the king of Egypt commanded them, but saved the men-children alive.

18 And the king of Egypt called for the midwives, and said unto them, Why have ye done this thing, and have saved the men-children alive?

19 And the midwives said unto ⁿ Pharaoh, Because the Hebrew women *are* not as the Egyptian women; for they *are* lively, and are delivered ere the midwives come in unto them.

---

m Ne. 5: 15.   n Jos. 2: 4.

With rigor.—Every service was exacted *with rigor, forcibly*, and with severity.

LESSONS.—The kingdom of darkness arrays itself against the kingdom of light. We see the early and violent opposition of the world to the Church. The wicked have often oppressed the good. The increase and prosperity of God's people often stir up relentless persecution. The presence of the good is an offence to the profligate wicked. God is on the side of His people. Powers of the world and gates of hell cannot prevail against the Church.

§ 3. THE MALE CHILDREN DOOMED TO DEATH. Ch. 1 : 15–22.

15. The monarch, failing in his policy of oppression to check the growth of the people, resorts to another and still more infamous plan —to command the nurses to destroy the male children at their birth, sparing only the female babes alive. *The midwives* were those who assisted, as a sort of female physicians, at the birth of a child. The plan was to have them take their opportunity in the time of delivery to kill the child, as could easily be done by suffocation or strangling. *Upon the stools.* (Lit.) *Upon the pair of stones.* This was, perhaps, an arrangement of some stone table (two leaved) for receiving the new-born child—or perhaps of a stone seat or a trough for washing the child. *When ye see them* (the babes, not the mothers), etc., in such condition, at the very delivery, as to allow of this act of violence without arresting attention. It was the *males* whom the king dreaded as allies of the enemy. The word *midwives* in Hebrew means those *bringing forth,* or giving delivery.

17. The obstacle in the way of this infamous plan was, that the midwives, being Hebrews, *feared God—(Elohim,* the Creator, and the true God of the Hebrews)—and such reverential fear led them to disobey the king's command. "So did not I, because of the fear of God." (Neh. 5: 15.) So sound a principle is worthy of universal adoption. No matter who commands us to do evil, we must obey God rather than men. (Acts 5: 29.) A true piety will so affect our conduct as to make us shun iniquity at whatever cost.

18, 19. The king found that his command was not executed, and he sent for the midwives to ascertain

20 Therefore God dealt well ⁰ with the midwives: and the people multiplied, and waxed very mighty.

21 And it came to pass, because the midwives feared God, that he ᵖ made them houses.

22 And Pharaoh charged all his people, saying, Every son that is born ye shall cast into the river, and every daughter ye shall save alive.

---

o Pr. 11: 18; Ec. 8: 12; Is. 3: 10; He. 6: 10.   p 1Sa. 2: 35; 2Sa. 7: 11; 1Ki. 2: 24; Ps. 127 :1.

---

the reason. They replied that the Hebrew women were unlike the Egyptians, and gave birth so readily as not to require the service of the midwives. It is very probable that this was more especially the case at this time, in the providence of God, for this very baffling of the monarch's plan. We cannot think the reply a mere pretext, or that it would have been justifiable to so deceive. Besides the women would delay to send for the midwives, or decline to do it altogether, so soon as they knew of Pharaoh's order, so that the birth would take place before their arrival. ¶ *Lively—full of life*—strong, vigorous. This is characteristic of the Orientals.

20. God did good to the midwives—prospered and rewarded them for their fidelity against the king's command, and the result was the great increase of the people and their growing power.

21. The fidelity and piety of the midwives led to the signal building up of the people, and of themselves specially—though the pronoun here is in the masculine—*he made them houses*. It is, therefore, to the honor of the midwives, and their firm and pious principle, that the building up of the Hebrew households went forward. This is the specific form, so important for the history, in which God signalized His favor—as the God of the households of His people. 2 Sam. 7 : 11.

22. The king, even more incensed at being thus baffled, made a still more desperate resort. He commanded all his people to cast into the river (Nile) every Hebrew son that was new-born. This command may have been specially given to certain officers, but it was also published in that district. They were already so strong and numerous as to make the king anxious thus to check and curb them, so as to prevent their rebellion and removal, or their alliance with his enemies. He valued them as slaves, but he feared lest they might become masters. And so the king issued his cruel edict, which, to the Old Testament Church in its infancy, was like that of Herod against the New Testament Church in its beginning, for the slaughter of the Bethlehem babes.

LESSONS. — No device formed against the people of God shall permanently prosper. (*b*.) "Wrath is cruel and anger is outrageous, (*a torrent*) but who is able to stand before envy?" (*Prov.* 27 : 4.) (*c.*) A pious woman may defeat a powerful king by faith and faithfulness. (*d.*) God will bless those who fear and serve Him; will protect the weak in dangers, and will prosper the nation by their means. (*e.*) "Evil men and seducers shall wax worse and worse." (*f.*) Affliction becomes, under God, a means of growth and strength. (*g.*) Trust in our covenant God is rewarded with deliverance. "None of them that trust in Him shall be desolate."

CHAP. II.

§ 4. BIRTH OF MOSES. Ch. 2: 1–10.

While God was developing the strength of the people by affliction,

CHAPTER II.

AND there went a man ^a of the house of Levi, and took *to wife* a daughter of Levi.

2 And the woman conceived and bare a son; and when she saw him that he *was a* goodly *child*, she hid him ^b three months.

3 And when she could not longer hide him, she took for him an ark of bulrushes, and daubed it with slime and with pitch, and put the child therein; and she laid *it* in the flags by the river's brink.

---

a ch. 6: 20.   b Ac. 7: 20; He. 11: 23.

He was, at the same time, preparing out of the affliction, to bring forth a Deliverer. While Pharaoh was seeking to cripple and check them, God was working to baffle Pharaoh, and to free them from his oppression, and this in the most unexpected manner. God also makes the wicked court of Pharaoh to aid indirectly in the preparation of Moses for the work of deliverance. *Bunsen* says, that "History herself was born on that night when Moses led forth his countrymen from the land of Goshen." *Strabo* gives a faithful outline of the Mission of Moses, in very brief terms, xvi: 760. So *Hecateus* and *Diodorus Siculus.*

1–4. The parentage of Moses is here given to show his purely Hebraic origin—of a Levitical family. Aaron and Miriam had already been born before Moses. Aaron was about 3 years old at Moses' birth, and as we do not read of his encountering any peril, we infer that the bloody edict was issued very shortly before Moses' birth. *Murphy* solves the chronological difficulty thus: Levi was 44 years old when he came down to Egypt, Jochebed was born to him say at 100, or 66 years after the immigration. Amram perhaps a little earlier. For his father, *Kohath,* (Exod. 6: 18,) may have been 20 when he came to Egypt, and hence 86 when Jochebed was born. Probably about 50 years after that, the nephew and aunt were married. There was, as yet, no law against such marriages. About 14 years after their marriage Moses was born, and he was 80 years old at the Exodus. These numbers (66 + 50 + 14 + 80 = 210.) make the period of the sojourn in Egypt. (p. 18.)

2. *A goodly* (Heb. *good.*) So Gen. 6: 2. Sept. αστειος. Stephen has it αστειος τω θεω, fair (or beautiful) *to God,* or before God—a phrase for exceeding fair—divinely beautiful —Acts 7: 20. Heb. 11: 23. There was probably a charm about his features which excited high hopes of the child from the beginning. *Delitzsch* says, that the very beauty of the child was to her a peculiar token of Divine approval, and a sign that God had some special design concerning him, Heb. 11: 23. ¶ *She hid him.* This was her instinctive impulse—to conceal the child from the oppressor. She succeeded in this for the space of three months. This is here attributed to the mother, but was the work of both parents "because they saw that he was a proper child"—(or beautiful) Heb. 11: 23. This act is ascribed to *faith*, and it was faith in God's covenant promise.

3. An end was put to this successful concealment, probably by the vigilant search of the officers; *and when she could not longer hide him, she took for him an ark* (chest) *of bulrushes.* It was a small box, or basket, made of the *papyrus*, or reed, which grew on the banks of

CHAPTER II.

4 And his sister stood afar off to wit what would be done to him.

5 And the daughter of Pharaoh came down to wash *herself* at the river; and her maidens walked along by the river side, and when she saw the ark among the flags, she sent her maid to fetch it.

6 And when she had opened *it*, she saw the child: and behold, the babe wept. And she had compassion c on him, and said, This *is one* of the Hebrews' children.

---

c Ps. 106: 43.

---

the Nile, to the height of ten feet, thick and strong. It was applied to various uses, chiefly of paper and boats. It is scarcely to be found, at this day. The word for '*ark*' is the same as in Gen. 6: 14. And here again, it is an ark of salvation. The mention of this article of bulrushes, is an evidence of the truth of the history. For in Egypt alone was it used in such manufacture. *Daubed it*, smeared it with asphaltum, or slime, the *bitumen* such as that of the Dead Sea—or perhaps, the mud of the Nile, which becomes hard and tough. This was used to cement it and fasten the reeds together compactly and fill up the crevices. The *pitch* was used to make it *water-tight*. The ark of Noah was also coated with pitch. She *put the child therein, and she laid* (it) *in the flags* (weeds) *by the river's brink*. This was her desperate resort—as the last and only hope—and yet, as it was done in faith it was owned and blessed of God. The basket was laid not in the water, but among the reeds, " by the side of one of the canals of the Nile, whence it floated down the stream," *Stanley*. The believing parent was led to place the child just where and how was best calculated to secure the issue. (The spot is marked by tradition as the Isle of Rodah, near old Cairo.) She knew perhaps that the King's daughter was accustomed to bathe there. Accordingly *his sister* (Miriam) *stationed herself* (*stood*) *afar off* (out of sight) to *witness what would be done to him*. The plan was laid with this end in view and in the hope to have the child taken in charge by the King's daughter. It was a true faith that used the means diligently while firmly trusting the issue to God.

5–10. Now occurs the anxiously awaited event, which proved the plan to be a success. The daughter of Pharaoh, came down to the river Nile *to bathe*. This is the meaning of the word here used, and not to wash clothes, as *Adam Clarke* supposes. We have here some clue to the residence of the Pharaohs and of Moses' family. The place must have been near the Nile—but not where crocodiles were found. Hence not at On, or Heliopolis, which is too far off, and not near Memphis, but—according to the traditions recorded by Eutychius—at the ancient *Avaris*—which name is traced to the name for *Hebrew—avar*—and which is the same with *Zoan*, on the Tanitic branch of the river near the sea, where crocodiles are never found, and which was probably the western boundary of the district occupied by the Israelites. The field of Zoan is the place associated by the Hebrews with the wonders which preceded the Exodus. Ps. 78: 43." *Quatremeres*. The Nile was regarded as *sacred*, and this female bathing in the river was the custom as appears from pictures on the monuments. *Wilkinson* III. p. 389. Ladies of high rank with their female attendants are represented as bathing in the sacred river, and it was regarded as an act

7 Then said his sister to Pharaoh's daughter, Shall I go and call to thee a nurse of the Hebrew women, that she may nurse the child for thee?

8 And Pharaoh's daughter said to her, Go. And the maid went and called the child's mother.

9 And Pharaoh's daughter said unto her, Take this child away and nurse it for me, ᵈ and I will give *thee* thy wages, and the woman took the child, and nursed it.

---

d Ps 27: 10.

---

of special sanctity and a religious solemnity;—sometimes an introduction of a sacred festival (as of the new moon). It was also supposed to impart health and vigor and to prolong life. This daughter's name (according to Josephus) was *Thermutis*. If Sesostris Rameses II) was the new king his daughter was *Thuoris*. "Thermutis was married to the infant heir of the throne of Lower Egypt, and thus became virtually regent over the Delta. She adopted a son in lack of any of her own. (Israel in Egypt, p. 285). *Her maidens walked along* (as attendants) upon the river bank awaiting her orders. *And she saw the ark (box) in the midst of the weeds* (or flags) *and she sent her body servant* (the word is different from the previous and means her special attendant) *and took it up.*

6. *And she opened (it)* · (uncovered the box) *and saw him, the child, —and lo! a male child, weeping.* She discovered it to be the child, and lo, a boy weeping! This vividly describes the scene in briefest terms. She saw that it was a Hebrew babe by the mark of circumcision, *and she was sparing of it—* carefully treated it—cared for it— *and said of the children of the Hebrews is this.*" "No tale of romance ever described a plot more skilfully laid or more full of interest in the development." "She is aware of the royal edict, and comprehends the whole affair at a glance," *Murphy.* We may suppose the scheme to have been due to a Divine suggestion, as the success was due to divine Providence, and the actuating principle was faith—the faith in the Divine Promise. Heb. 11 : 23.

7. *Then,* upon hearing the exclamation of the King's daughter— *his sister said unto her, Shall I go etc.* A most natural and timely suggestion, to procure a nurse from the Hebrew women for this Hebrew child. The suggestion was approved. *She said go! And the maid went and called the child's mother.* This plan seems, at least, worthy of a Divine origin. The babe is thus restored to its natural nourisher and protector. And the glad mother rejoices in the welcome task. And God's purpose is accomplished by these various and complicated agencies; weaving the network of His eternal counsels by so many threads and bringing out so beauteous a picture. *Murphy* supposes that the sister Miriam was about 13 years old at this time.

9. Pharaoh's daughter, at once, engages this Hebrew woman to nurse the child, not knowing, however, of the relation between them, —*Take this child away and nurse it for me, and I will give thee thy wages.* The glad mother is only too happy to do this, and her wages already will be found in the welcome maternal service. The dear doomed boy is in her arms again—rescued from a watery grave. "A literary education was the prime condition for admission to the public service," Sp. Com.

10. The woman was the best

10 And the child grew, and she brought him unto Pharaoh's daughter, and he became her son. And she called his name Moses; and she said, Because I drew him out of the water.

nurse that could have been found—and no wonder that *the child grew—and she brought him*, in course of time, *unto Pharaoh's daughter*. The verb is used in Gen. 21: 8, of *being weaned*. But it would seem that he was early trained in the divine religion, and was old enough to receive such impressions as were never lost in all his Egyptian living. And he became her son, was adopted by the King's *daughter*. The mother, doubtless, brought him to her with a lawful pride, and with faith also in his high calling—though, she must have grieved to let him go from her side to become an heir of the heathen court. *And she called his name Moses*, etc. The Hebrew word bears this meaning from the verb to *draw out*. *Gesenius* says it means *drawing out*, not *drawn out*. Sp. Com. says the exact meaning is "Son" but the verbal root means 'draw forth.' He was named by his mother at his circumcision, but by what name is not stated. Tradition has it *Joachim*. This name—Moses—would naturally be Egyptian, and the reason for giving this name is stated, *because I drew him out of the water*. Josephus states that the word for *drawn out of the water* is *Mouses*, in Egyptian they call water *Mo;* and one drawn out *Uses*. And so the Coptic, where *Oushe* means to save. The Sept. has it *Mouses*. But the Hebrews lived so long in Egypt, that there would be some mingling of terms; and the languages are cognate, and would easily have the same root in both *Heb*. and *Egyptian*. Some think that a Hebrew name was designedly given to the child. *Hartz* says in the transformation of the name from Egyptian *Mouje* to the Heb. *Moshe*, " there was an unintentional prophecy; for the person *drawn* out did become, in fact, the *drawer out*"—that is the deliverer of his people, or "The Israelites afterwards formed out of the Egyptian word the name *Mo-scheh* which signifies a leader out." *Von Gerlach*. He was educated in all the wisdom of the Egyptians (Acts 7: 22) and so "the wisdom of Egypt was employed by the wisdom of God for the establishment of the kingdom of God," *Del. Brugsch* (hist. d'Egypte) renders the name *Mes*, or *Messon* "*child*" as borne by one of the Princes of Ethiopia under Rameses II, as also in the names Amosis and Thuth *mosis*.—*Stanley*.

At a recent convention of Philologists at Wurzburg, Dr. Lanth, of Munich, read a paper upon some discoveries which he had made in translating Egyptian papyrus rolls—an account of a personage whom he believed to be Moses. He finds, for instance, that the writer, Hui, accuses a person of some consequence, whose name is *Mesu*, of having taken a sea-bath, eaten fish, and done other acts forbidden to the priesthood. It is further related that *Mesu* had made a secret journey to Syria; that he had studied in On (Heliopolis), and had commanded five thousand men during a miltary campaign; but that he was too much given to say new things upon religious matters. He is described as handsome, and of irascible temperament. In addition to his name of *Mesu*, which means "child," he has another which may be translated "basket of rushes." The date of the report is the fifty-second year of Rameses, corresponding to 1525 B. C.

§ 5. MOSES' PATRIOTISM AND HIS FLIGHT. Ch. 2: 11-25.

11. *In those days*, etc. The historian passes at once to a great crisis

EXODUS.

11 And it came to pass in those days, when Moses was grown, that he went out unto his brethren, and looked on their burdens : e and he spied an Egyptian smiting an Hebrew, one of his brethren.

12 And he looked this way and that way, and when he saw that *there was* no man, he slew the Egyptian, and hid him in the sand.

---

e ch. 1: 11; Ac. 7: 23-24; He. 11: 24-26.

---

in the life of Moses, when his love of country and people broke out. An interval is here passed over which is filled up by the narrative of Stephen (Acts 7.). More than forty years had elapsed, and he was grown. The *Sept* has it—*In those many days*—*Heb.* And *Moses grew* (to maturity). Stephen says, "He was mighty both in word and deed." He was moved—as probably for many years past—to *go out unto his brethren* and *look on their burdens*. His maturity and position at Court were such, now, as to make this a most natural and most important step. And it was the free prompting of his patriotism which he drew in with his mother's milk, and of the strong faith by which he was moved to great thoughts and deeds. (Heb. 11 : 24-26.). He would also be drawn toward his oppressed brethren, hearing of their *burdens*, and would be prompted to examine into their case and commiserate it. It so occurred, in the Providence of God, that he was witness to a personal conflict which represented the whole matter. He spied an Egyptian smiting an Hebrew. It was an Egyptian taskmaster scourging one of his *Hebrew brethren* without just cause, and so cruelly that he seems to have died under the treatment (Acts 7 : 24.). It may indeed have been a private individual undertaking arrogantly to chastise (bastinado) a Hebrew, as they felt bold to do after Pharaoh's oppressive commands. At any rate Moses felt called upon to interfere in the defence of his brother. (1.) This was the well-established usage among the people of his time. Avenging the blood of nearest of kin and so, of one's own people or tribe, against one of another tribe, was held to be a sacred duty. (2.) He was conscious of acting under a prospective commission as Deliverer of his people. This we learn from Stephen's narrative (Acts 7 : 23-25.). "For he supposed his brethren would have understood how that God, by his hand, would deliver them." He was not "impelled by a carnal ambition"—but he had high aims, full of patriotic ardor, and in the impulse of a lofty faith. *Stephen* cites the fact not to condemn Moses, but to condemn the Jews who understood not Moses' action and relation as coming Deliverer (Acts 7 : 25, 26.). He is therefore not to be judged as an assassin, as though this had been done in our time, or without strong extenuation, and something of a Divine call. *Augustin* says, that "the Egyptian though criminal and the offender in the case, ought not to have been slain by Moses without lawful authority." Yet it was the Spirit of the Coming Deliverer rising within him, and only needing the formal Commission to go forth to his work. Moses was a high personage at Court, and may have claimed authority to interfere in a case of grievous oppression and wrong. But his patriotic ardor and warm fraternal sympathy "were precipitated into action" by a flagrant case before his eyes, suddenly sprung upon him. We cannot know all the palliating facts. But Stephen refers to the act without con-

CHAPTER II.

13 And when he went out the second day, behold, two men of the Hebrews strove together; and he said unto him that did the wrong, Wherefore smitest thou thy fellow?

14 And he said, Who made thee a prince and a judge over us? intendest thou to kill me, as thou killedst the Egyptian? And Moses feared, and said, Surely this thing is known.

15 Now when Pharaoh heard this thing, he sought to slay Moses. But Moses fled from the face of Pharaoh, and dwelt in the land of Midian: and he sat down by a well.

---

demnation of it, and rather ranking it as an act of faith in the Divine Promise of Deliverance to the covenant people. This act is compared by some with that of Peter, whose hot impulse drew his sword upon a servant of the High Priest, in defence of Jesus, but was rebuked by the Master. *Diodorus Siculus* quotes an Egyptian law which made it a capital crime not to interfere for rescue in case of assault, or not to apprehend the murderer. The Law provided (afterward) the Cities of Refuge for cases of manslaughter (Lev. 35: 9.). The person slain, in this case, being probably a government officer, Moses was liable to punishment. *Diod. Sic.* He sought to escape detection by concealing the corpse. Some have objected that there was not sand enough in this quarter to bury a body. But we took a carriage and two horses to drive out from Cairo to Heliopolis—a few miles—and we found the sand so deep that we were forced to leave the carriage on the road, and mount the horses. Besides at Memphis, near by, we saw an immense Sphinx, almost entirely buried in the sand. We found the French Engineers excavating some 40 feet in the sand, to discover the lost Temple of the Serapion, in that vicinity—the loose sand being carried on their heads in baskets by a train of little girls, and emptied at the brink of the excavation. *He looked this way and that way*, perhaps to see if any one would come to his help, or, taking every precaution against detection. If he was acting in mere anger, this would have shown the foul spirit of an assassin. But he was a meek man and a man of faith. Mohammed, in the Koran, follows a Jewish tradition that Moses repented of this wrong and was forgiven.

13, 14. *The second day*, etc. Moses was fairly committed now to this great undertaking. His soul was fired with this passion for his people's deliverance in which he was to find his life work. Two Hebrews were now seen by him in a personal conflict—He interfered by a fair and firm expostulation with the wrong-doer. But he was answered sharply and in a way to show that this Hebrew had no idea of him as their future Deliverer, but was rather prejudiced against him. Besides, his bloody interference on the previous day was thrown in his teeth by this enraged Hebrew: showing that the people were not ready for the idea of deliverance. The reply of the wrong-doer to Moses betrays a violent spirit— *Who made thee* or (Heb) *Who put thee for a man, a prince and a judge over us?* Prince implies the power, and Judge, the right of judging. Moses saw, by his further questions, that his deed of yesterday was known, and he was alarmed for his life. The Hebrews themselves, had now betrayed him. Still he had faith in their covenant relations to God. ¶ *Thy fellow*, more exactly, *thy neighbor*. "The reproof was that of a legislator who established moral obligation on a recognized principle," *Sp. Com.*

16 Now the priest of Midian had seven daughters: and they came and ᶠ drew *water*, and filled the troughs to water their father's flock.

17 And the shepherds came and drove them away: but Moses stood up and helped them, and watered their flock.

18 And when they came to Reuel their father, he said, How *is it that* ye are come so soon to-day?

19 And they said, An Egyptian delivered us out of the hand of the shepherds, and also drew *water* enough for us, and watered the flock.

20 And he said unto his daughters, And where *is* he? Why *is* it *that* ye have left the man? call him that he may ᵍ eat bread.

---

f Ge. 24: 11; 29: 10; 1Sa. 9: 11.   g Ge. 31: 54.

15. Pharaoh, on hearing of Moses' bloody deed, sought to slay him. Accordingly he fled for his life. He had cut loose from the Court, and had been rejected and betrayed by his own people, and what can he do? He found his way to *Midian*. It was on the W. shore of the Elanitic Gulf of the Red Sea, and was the land of Moses' kindred—as Midian was the son of Abraham (Gen. 25: 2–4.). Midian lay S. W. of Moab, and extended far across the Peninsula of Sinai. *He sat down*—lonely and disheartened—*by the well*—the well-known resort of travellers, as well as natives.

16–20. This was a pastoral country—flocks were kept—and, as in Syria, the females were wont to take them out to water, Gen. 29: 6. *The Priest of Midian.* He seems to have been the religious head of the tribe, or branch of the Midianites there located. In v. 18 he is called *Reuel* (*Raguel*), Num. 10: 29, but in ch. 3: 1 the priest is called *Jethro*. *Delitzsch* thinks it the same person, as seems plain from Num. 10: 29. He may have been also an Elder in the civil government, combining the two functions in one, as the word means both prince and priest. He retained the true faith and the worship of God. Some wrongly suppose that *Jethro* was the official name. *Gerlach* suggests that Jethro and Hobab were the same person. *Sp. Com.* supposes Hobab to have been a young brother of Jethro, and that Jethro was brother-in-law of Moses. The *seven daughters* of Jethro, or Reuel, were tending the flock, and bringing them to water. *And the shepherds came and drove them away.* This was a grievance to which the female shepherds were liable—the stronger party driving away the weaker. Moses interfered, on their behalf, against the shepherds, and watered their flocks. They returned to their father, and explained to him their early arrival by reporting this service rendered them by Moses, in their need. They called him an *Egyptian*, because he probably wore their dress, and spoke their tongue, or dialect. Moses seems to have had a strong passion for delivering the oppressed, though he was the meekest man. The father naturally inquired after this benefactor of his helpless and exposed daughters, and is eager to show him favor in return. He complains of them for having left their helper behind. But they may have been restrained by a natural and becoming modesty from inviting him to their home. *Call him that he may eat bread.* He will have them invite him to take a meal, and be provided for. So Jacob was the gainer by a like service.

CHAPTER II. 41

21 And Moses was content ^h to dwell with the man; and he gave Moses ¡ Zipporah his daughter.

22 And she bare *him* a son, and he called his name Gershom; for he said, I have been a stranger in a strange land.

23 And it came to pass, in process of time, that the king of Egypt died; and the children of Israel ^k sighed by reason of the bondage, and they cried; and their cry came up unto God, ^l by reason of the bondage.

24 And God heard their groaning, and God remembered his covenant ^m with Abraham, with Isaac, and with Jacob.

25 And God looked upon the children of Israel, and God had respect unto *them*.

---

h Ph. 4: 11. i ch. 18: 2. k Nu. 20: 16; De. 26: 7; Ps. 12: 5. l Ge. 18: 20; ch. 3: 9; 22: 23–27; De. 24: 15; Is. 5: 7. m Ge. 15: 14; 46: 4; Lu. 1: 72–74.

---

21. Moses was so well treated as to be satisfied to abide with Reuel. *Was content*—was willing, or pleased, *to dwell with the man. And he gave Moses Zipporah*, his daughter. The name means *birdie—a little bird.* He probably acquired her by service as Jacob gained Rachel and Leah.

22. *Gershom*, one of Moses's sons by this Zipporah, means *banishment*, or *a stranger there.* This expressed his fixed feeling of exile, for he said, "*I have been a stranger in a strange land.*"

23–25. The condition of the people immediately prior to the deliverance is here recorded. *In process of time* (Heb.). *And it came to pass* (in) *after those many days.* The interval is the forty years' period of Moses' residence in Midian; in the course of which time the king died. This may have occurred soon after Moses left the country, but his policy of oppression was sharply followed up by his successors; and as their bondage began before Moses' birth, so it lasted during more than eighty years. *They sighed and cried* by reason of the bondage, or hard slave-labor. This king who died was the same probably as in verse 15; but whether the same with the new king (Ch. 1 : 8) or not, does not appear; but it was most likely a successor. The Israelites may have hoped for some relief in the change of kings, and when disappointed in this they cried in despair of such help, and *their cry came up unto God*, Deut. 26 : 7. It is thought that when Moses declined the honors of the court, the king's daughter (*Thuoris*) having come to the throne, withdrew in disappointment to Upper Egypt, and reigned as guardian of her infant nephew Sethos, whom she now made his heir. Seven years afterwards she died, and Sethos took the throne of Upper Egypt, and on the death of Si-phtha several years later (v. 23) he succeeded to the sovereignty of Lower Egypt also. He was a shameless tyrant, who increased the burdens of the Hebrews, "their wages being chiefly paid by the bastinado."—*Crit. Com.*

25. *God heard . . . remembered His covenant.* This was a covenant people, and they were beloved for the fathers' sake. Promises made to faithful Abraham were to be fulfilled in them. The Messianic hope was the ever abiding foundation of trust and solace to them in their bondage. Accordingly God *looked upon them and had respect unto them.* (Heb.) *He saw them and knew them*—approved them—recognized them approvingly. Luther— *He accepted them.*

Prayer is mighty. God is almighty to save. God never forgets

CHAPTER III.

NOW Moses kept the flock of Jethro his father-in-law, the priest of Midian ; and he led the flock to the back side of the desert, and came to the mountain of God, ª *even* to Horeb.

2 And the angel of the Lord appeared unto him in a flame of fire, out of the midst of a bush ; ᵇ and he looked, and, behold, the bush burned with fire, and the bush *was* not consumed.

---

a ch. 18: 5; 1Ki. 19: 8.   b De. 33: 16; Is. 63: 9; Ac. 7: 30.

His covenant. The prayer that pleads God's covenant finds Him a covenant God. God's covenant is a household covenant, and the baptismal sacrament is precious.

CHAP. III.

§ 6. CALL AND COMMISSION OF MOSES. Ch. 3: 1-10.

The proverb is "When the tale of bricks is doubled then comes Moses." Moses, who had been so marvellously preserved and led forward by Providence as a deliverer of his people, now receives a Divine call and commission to this work. He became a shepherd in the employ of his father-in law as Jacob had been under Laban (Gen. 30: 28), see ch. 2: 21. Jethro was *priest of Midian* (ch. 2: 18) and was the same probably as Raguel or Reuel. See Numb. 10: 29. Moses *led (was feeding,* or *shepherding) the flock to the back-side of the desert*—lit.—*after the desert* or *beyond it*—(after passing through the desert)—west of the desert.—Gesenius. Tradition points to a valley N. of *Jebel Musa* as Jethro's Valley—(Wady Shuweib or Shoaib-Hobab). Jethro's home was east of the wilderness and of Horeb. '*The mountain of God*' is the name given to Mt. Horeb, by the historian Moses because it was known by that name at the time of his writing, late in life, and after these events, here recorded. It may, indeed, have already received this name. It means, *dryness,* from the barren, rocky region where it is—the region of Sinai. Sp. Com. reads, "the mountain of God, towards Horeb."

2. *The Angel of the Lord—an angel of Jehovah*—is the covenant angel, see Gen. 16: 7. God now began to appear, not as heretofore, in human form, to the patriarchs, but in symbols, as here—*in a flame of fire*, see Ps. 104: 4. " It was in that wonderful region of the earth where the grandeur of mountains is combined, as hardly anywhere else, with the grandeur of the desert"—Stanley. ¶ *A bush*, lit.—*The bush,* well-known and often spoken of by Moses. "A flame of fire like that which seemed to consume and waste away His people in the furnace of affliction, shone forth amidst the dry branches of the thorny tree, and behold ! the bush, the massive thicket, burned with fire and the bush was not consumed." This was the *thorn bush*, the wild acacia, like that, we suppose, which we have seen growing in the neighborhood of the Dead Sea, only of greater height. The meaning intended was that God's presence in the midst of their fiery afflictions preserved them from being consumed. " He chastens His people by sore judgments but does not give them over to death." Others, as *Kurtz*, think it symbolical of the future history of Israel, in which God, as a holy God, would be consuming to them in their sins, but for a constant miracle. *Not consumed,* meaning not *burned,* not at all injured by the fire. Fire had done its utmost upon

CHAPTER III.

3 And Moses said, I will now turn aside, and see this great sight, why the bush is not burned.

4 And when the Lord saw that he turned aside to see, God called unto him out of the midst of the bush, and said, ^c Moses, Moses. And he said, Here *am* I.

5 And he said, draw not nigh hither; put off thy shoes ^d from off thy feet, for the place whereon thou standest *is* holy ground.

6 Moreover he said, ^e I *am* the God of thy father, the God of Abraham, the God of Isaac, and the God of Jacob. And Moses hid his face; for he was afraid to look upon God.

---

c Ge. 22: 1-11; 46: 2.   d ch. 19: 12; Jos. 5: 15; Ec. 5: 1.   e Ge 28: 13; 1Ki. 18: 36; Matt. 22: 32.

---

it; the bush blazed with fire; was wrapped in flame; but was not damaged by the fire. *Delitzsch* says, It also served as a prelude to God's manifestation on Sinai for the establishment of the covenant (ch. 19 and 20) and therefore was on that spot.

3. Moses' attention was fixed on this strange sight. It was to him, indeed, "*this great sight—why the bush is not burned.*" What made the sight so great and notable was the mystery why the bush was not consumed—destroyed by the flame.

4. *The Lord Jehovah* is here the same as "the Angel of Jehovah," v. 2. "Jehovah" is the name of God used to denote God in redemption; while *Elohim*, rendered "God," is the term to denote God in creation. The divine names are here interchanged with a significance in the mind of the writer. *Delitzsch* remarks that this precludes the idea of Jehovah being merely a national God. See ch. 6: 2, 3. God appears here in nature as controlling nature. Law implies a lawgiver, who is higher than the law.

It was God in nature—the Creator—in the midst of the bush.

5. This was the direct personal call to Moses, out of the midst of this miraculous manifestation. Moses responded as ready to obey the call.

5. *Draw not nigh*, etc. At the East, among Mohammedans, no one is allowed to enter a mosque without removing his shoes or sandals. In Egypt we found this much insisted on—even at the College of the Howling Dervishes at Cairo. We were obliged to put off our boots or shoes at the door of the mosques, but were commonly furnished with straw slippers, to protect the feet from the cold stone pavement. Sometimes it is allowed to slip these over the shoes, but not commonly, as the shoes or sandals in that dry country are supposed to be filthy with dirt. Even in Grecian temples the priests and priestesses were barefooted in their services. So the Arabs and Samaritans, and even the Yezidis of Mesopotamia take off their shoes on entering the sacred places. See *Delitzsch* for citation. This removal of the shoes is a confession of personal defilement in the presence of the Holy Being dwelling there. The place was made holy by the Divine Presence.

6. God now announces Himself as the covenant God of his fathers, and thus reminds him of the promises made to the patriarchs, now about to be fulfilled. According to the term fixed (Gen. 15: 13) [400 years], it was now in the last year of the predicted exile and oppression. All this was most deeply impressive to Moses, and he *hid his face*, awe-struck by the presence of

7 And the Lord said, I have surely seen the affliction of my people ᶠ which *are* in Egypt, and have heard their ᵍ cry by reason of their task-masters; for I know their sorrows;

8 And I am come down to deliver them out of the hand of the Egyptians, ʰ and to bring them up out of that land unto a good land ⁱ and a large, unto a land ᵏ flowing with milk and honey; unto the place of the Canaanites, and the Hittites, and the Amorites, and the Perizzites, and the Hivites, and the Jebusites.

9 Now therefore, behold, the cry of the children of Israel is come unto me: and I have also seen the oppression wherewith the Egyptians oppress them.

10 Come now, therefore, and I will send ˡ thee unto Pharaoh, that thou mayest bring forth my people, the children of Israel, out of Egypt.

---

f Ne. 9: 9; Ps. 106: 44; Is. 63: 9.   g Ex. 22: 23; Ps. 145: 19.   h ch. 6: 6–8; 12: 51.
i Nu. 23: 19; De. 1: 25.   k De. 26: 9; Je. 11: 5; Eze. 20: 6.   l Ps. 105: 26; Mi. 6: 4.

God, and afraid to look up. 1 Kings 19: 12; Gen. 16: 13; Isa. 6: 1, 5; Rev. 1: 16. No man hath seen, nor can see God; and any visible manifestation of Himself, as in the glory of the bush, he was afraid to gaze upon, now that he heard the voice, and knew the fact of the Divine Presence.

7. *I have surely seen.* Heb., *Seeing I have seen.* I have closely, carefully noticed and watched. God assures Moses that He has all along attentively considered the case of His people, and *has heard their cry* under the oppressive *task-masters;* and the proof of this is, *for I know their sorrows,* as having taken exact account of them.

8. And this is given as a reason for the Divine interposition. The case was known to call for such. God has a plan of salvation which includes deliverance from bondage and introduction to the better land, and comprehends all the intervening particulars. The Land of Promise is described as superior to Goshen—*a good land and a large*—of large extent as compared with Goshen—*flowing with milk and honey*—abounding in pasturage for milk and in flowers for honey. The phrase is a proverbial one for luxuriant fertility and richness of produce, while these were articles yielded in large abundance by the land of Canaan, ch. 13: 5; 16: 14. Deut. 8; 7–9. Isa. 7: 15, 22. John the Baptist fed on wild honey. I have seen, at Heliopolis, the great obelisk, covered, towards the sun, with the honey of the bees, and that it is common to see this wild honey on rocks and trees. ¶ *Unto the place of,* etc. Six tribes inhabiting the land, would give some idea of its breadth. See Gen. 10: 15–18; 15: 18, 20. There were in Abraham's time, ten tribes inhabiting the land. The Canaanites sometimes include the whole—though only five were descended from Canaan. These names are in the singular—the *Canaanite,* etc.

9, 10. God here repeats the fact which impelled Him to this movement of deliverance, and states the plan for sending Moses to Pharaoh, and the object in view.

§ 7. MOSES' OBJECTIONS AND GOD'S ANSWER. Ch. III: 11–22.

11. Moses demurs at this Divine commission, though he had been

CHAPTER III.

11 And Moses said unto God, Who *am* I, ᵐ that I should go unto Pharaoh, and that I should bring forth the children of Israel, out of Egypt?

12 And he said, Certainly I will be with ⁿ thee; and this *shall be* a token unto thee, that I have sent thee: When thou hast brought forth the people out of Egypt, ye shall serve God upon this mountain.

13 And Moses said unto God, Behold, *when* I come unto the children of Israel, and shall say unto them, The God of your fathers hath sent me unto you; and they shall say to me, What *is* his name? what shall I say unto them?

---

m Je. 1: 6. n Ge. 31: 3; Jos. 1: 5; Ro. 8: 31.

---

so ready to go at his own impulse. He was awed by the Divine Majesty, and could see no reason why he should be chosen by God for such a work. This may have been in part owing to his humble condition as a shepherd in Midian. But when one sees God, he shrinks at a sense of his own insignificance. *Who am I?* This was most natural, considering that he knew the haughtiness and power of Pharaoh, and besides he knew of his having been sought for his life by the monarch for having interfered on his brethren's behalf, and of his having been rejected by his own people, at his first attempt. Going to Pharaoh and bringing forth the people of Israel from his power, would, of course, seem to him a thing impossible. But this was from the human side, and from his own point of view. They who are best fitted for God's work, commonly have the humblest estimate of themselves and their fitness.

12. Another aspect is put upon the commission by this pledge of the Divine Presence to accompany him. The same Apostle who said he was not able to think anything as of himself, said, also, "I can do all things through Christ which strengtheneth me," (Phil. 4: 13). *God with us* is our surest warrant for all undertakings, and our purest comfort in all affliction. God was ready also to furnish to the timid man *a token*—for his most ample and positive assurance in the event itself—the promised result of his mission—that after he had achieved the deliverance—*ye* (the Israel) *shall serve God upon this mountain.* For the present, he had the miraculous token in the burning bush—and for the future, he should be sustained and strengthened by the fulfilled prophecy now uttered. So that both by prodigy and by prophecy God's hand should be made known. So surely as God appeared to him at Horeb so surely should Israel serve Him there, on their way from Egypt to Canaan. (See ch. 24.) They entered into covenant with God there, and gave proof of their obedience, ch. 36: 1-7, Numb. 7.

13. Moses begins to contemplate the work so far as to anticipate the practical difficulties. They would probably ask him for the name of Him who sent him. By this he means, that they would ask, not for His common title, but for His plan of manifestation, or the mode of His action or dispensation towards them. A name is that whereby one makes himself known—and here the question likely to be asked is—How will God display Himself or make Himself known? What does He propose to do?

14, 15. *I AM that I am*—Heb.—*I will be what I will be. Sept.*—*I am He who is*—or the Existing One. Essential Being not only, but with reference to further revelation, the

46

EXODUS.

14 And God said unto Moses, I AM THAT I AM ; ᵒ and he said, Thus shalt thou say unto the children of Israel, I AM hath sent me unto you.

15 And God said, moreover, unto Moses, Thus shalt thou say unto the children of Israel, The Lord God of your fathers, the God of Abraham, the God of Isaac, and the God of Jacob, hath sent me unto you; this *is* my name for ever, and this *is* my memorial ᵖ unto all generations.

16 Go, and gather the elders of Israel together, and say unto them, the Lord God of your fathers, the God of Abraham, of Isaac, and of Jacob, appeared unto me, saying, I have surely visited ᑫ you, and *seen* that which is done to you in Egypt.

17 And I have said, I will bring ʳ you up out of the affliction of Egypt unto the land of the Canaanites, and the Hittites, and the Amorites, and the Perizzites and the Hivites, and the Jebusites, unto a land flowing with milk and honey:

18 And they shall hearken to thy voice; and thou shalt come, thou and the elders of Israel, unto the king of Egypt; and ye shall say unto him, the Lord God of the Hebrews hath ˢ met with us ; and now let us go, we beseech thee, three days' journey into the wilderness, that we may sacrifice to the Lord our God.

---

o ch. 6 : 3; Jno. 8 : 58; He. 13 : 8. p Ps. 102 : 12; 135 : 13; Ho. 12 : 5. q Ge. 50 : 24 ; Lu. 1 : 68. r Ge. 15 : 13–20; 46 : 4. s Nu. 23 : 3, etc.

Supreme Being as about to display Himself in Redemption—So that Elohim and Jehovah are combined, as in Gen. 2. The Lord God, who in Gen. 2, moved to Redemption, here moves in another grand stage of the Redeeming work as a Covenant God. In the Apocalypse it is "I am He which is, and was, and is to come—the Almighty (Rev. 1 : 8). And on the veil which overhung the Temple of the Egyptian Sais was written " I am that which has been, and which is, and which is to be, and my veil no mortal hath yet drawn aside." It was not merely God's self-existence which was expressed in the wonderful name, but His Redeeming Providence and Grace also. So it is further expanded—*This* (is) *my name forever, and this* (is) *my memorial unto all generations*—the principle and style of His further manifestation as to be recognized among men. (Ps. 135.) I will make myself known in this capacity of a covenant God and Redeemer to all future generations of His people. Literally it reads— " Jehovah, God of your fathers, God of Abraham, God of Isaac and God of Jacob."

16, 18. Moses is now directed to the first step to be taken. He was to go and *assemble the Elders*—So in *Joel*, 2 : 16. They were the heads of the people, and the office has been preserved in the synagogue, and handed down as the only permanent office in the Church, (Gen. 50 : 7.) *The Lord God*—Jehovah God—the two names comprising the whole idea of a Supreme Covenant God. Moses is to assure the people of all that had been assured to him. He is warranted that they shall hearken to him, and not reject him, as at first. Accompanied by

CHAPTER III.

19 And I am sure that the king of Egypt will not let you ᵗ go, no, not by a mighty hand.

20 And I will stretch out my hand, and smite Egypt with all my wonders,ᵘ which I will do in the midst thereof; and after that he will ᵛ let you go.

21 And I will give this people ʷ favor in the sight of the Egyptians; and it shall come to pass, that, when ye go, ye shall not go empty;

22 But every woman shall borrow ˣ of her neighbor, and of her that sojourneth in her house, jewels of silver, and jewels of gold, and raiment; and ye shall put *them* upon your sons, and upon your daughters; and ye shall ʸ spoil the Egyptians.

---

t ch. 5: 2. u ch. 7: 3; 11: 9; De. 6: 22; Ne. 9: 10; Ps. 105: 27; Je. 32 20; Ac. 7: 36.
v ch. 12: 31. w ch. 11: 3. x ch. 12: 36. y Job 27: 17; Pr. 13: 22; Is. 33: 1.

---

these Elders as the official representatives of the people—and not alone as he had feared—they should present the case to Pharaoh. *The Lord God of the Hebrews*—So God already encourages the people by a title that insures His covenant relation and protection. They were to assure the monarch of the Personal Existence of their God, by mentioning His meeting with them, as had been seen by Moses. *Let us go*—This request is not at first for manumission, which the monarch had been so guarding against, but it was a religious request for leave of a *three days' journey to sacrifice* to their God. It was no pretence (ch. 8: 27). It was reasonable, moderate, fair, that he might have no good ground for refusing. God will have it appear how utterly unyielding and oppressive Pharaoh is. What God purposes in the future has nothing to do with Pharaoh's action, for He does not disclose His plans. God's eternal purposes are hidden from us and therefore they cannot be pleaded in extenuation of our sin. It will be seen that Pharaoh is free in his action, while God accomplishes His own eternal purposes of Redemption in perfect consistency with the freedom of the creature. Besides, it is only the immediate duty that is provided for, and the sequel shall be met in its time. The three days' journey would carry them quite outside of Egypt. And as their sacrifice would be of animals held sacred among the Egyptians, it would be proper to get out of the land for the purpose. God will have us attend to present duty and leave the sequel to come upon us in its own time.

19. God at the same time knows the end from the beginning, and is *sure* of the result. But this does not at all affect Pharaoh's responsibility. Pharaoh shall be dealt with so as to have his own free choice; and so as to show his wickedness and to open the way for God's gracious interposition.

20. God now reveals to Moses, for his encouragement, the outline of His plan for deliverance, and the effect upon Pharaoh. ¶ *Not by*—*Not even by means of a strong hand*. All the mighty works of God would not induce him. He would resist to the end, and thus his destruction would be the fruit of his obduracy. The ultimate release would be against his will—by severe compulsion and perdition. See ch. 10: 27. See also ch. 12: 31 and 14: 5, etc., or the other rendering of some, "*But by a mighty hand*," is sustained by the reading ch. 6: 1. *And after these things* (the miracles) *he will let you go.*

21–22. *Favor* from the Egyptians

CHAPTER IV.

AND Moses answered and said, but, behold, they will not believe me, nor hearken unto my voice: for they will say, The Lord hath not appeared unto thee.

2 And the LORD said unto him, What *is* that in thine hand? And he said, A rod.

---

is also promised to them for their departure, securing a supply of treasure for the journey. *Shall borrow.* The word means, *shall ask*, or claim as a right—shall *demand*. It was their right. Some think it means *shall ask as a favor* and it should be granted as such. This was in fulfilment of the promise (Gen. 15 : 14) that they should come out with great substance. The Egyptian people should be well disposed towards their Hebrew neighbors, and would grant their request or demand of jewels and raiment. This might be from neighborly feeling, or from joy at their departure on account of fear of God's tokens. " Egypt was glad when they departed—for the fear of them fell upon them," (Ps. 105 : 38.) So the Israelites are directed to ask, ch. 11 : 2, 3. So ch. 12 : 35, 36 it was done. *Asking of her that sojourneth in her house* would imply that they lived with the Egyptians in some cases (see ch. 11 : 2) as servants or otherwise. The jewels and clothes they should put upon their sons and daughters —and so they should *spoil the Egyptians* (Egypt). Objectors have made this to be a *borrowing and stealing* of treasure; but the whole connection here shows that the sense in which it must have been understood was that of asking and of receiving, whether as a mere favor or as a right also, an amount which would be a serious draught upon the Egyptians, and which yet would be conceded; for it was to come from the favor which God would give them in the sight of the Egyptians. The term for *borrowing* in the Hebrew, is quite different from this.

CHAP. IV.

§ 8. MOSES' DOUBTS REMOVED, FURTHER OBJECTION MET BY A SIGN. Ch. IV : 1-9.

1. Moses now foresees the difficulty which he must meet from the unbelief of the people in his Divine commission. Pharaoh's refusal had already been provided for in the plan of God, (ch. 3 : 19-22), yet, he needs further confirmation of his own faith on the spot, and further provision for his probable repulse by his own people (v. 5). God furnishes to him the most satisfactory signs, and his difficulties are thus effectually removed. *But, behold.* The *Gr.*, has—*If.* Moses may, however, well be certain of his ill-success, considering his recent experience with his brethren. The last instance of the Divine appearing to Israel was Gen. 46 : 2. And besides Moses had now been an exile in Midian forty years, and would be a stranger to most of his people.

2. Moses' rod was the shepherd's staff. Upon being thrown down, it is turned into a serpent, and on being taken up again it becomes a rod, as at first. This miracle is suggestive and full of meaning as to the matter in hand. The throwing down of his shepherd office was repugnant to him and would involve him in difficulties from which he would desire to escape, —difficulties especially in connection with Egypt's wicked, Satanic power. But God would enable him to seize this fearful thing and it should turn to be in his hands the rod of power whereby he should smite the Egyptians. For the serpent was the symbol of

3 And he said, Cast it on the ground. And he cast it on the ground, and it became a serpent; and Moses fled from before it.

4 And the Lord said unto Moses, Put forth thine hand, and take it by the tail. And he put forth his hand, and caught it, and it became a rod in his hand:

5 That they may ª believe that the LORD God of their fathers, the God of Abraham, the God of Isaac, and the God of Jacob, hath appeared unto thee.

6 And the LORD said furthermore unto him, Put now thine hand into thy bosom. And he put his hand into his bosom; and when he took it out, behold, his hand *was* leprous [b] as snow.

7 And he said, Put thine hand into thy bosom again. And he put his hand into his bosom again, and plucked it out of his bosom; and, behold, it was [c] turned again as his *other* flesh.

8 And it shall come to pass, if they will not believe thee, neither hearken to the voice of the first sign, that they will believe the voice of the latter sign.

---

a ch. 19: 9.   b Nu. 12: 10; 2 Ki. 5: 27.   c Matt. 8: 3.

royal power. The Pharaohs wore this on their diadem, as the sign also of Divine authority—and the coiled serpent forming a circle was the token of eternity. This change of the rod to a serpent was to him a pledge of victory over the Kings and gods of Egypt. This miracle was given to him for his own assurance, and also to be performed before the people, *that they may believe in his* Divine commission (ch. 7: 10). The working of a miracle was understood and accepted among the Israelites as a criterion of a Divine call and authority, (John 3: 2, 3.) A miracle was a *sign* of the Divine presence. " The shepherd's rod was the symbol, of his simplicity, of his exile, of his lowliness."—Stanley.

6. A second sign is given to Moses to add to the attestation of the first. It was also full of significance. The hand of Moses was the symbol of action. As his efficiency and power in Egypt had become blighted by his exile, as by leprosy, yet it should become perfectly restored again. What seemed to him at first to be utterly disabled, as if smitten with leprosy, should, at the Divine bidding, become a restored hand of power. And further, the people should see by this sign, that as God could make Moses' office what He pleased, so He could make Moses' hand what He chose, and purge it of all defilement and disability. And so He could make Pharaoh leprous and Moses whole. And He could make Israel free from defilement and exile by the cleansed hand of Moses. The first sign had reference to Moses' call—the second to his power in executing the call. *If they will not hearken,* etc. If they will not accredit Moses' office, they will be forced to believe his work. The sign has a *voice*—and speaks, as a witness of God's presence and power, (Ps. 105: 27, John 3: 3.) ¶ *Leprous as snow.* White from the color of the parts affected, in the most malignant leprosy. I have seen lepers in Palestine, with white, scabby blotches on the face and wrists.

9. Further provision is now made for the persistent unbelief of the people, if necessary. It has a most significant reference to the consequences of rejecting God's

50 EXODUS.

9 And it shall come to pass, if they will not believe also these two signs, neither hearken unto thy voice, that thou shalt take of the water of the river, and pour it upon the dry *land:* and the water, which thou takest out of the river shall become d blood upon the dry *land.*

10 And Moses said unto the LORD, O my Lord, I *am* not eloquent, neither heretofore, nor since thou hast spoken unto thy servant: but I *am* slow of speech, and of a slow tongue.

11 And the LORD said unto him, Who hath made man's mouth?e or who maketh the dumb, or deaf, or the seeing, or the blind? have not I the LORD?

---

d ch. 7: 20.   e Ps. 94: 9; Jc. 1: 6,9.

---

messenger. The water of the sacred river, the Nile, which was everything to the Egyptians, was by the hand of Moses to become blood. One of the plagues with which God afterward smote Egypt, was to be enacted in miniature before the Israelites to fortify his faith and courage, and to satisfy their doubting minds. It is an intimation to him of the Divine power with which he should be armed. The miracle wrought before the Egyptians (ch. 7: 20,) was on a larger scale, and not by handful, but in mass. The water on which they relied for drink, and for watering the soil (having no rain) was thus, in the power of Moses to turn it into a stream of blood. Moses was the first God-sent Prophet, and the first miracle-worker, and so he was a type of the Apostle and High Priest of our Profession Jesus Christ. (Heb. 3: 1.)

LESSONS—(1) God can clearly signify to His servants His will and His warrant. (2) God uses His absolute control of nature to serve His purposes of grace. (3) The supernatural act is natural to the Supernatural Being, who is God over all. (4) God suits His miracles to the occasion so as to make the truth most clear.

§ 9. MOSES' FURTHER OBJECTION AND GOD'S ANSWER. Ch. IV: 10-31.

10. Moses finds yet another difficulty in the way of his success. He says, *I am not eloquent*—Heb.—*a man of words*—of fluent speech—(Gr.—not sufficient—fit)—*even from yesterday and from the third day* (or, the day before yesterday), that is, from the very first—(Gen. 31: 2.)—*and even from the time of thy speaking to thy servant.* "I do not possess the gift of speech, either by nature, or since thou hast addressed me." He could not summon courage to plead his cause before Pharaoh, but felt his incompetency as to freedom and facility of speech, and strength of argument. He had failed even before his oppressed countrymen, to impress them with his claim to their confidence. I am *heavy of mouth and heavy of tongue.* There may be a reference to his deficiency in the Egyptian tongue after his absence of forty years.

11. *Who hath made*—Heb. *Who hath put the mouth to man.* God here reminds Moses of His prerogative, who created all man's organs and powers. All the needed gifts are at the Divine command, and will be supplied as they are needed. He can make the speech and the senses or can take them away.

12. He is now bidden to go forward, with the assurance *I will be with thy mouth.* While he shall speak, God will aid his natural powers to the full extent of the necessity. God is said to have

12 Now therefore go, and I will be with thy mouth, and teach thee what ᶠ thou shalt say.

13 And he said, O my Lord, send, I pray thee, by the hand *of him whom* thou wilt send.

14 And the anger of the LORD was kindled against Moses; and he said, *Is* not Aaron the Levite thy brother? I know that he can speak well. And also, behold, he cometh forth to meet thee; and when he seeth thee, ᵍ he will be glad in his heart.

15 And thou shalt speak unto him, and put words ʰ in his mouth: and I will be with thy mouth, and with his mouth, and will teach you what ye shall do.

16 And he shall be thy spokesman unto the people: and he shall be, *even* he shall be to thee instead of a mouth, and thou shalt be to him instead ⁱ of God.

17 And thou shalt take this rod ᵏ in thine hand, wherewith thou shalt do signs.

---

f Is. 50: 4; Matt. 10: 19. g Ver. 27. h Nu. 22: 38; 23: 5, etc.; De. 18: 18; Is. 51: 16; Jo. 1: 9; Lu. 21: 15. i ch. 7: 1; 18: 19. k Ver. 2.

---

spoken by the mouth of David, etc. This is the doctrine of inspiration that the Scripture is the word of God in the very words of men. God would teach him what to say. —So also the apostles.

13. *Send, I pray thee, by the hand thou wilt send.* That is, send by whomsoever thou wilt, meaning that he had rather any other should be sent than he, and that if he must go, he would, yet reluctantly, and by constraint.—Do as you please.

14-17. No wonder that *the anger of Jehovah was kindled against Moses*, when the man demurs so, and objects to the last. Yet God had been most patient and forbearing towards him. It is only a misnamed humility that declines to accept God's provisions and promises, under any deep sense of our deficiency and ill-desert. Moses' objections however, were not in any spirit of opposition toward God, but only of shrinking and of self-distrust. Accordingly God provides even for this last difficulty by appointing his brother Aaron as his colleague. (Heb.) *Is not Aaron thy brother, the Levite.* Delitzsch thinks there is no reference here to the future calling of the tribe of Levi, and that it is intended, by these terms, merely to designate Aaron more fully. He is of the same tribe with Moses and therefore most fit to be his associate. Aaron is coming forth already willingly to the work, and will be glad to see thee, instead of shrinking, as you have done. Although the elder brother he will gladly act under Moses. In v. 27 God gives him the direction as to the route. Moses was to dictate, and Aaron was to speak. And God was to guide and guard the lips of both of them. Aaron was to be the *spokesman* of Moses *unto the people,* to serve instead of a mouth to Moses, and Moses was to be to him instead of God. "Aaron would stand to Moses in the same relation as a prophet to God." "What God is to Moses, that Moses is to Aaron in regard to the matter and authority of his message (ch. 7: 1). *This rod in thine hand. The rod* and *the hand* had both been miraculously wrought upon, and now Moses could understand the meaning—*wherewith thou shalt do signs.*

18. *Moses went and returned*—from the burning bush of Horeb, to Jethro. (See ch. 3:1.) Moses now

18 And Moses went, and returned to Jethro his father-in-law, and said *unto him*, Let me go, I pray thee, and return unto my brethren which *are* in Egypt: and see whether they be yet alive. And Jethro said to Moses, Go in peace.

19 And the LORD said unto Moses in Midian, Go, return into Egypt, for all the men [l] are dead, which sought thy life.

20 And Moses took his wife and his sons, and set them upon an ass, and he returned to the land of Egypt: and Moses took the rod [m] of God in his hand.

21 And the LORD said unto Moses, When thou goest to return into Egypt, see that thou do all those [n] wonders before Pharaoh, which I have put in thine hand: but I will harden [o] his heart, that he shall not let the people go.

---

l ch. 2: 15, 23; Matt. 2: 20.   m ch. 17: 9; Nu. 20: 8-9.   n ch. 3: 20.   o ch. 7: 3, etc.; De. 2: 30; Jos. 11: 20; Is. 6: 10; 63: 17; Jno. 12: 40; Ro. 9: 18; 2Th. 2: 10-12.

---

finds all his objections met, and he takes preparative steps at once for entering upon the work. As in duty bound so he asks leave of his father-in-law, in whose service he was employed. He states to him, only in most general terms, the object of his mission—*to see whether they be alive*—and to look after their interests under their crushing bondage, if, indeed, it has not crushed them utterly. Jethro, understanding the earnestness of Moses' request, consents. (Heb.) *Go in [for] peace.* Moses makes no unfair concealment.

19, 20. The Greek here inserts a passage—"And after those many days the King of Egypt died,"—which is not found in the Hebrew, but is added by the *LXX* to accommodate the next sentence. While he was in Midian, God directs him to set out for Egypt now that the hostile Pharaoh and others who *had sought his life were dead*. This is after he had obtained Jethro's consent, and was in waiting perhaps for such Divine direction as to the fitting time for his departure.

20. He now sets out upon his journey. His wife and his two sons (ch. 18: 4 tells us of the second) are set upon an ass. I have seen children swung in a pair of baskets on an ass, and the parents walking alongside, or one or the other riding by turns. This is common in the pilgrimages to Jerusalem. Moses goes in the faith of all that he was to accomplish under God—*taking the rod of God in his hand*—the rod which was transformed by God's power so as to be the symbol of His Omnipotence.

21. God now gives to Moses a solemn charge to do all the miracles as directed—Heb.—*In thy going to return to Egypt, see all the miracles* (wonders) *which I have put* (ordered) *by thy hand, and do them before Pharaoh.* He will have him use all the Divinely appointed means, all of them so eminently calculated to impress Pharaoh and constrain him to compliance. *But I will harden his heart that he shall not release the people.* The word means, to *make strong*, firm, obdurate—so that his heart will not yield, nor relax for the release of Israel. In ch. 7: 3, it is another word meaning I will make his heart unfeeling. And in ch. 10: 1, it is still another word, I have made his heart *heavy*, stupid, insensible. In these different forms the hardening of Pharaoh's heart is ascribed to God, ten times:—Ch. 9: 12, 10: 20, 27, 11: 10, 14: 8, 14: 4, 17. But just as many times it is said that Pharaoh hardened his own heart, or

22 And thou shalt say unto Pharaoh, Thus saith the Lord, Israel *is* my son, p *even* my first-born:

23 And I say unto thee, Let my son go, that he may serve me: and if thou refuse to let him go, behold, I will slay q thy son, *even* thy first-born.

p De. 14: 1; Je. 31: 9; Ho. 11: 1; Ro. 9: 4.　　q ch. 11: 5; 12: 29.

what is the same, that it became hard—ch. 7: 13, 22, 8: 15, 9: 35, ch. 7: 14 *was* (became) *heavy*, ch. 9: 7, 8: 11, 28, 9: 34. In ch. 7: 13, the English version reads: "And he hardened the heart of Pharaoh." But it should read the same as in verse 22, where the Hebrew phrase is exactly the same. And in ch. 13: 15 expressly—*for Pharaoh made his heart hard*. So that it is represented in the Scripture as quite as much the work of Pharaoh as of God. In different senses it may be understood to be the work of one or the other—of Pharaoh, as the free moral agent, acting from motives and without any sense of compulsion—or of God, as acting in and by Pharaoh because the free acts of men enter into His plan, and His decree secures their freedom, while it ordains the means along with the ends, and the ends in connection with the means. This heart-hardening was neither unknown to God from the beginning, nor independent of God's working in the case, much less was it any baffling of God's plan; but God's plan comprehended it, as the free act of the man, no less than part of the all in all of God's working—in all, through all, and above all. In Josh. 11: 20, the same term is applied to other cases. God is not the author of sin, but God works in a world of sinners so as to weave every thread of human agency into the wondrous fabric of His designs in the great scheme of Redemption. It is remarkable here that not only after the first sign wrought before Pharaoh, ch. 7: 13, 14, but after the first five judicial miracles the heart-hardening is ascribed to Pharaoh. After each of these miracles it is recorded that *his heart was* (or *became*) *hard*, or stupid—unmoved by the Divine wonders, ch. 7: 22, 8: 8, 15, 28, 9: 7. It is not till after the sixth plague that it is said *that Jehovah made the heart of Pharaoh hard*, or strong, firm, unyielding—ch. 9: 12. Then at the seventh it is *Pharaoh made his heart heavy*, ch. 9: 34, 35, but after the eighth and ninth his continued refusal, and his resolution to follow the Israelites and bring them back, are ascribed to Jehovah's hardening his heart—ch. 14: 8, comp. vs. 4 and 17. The Divine dealing affected Pharaoh in this way and so resulted—and may be looked upon as working this result. The Divine hardening however was plainly a result of the human self-hardening. God is looked upon as giving up the man to the hardening, obdurating influence of this Providential dealing. It is only as a necessity of the Divine contact, with such increasing pride and haughtiness and self-will, that God can be said to produce the hardening—even as the sun hardens some materials while he melts other substances—"melts the wax and dries the clay." It is the just curse of sin and its necessary working that it renders the heart harder, and this is by a Divine law in which God may be said to act. And Moses is here informed that not only could not Pharaoh act independently of Him, but that even his very heart-hardening should come within the domain of the Divine action, and therefore was most fully provided for in His plan (*See Delitzsch*). Moses is now furnished with the *ultimatum* which he was to lay be-

54 EXODUS.

24 And it came to pass, by the way in the inn, that the Lord ʳ met him, and sought to ˢ kill him.

25 Then Zipporah took a sharp stone, and ᵗcut off the foreskin of her son, and cast *it* at his feet, and said, Surely a bloody husband *art* thou to me.

---

r Nu. 22: 22.   s Ge. 17: 14.   t Jos. 5: 2, 3.

---

fore Pharaoh, in all his hardness and obstinate refusal. He was to declare to him the relation in which this people stood to God, and the Divine demand for their release, and the penalty which the King should incur by refusing to let the people go. *Israel is my son.* The covenant people are represented in the Old Test. as the son and servant of Jehovah. And the Messiah is also thus described. It is the complex Person, of which Christ is the Head, and His people are the members So that in the New Testament the return of the Infant Christ from Egypt is referred to as a fulfilment of this typical prophecy in the Exodus. So in Hos. 11: 1. " Out of Egypt have I called my Son."—Matt. 2: 15. " Wherever Jehovah is called the Father, Begetter, or Creator of Israel, even in Deut. 32: 18, Jer. 2: 27, Isa. 64: 8, Mal. 1: 6; 2: 10, the Fatherhood of God relates to the election of Israel as Jehovah's people of possession." The choosing of Israel as the Son of God was an adoption flowing from the free grace of God, which involved the loving, fatherly treatment of the Son, and demanded obedience, reverence and confidence towards the Father.—Mal. 1: 6. Paternal discipline (παιδεια) was also involved in the covenant relation. Israel was, however, not only *Son*, but *first-born Son* of Jehovah. In this title the calling of the Gentile nations is *implied.* Israel's was the first place among the nations, by virtue of this election. So Israel was the queen at the right hand of the King, arrayed in gold of Ophir, but accompanied by Kings' daughters as her honorable women, and typically inferior brides.—Ps. 45. So Ps. 89: 26, 27. This demand is now to be made upon Pharaoh, and the penalty of refusal is plainly to be set forth. Release my son, if not, *I will slay thy son, even thy first-born.* This was the form of penalty which would most vividly remind Pharaoh of Israel's relation to God. —Ch. 11: 5; 12: 29. Some think that this is God's language to Moses, demanding the circumcision of one of his sons, and thus connecting with the next verse.

24. Moses is now to be taught that he must first rule well his own house, and obey in his own house the Divine ordinance, before he can enforce obedience upon others. Their son, perhaps the younger, was uncircumcised. It was by some fault of the parents, and probably of the wife, who here, at once, performs the ceremony. *By the way*— on the route to Egypt—*in the inn*— or *caravanserai,* for lodging at night, such as travellers at the East were accustomed to—a walled enclosure for protection from beasts. *Jehovah met him,* literally—*rushed upon him,* in a hostile attitude—to attack him —*and sought to kill him.* This was the aspect of the case. Whether it was by some apparition threatening death with drawn sword, as in the case of Balaam's beast, we do not know, but suppose it was a fearful manifestation, as with a sword, or a threatening voice, and not a mere matter of sudden disease. He was brought to see how dangerous it must ever be to disobey the Divine command, or to slight God's holy ordinances.

25. *Then Zipporah.* How promptly his wife Zipporah understood the

26 So he let him go: then she said, A bloody husband *thou art*, because of the circumcision.

27 And the Lord said to Aaron, Go into the wilderness to meet Moses. And he went, and met him in the mount[u] of God, and kissed him.

---

u ch. 3: 1.

---

controversy which God had with them and performed the sacred rite, is here related. Only by hastening to obey can we avert the Divine displeasure. And they who go in God's name to preach obedience ought to be, themselves, a pattern of it to others. Some think that it was the lad whose life was here threatened, and that this brought the fond mother so promptly to obey. As they had two sons, the one probably the older had already been circumcised. This ordinance had been commanded to Abraham as a seal of the Divine Covenant and the neglect of it was punishable with death.—Gen. 17: 14. *A stone.* The sharp flint was sometimes used as a knife, in the absence of metallic ones, some suppose as being safer, and others as being symbolical, but probably as more available. In some localities the flint implements preceded the metallic. But see Gen. 4: 22. As Zipporah was a Midianitish woman, she was most probably averse to this bloody and painful duty. She said, a *bridegroom of blood* thou art to me. Moses, as a husband, was now associated in her mind with blood, as the blood was the price of his life, or as her marital relation with a Hebrew was now sealed with blood. But others, (as *Gesenius*,) understand this to be said of the lad, and suppose that circumcision, as the sign of the Divine covenant, is compared with marriage. The term here used for bridegroom is used of circumcision, as having some affinity. *Stanley* understands it—" A bloody husband thou art to cause the death of my son—fearing that her child would die (as smitten of God). Then when the recovery from the illness took place (whether of her son or her husband) she exclaims again—" A bloody husband still thou art, but not so as to cause the child's death, but only to bring about his circumcision." And it is more natural to refer it to Moses than to the boy. *So he let him go.* As if God had arrested or seized Moses, and now lets him go, because the required duty was performed. *Then she said*—repeating the significant language—*because of the circumcisions*, because she had been thus compelled to undergo this painful duty of circumcising the lad, casting a reproach upon Moses, as having been the occasion to her of this blood-shedding of her boy. She uses the plural as referring to *circumcisions*, as enjoined in all cases, or as in the case of both her sons. This was probably on the first night of their journey, as they had not come to Horeb, v. 27. And as the child was now unable to travel, the mother and sons were sent back to Jethro's house from this point.—Ch. 18: 2.

27. Aaron had already been announced to Moses as setting forth to meet him, and here it would seem to be God's direction as to where Moses should be met. *Go into the wilderness.* It was where God had appeared to Moses in the bush—(ch. 3: 1.) *Kissed him.* This was the token of that gladness which had been predicted of him, in meeting Moses (v. 14). They had been now forty years separated, and what wonder that both should be glad. The kiss is still the salutation of Arab friends meeting in the desert. Often it is on both sides of the face.

56 EXODUS.

28 And Moses told Aaron all the words of the LORD who had sent him, and all the signs which he had commanded him.

29 And Moses and Aaron went and gathered together all the elders of the children of Israel:

30 And Aaron spake[v] all the words which the LORD had spoken unto Moses, and did the signs in the sight of the people.

31 And the people believed; [w]and when they heard that the LORD had visited the children of Israel, and that he had looked upon their affliction, then they bowed their heads [x] and worshipped.

CHAPTER V.

AND afterward Moses and Aaron went in and told Pharaoh, Thus saith the LORD God of Israel, Let my people go, that they may hold a feast [a] unto me in the wilderness.

---

v Ver. 16   w ch. 3: 18; ver. 8, 9.   x Ge. 17: 3; 24: 26; ch. 12: 27; 1Ch. 29: 20; 2Ch. 20: 18.   a ch. 10: 9.

(*Gr.*—They kissed each other.) OBSERVE. The distance to Egypt was about 200 miles.

28–31. Moses told Aaron all as God had commanded him to do. (v. 15.) They assembled all the Elders of the people of Israel in Egypt. Aaron was now about 83 years old. Everything goes forward according to the Divine programme. *And Aaron spake* (as directed in v. 16) *and did the signs, in the sight of the people.* These were such signs as had been directed to secure the faith of the people of Israel.—vs. 1–4. *And the people believed.* The signs were expressly given for this purpose (v. 5). All this strong evidence of God's interposition on their behalf, and of His regard for His people in their distress, filled them *with the spirit of devout worship.*

LESSONS.—(1) God's merciful visitations should provoke our grateful devotion. (2) Especially God's gracious interposition through Jesus Christ for our deliverance from the bondage of Sin and Satan ought to prompt our grateful praise. (3) God's servants are to do duty fearlessly and faithfully, and to leave results in His hands. (4) If the people truly believe, it is by a greater work than these miracles— even the Spirit's miracle upon the mind and heart. (5) How blessed in trouble is it to mark God's gracious presence and blessing. (6) We ought reverently to adore and worship our Great Deliverer and Saviour.

CHAP. V.

§ 10. MOSES AND AARON BEFORE PHARAOH AND THE SAD RESULTS. Ch. V. 1–23.

1. The first step has been taken. The covenant people believe in God. The Divinely commissioned brothers appear before Pharaoh and make their demand, according to the direction given by God Himself (ch. 4). *Thus saith the Lord God of Israel.* They had been told to speak of God as *the God of their fathers* (chs. 3, 4). It is probable that some of the elders accompanied them (ch. 3: 18). The immediate object only is mentioned to Pharaoh. To demand more, might have seemed extravagant. If he will not consent to the less, he will not consent to the greater. If he will grant this request, then, after that, they would

CHAPTER V.

2 And Pharaoh said, b Who *is* the LORD, that I should obey his voice to let Israel go? I know not the LORD, neither will I let Israel go.

3 And they said, the God of the c Hebrews hath met with us: let us go, we pray thee, three days' journey into the desert, and sacrifice unto the LORD our God; lest he fall upon us with pestilence, d or with the sword.

4 And the king of Egypt said unto them, Wherefore do ye, Moses and Aaron, let the people from their works? get you unto your burdens.

---

b 2Ki. 18: 35; Job 21: 15; Ps. 12: 4.   c ch. 3: 18.   d De. 28: 11; Eze. 6: 11.

---

ask more, and would more fully express their wishes. It is probable that Pharaoh would understand this as a simple request for religious service to their God, since all nations were wont to pay homage to their deities in festivals and sacrifices and in special places. *The wilderness*—outside of Egypt towards Canaan, as being retired and best suited for religious ceremonies. The King probably resided at *Zoan*, called *Avaris*. *A feast* would include all the service of sacrifice, etc. It is more fully explained in v. 3. The request was perfectly reasonable.

2. Pharaoh's reply is full of stubbornness and bravado, and indicates the hostility of his heart. *Who is Jehovah*, etc. He denies any relation or obligation to Jehovah; *I know not Jehovah*. Pharaoh denies all knowledge of this name, as though he had not heard of such a Being. It was the peculiar Redemptive name of God. He was a worshipper of the gods of Egypt. But his predecessors knew the God of Israel (Gen. 12: 17, 41; 43: 23). He may only not have known Him by this peculiar name. He positively refuses their request. The policy of the Pharaohs had been to keep this people in bondage.

3. These ambassadors reply in a way to enlighten him, explaining and adding particulars. *The God of the Hebrews*. This title he would understand. Besides it would show why they needed to go out of Egypt to sacrifice. *Hath met with us*. Another form of the word in ch. 3 · 18, rendered the same in both places. The *Gr*. and *Vulg*. render *hath called us*, hath revealed Himself to us. The distance is now given as the limit of this request (ch. 3: 18). And this is according to the Divine direction, so that there is no wicked dissembling. The request is made moderate, and Pharaoh knows of no ultimate plans, so that he is not irritated by any extravagant demand, and has full opportunity to show his wicked obstinacy and defiance. They plead as humble petitioners. *We pray thee—Lest*. They now declare themselves moved to this worship by the fear of all that God could do in punishing their neglect of His command, intimating thus to Pharaoh what he might expect if he should resist God. *With pestilence, or with the sword*. Such resources of penalty God has at command. Therefore it is no light thing to resist His claim.

4. Instead of granting them anything, the wicked King treats them with despotic severity—accuses Moses and Aaron, God's messengers, of *letting*—or hindering the people from their works as bond-slaves—and commands them and those who were with them (the elders) to get to their burdens—and go about their business as slaves, instead of agitating such a question of withdrawment from work for purposes of worship, or on such pretence.

5. Pharaoh now rebukes the

58   EXODUS.

5 And Pharaoh said, Behold, the people of the land now *are* many, and ye make them rest from their burdens.

6 And Pharaoh commanded the same day the task-masters of the people, and their officers, saying,

7 Ye shall no more give the people straw to make brick, as heretofore: let them go and gather straw for themselves.

8 And the tale of the bricks, which they did make heretofore, ye shall lay ᵉ upon them; ye shall not diminish *ought* thereof: for they *be* idle; therefore they cry, saying, Let us go *and* sacrifice to our God.

---
e Ps. 106: 41.
---

messengers, Moses and Aaron, as stirring up idle schemes among the numerous *people of the land*—of Goshen—or *land-people*—working people—in distinction from the ruling classes of the Egyptians (Ezek. 7: 27). Cessation from work, among so large a multitude, was, in the King's view, dangerous to the state. 6–9. The King would now rebuke the spirit of idleness and freedom which he suspected at the bottom of this movement. He will take prompt measures for crushing out the rising spirit of the people by increasing their burdens. *He commanded, the same day, the task-masters.* No time was to be lost, and his despotic passion, excited by the dignified attitude of the messengers, would be satisfied with no delay and no half measures. The *task-masters* were those Egyptian overseers who urged on the workmen with the whip or club. *And their officers* were the clerks of these task-masters, or overseers, who kept the accounts and gave out the allotment of work—the tale of brick. (See v. 14). These were Hebrews, who were placed over their brethren as *foremen*—like the Arab officers set over the Arab fellahs—the poor laborers in modern Egypt—as subordinates of Government officials —and held responsible for the performance of prescribed labor.— *Hengstenberg.* (See Deut. 20: 1 etc.) *Straw* was no longer to be supplied to the people *to make brick*. It was chopped straw mixed with the clay, which helped to make the brick and gave it firmness. The brick was not burnt, but dried in the sun. Such fine straw is found in the composition of Egyptian brick. *Rosellini* says, "The bricks which are now found in Egypt belonging to that period always have straw mingled with them, although in some of those that are most carefully made, it is found in small quantities." *Prokesch* says, "The bricks of the first Pyramid of Dashow, are of fine clay from the Nile mingled with chopped straw, which gives them an astonishing durability." We have handled these bricks, or such like in Egypt. The people were now to be compelled to gather their own straw and thus their burdens would be increased, while they were required to make the same *tale* (or account) of brick, as before. This was in order to oppress them more severely, and to crush their spirits; so as to discourage any plans for release. Their application was judged to be a mere pretence for getting rid of work. Much idleness and license is pleaded for in the name of religion. But irreligion also falsely accuses God's people of hypocrisy when they plead for their worship. *Let the work be heavy upon the men* —(more work be laid) *and they shall do in it* (stick to their work) *and not give heed to lying words.* So tyrannical is the world-power towards the people of God, willing to

CHAPTER V.

9 Let there more work be laid upon the men, that they may labour therein; and let them not regard vain ᶠ words.

10 And the task-masters of the people went out, and their officers, and they spake to the people, saying, Thus saith Pharaoh, I will not give you straw.

11 Go ye, get you straw where ye can find it: yet not ought of your work shall be diminished.

12 So the people were scattered abroad throughout all the land of Egypt, to gather stubble instead of straw.

13 And the task-masters hasted *them*, saying, Fulfil your works, *your* daily tasks, as when there was straw.

14 And the officers of the children of Israel, which Pharaoh's task-masters had set over them, were beaten, *and* demanded, Wherefore have ye not fulfilled your task in making brick, both yesterday and to-day, as heretofore?

15 Then the officers of the children of Israel came and cried unto Pharaoh, saying, Wherefore dealest thou thus with thy servants?

16 There is no straw given unto thy servants, and they say to us, Make brick: and, behold, thy servants *are* beaten, but the fault *is* in thine own people.

17 But he said, Ye *are* idle, *ye are* idle, therefore ye say, Let us go *and* do sacrifice to the LORD.

---

f 2Ki. 18: 20.

---

crush out the Church from the earth. The "lying words" were the statements of the messengers which were pronounced false by Pharaoh. So the Scripture is charged with being unhistorical, or fabulous, or a mere religious tradition, by scoffers of our day.

10-14. The command of Pharaoh was promptly made known to the Israelites. *Go ye, fetch to you straw from where you shall find it—for it is not diminished from your work, a thing*—anything. *So the people were dispersed in all the land of Egypt to gather stubble for the straw* (for this purpose)—the stubble left in the cornfields. Not *instead of* straw, but *for this purpose. The taskmasters were urgent* saying, *Fill up*—complete—*your works*—(Heb.) *the matter* (or business) *of a day in his day — your daily task — like as in there being the straw*—the same as when the straw was supplied to you. *The officers*—clerks, accountants, foremen—*of the children of Israel, were beaten.* These were Israelites, whom the taskmasters had set over the people as overseers, responsible for the full amount of work. The beating was by the *bastinado*, as is shown in the pictures found upon the Egyptian monuments. "Men and boys are laid prostrate on the ground and frequently held by the hands and feet, while the punishment is administered."—*Wilkinson, Rosellini,* cited by *Hengstenberg.* The time was in early spring—about April—when the *Chamsin*, or *sand-wind*, blows over Egypt, which would increase their suffering.

15-19. Complaint is now made by the foremen, of this cruel treatment, and the case is stated to the King, that the refusal to supply

EXODUS.

18 Go therefore now, *and* work; for there shall no straw be given you, yet shall ye deliver the tale of bricks.

19 And the officers of the children of Israel did see *that* they *were* in evil ᵍ case, after it was said, Ye shall not minish *aught* from your bricks of your daily task.

20 And they met Moses and Aaron, who stood in the way, as they came forth from Pharaoh;

21 And they said unto them, The LORD look upon you, and judge; because ye have made our savour to be abhorred ʰ in the eyes of Pharaoh, and in the eyes of his servants, to put a sword in their hand to slay us.

22 And Moses returned unto the LORD, and said, Lord, wherefore hast thou *so* evil-entreated ⁱ this people? why *is* it *that* thou hast sent me?

23 For since I came to Pharaoh to speak in thy name, he hath done evil to this people; neither hast thou delivered thy people at all.

g De. 32: 36; Ec. 4: 1; 5: 8. h Ge. 34: 30; 1Sa. 13: 4; 27: 12; 2Sa. 10: 6; 1Ch. 19: 6.
i Je. 20: 7; Ha. 2: 3.

straw, required their time and labor to gather it, and they could not fulfil the same task of brick as before. The charge of idleness and hypocrisy was repeated, as the only reply; while the demand of work was to be insisted on without any abatement. The Israelitish *officers* (*foremen*) saw the evil (case) they were in—(Heb) *saw them in evil, saying,* The King's unrelaxed order was the bitter cup for them, cutting off all hope from that quarter. 16. *The fault,* lit. *Thy people sin.* This was their complaint.

20, 21. *They met*—Heb.—*fell upon* —implying severity or hostility—the same verb as in v. 3. Moses and Aaron seem to have been waiting outside, to learn the result of their mission. The blame of their new hardships was cast upon Moses and Aaron. *Jehovah look upon you and judge*—condemn—*because ye have made the smell of us to stink before Pharaoh.* Their odor or repute was made most disgusting and repulsive to the King and *his servants*—the task-masters—*to give a sword into their hand to kill us.* This was declared to be the fatal working of Moses' and Aaron's mission. They had prejudiced the King by this application and had made him enraged against them as idlers, agitators, and vain pretenders, and so had only armed him with a sword for their ruin.

22, 23. Moses now brings the matter before Jehovah for explanation. *Wherefore hast thou done evil to this people.* He sees all his mission seemingly working damage instead of deliverance to the Israelites, and naturally he inquires why God has sent him. *Augustine* says " These are not words of contumacy or indignation, but of inquiry and prayer." The question and complaint, says *Delitzsch*, proceeded from faith which flies to God when it cannot understand the dealings of God. Trouble drives God's people to prayer,—and prayer brings the relief. Often God seems to work adversely at first in order to make the coming blessing more valued. The darkest moment is immediately before the dawn. " In the mount the Lord will be seen." We are prone to be impatient, and to take delays on God's part to be the evidences of

CHAPTER VI.

THEN the Lord said unto Moses, Now shalt thou see what [a] I will do to Pharaoh: for with a strong hand [b] shall he let them go, and with a strong hand shall he drive them [c] out of his land.

2 And God spake unto Moses, and said unto him, I *am* the Lord:

3 And I appeared unto Abraham, unto Isaac, and unto Jacob, by *the name of* God [d] Almighty; but by my name [e] JEHOVAH was I not known to them.

---

a 2Ch. 20: 17; Ps. 12: 5.   b Ps. 89: 13.   c ch. 11: 1.   d Ge. 17: 1; 35: 11; 48: 3.
e ch. 3: 14; Ps. 63: 4; 83: 18; Is. 42: 8; Jno. 8: 58; Re. 1; 4.

His unfaithfulness. So Moses and Aaron complain that all had worked badly since their coming, and that God had not delivered His people at all.

CHAPTER VI.

§ 11. JEHOVAH'S PROMISE—Ch. VI, 1—8.

The time has now come for God to work. Jehovah replies to Moses' complaints, *Now thou shalt see what I will do to Pharaoh.* This at once answers the complaints and shows that He has a plan for requiting Pharaoh. God does not move before the time to meet any cavil, but at the proper time He moves, and silences cavil and the caviller. "Only with thine eyes shalt thou behold and see the reward of the wicked."—Ps. 91. *With, or by a strong hand* he shall let them go (ch. 3: 19). The phrase is repeated with emphasis and applied to Pharaoh's actually driving them out of the land for fear of them. "Egypt was glad when they departed, for the fear of them fell upon them."—Ps. 105: 38.

2, 3. God deems it worth while at this solemn crisis of His judgment to announce Himself by His peculiar redemptive name, *I Jehovah.* He further associates this dealing with all the past covenant dealings, as all along moving forward in the sphere of Redemption. To the patriarchs He had not so fully revealed Himself as a personal Redeemer, but *By the name of God Almighty* Heb. *El Shaddai* (Gen. 17: 1.) This is the name which reveals God as Omnipotent. *Ewald* admits this name to be the expression of the thought of the Patriarchs, finding in it the truth, that "He who is alone rightly called the Almighty God, can only be One before whom all plurality and distinctions of Divine natures disappear." He was known to them as *El Shaddai, the Potent,* but not as Jehovah, *the Agent.* This peculiar name Jehovah was surely in common use before this time, (Genesis, ch. 2: 4,) where it appears first in combination with Elohim, (Gen. 4: 1) as used by Eve. So Exod. 3: 14, 16; 4: 1, shows it to have been familiar. At the institution of the covenant with Abraham, God said to him, I am *El Shaddai,* God Almighty—Omnipotent to perform. This incited faith in the promise. And so God wrought for him, to prove His omnipotency. Now there is a second step to be taken in the covenant working and in the development of God's Redeeming Plan. God is now and henceforth to show Himself as JEHOVAH, acting in the capacity of Redeemer in the first

4 And I have also established my covenant ᶠ with them, to give them the land of Canaan, the land of their pilgrimage, wherein they were strangers.

5 And I have also heard the ᵍ groaning of the children of Israel, whom the Egyptians keep in bondage ; and I have ʰ remembered my covenant.

6 Wherefore say unto the children of Israel, I *am* the LORD, and I will bring you out ⁱ from under the burdens of the Egyptians, and I will rid you out of their bondage; and I will ʲ redeem you with a stretched-out arm, and with great judgments :

7 And I will take you to me ᵏ for a people, and I will be to you a God : and ye shall know that I *am* the LORD your God, which bringeth you out from under the burdens of the Egyptians.

---

f Ge. 17: 7, 8.   g ch. 2 : 24; Ps. 106:44.   h Ps. 105: 8.   i De. 26: 8; Ps. 81: 6.
j ch. 15 : 13; De. 7: 8; 1Ch. 17: 21; Ne. 1: 10.   k De. 4: 20; 2Sa. 7: 24; Je. 31: 33; Ho. 1: 10; Re. 21: 3, 7.

---

great act of Redemption by means of a Personal Leader (Moses) as the type of the Personal Deliverer—the Messiah. - The meaning then is not that this name Jehovah had not been known, but that He was not known to them in this capacity, or with such Redeeming display as was now to be manifest. They had often used this name. Gen. 12: 1, 7, 8; 14: 22; 15: 2, 6; 17: 1; 18: 27; 31: 33; 22: 14; 25: 21; 28: 13, 16, 21. The name Jehovah already known is now to be made more fully and gloriously manifest.

4, 5. This name implies fidelity to a covenant. This is fixed as the basis of proceeding. He will act according to it, and will act up to it. And in making known His *name*, He will deliver them from bondage and will *give to them the Land of Canaan*. This latter, which is the result of the deliverance, is put first, for that is the great object and end in view. The fulfilment of promises already made would confirm their faith for the future. *I have established my covenant with them* (the fathers) Gen. 15 : 18 ; 17: 4, 7, *to give them*—this was the Divine territorial grant—*the Land of Canaan*—to them as a people—the land of their pilgrimage—where they dwelt in tents and had no inheritance (Heb. 11 :9 :) though heirs together of the country. There was to be a display of God's nature and purposes in the sphere of grace and Redemption more glorious than by any displays of miraculous powers. Besides the time had come for God to work and fulfil his covenant promise—'*For I have heard the groanings*,' etc. 'Man's extremity is God's opportunity.' *Whom the Egyptians keep in bondage*—so persistently—*and I have remembered my covenant*. It had not passed from His mind. He kept it in vivid remembrance both as to the thing promised and as to the time for the performance.—Gen. 15: 10, 11.

6, 7. *Wherefore say*—God now authorizes the public announcement of His purpose prefacing the declaration by His Redemptive *Name*. *I am Jehovah*—and in pursuance of this title, *I will bring you out*, etc.—with *a stretched out arm*, v. 1. This indicates the *great* '*judgment*' which he undertakes to execute. *And I will take you to me for a people*. This is the covenant relation which He now is to establish with them *as a people*. It had been instituted with their fathers

CHAPTER VI.   63

8 And I will bring you in unto the land, concerning the which I did swear to give it to Abraham, to Isaac, and to Jacob; and I will give it you for an heritage: I *am* the LORD.

9 And Moses spake so unto the children of Israel: but they hearkened not ¹ unto Moses for anguish of spirit, and for cruel bondage.

10 And the LORD spake unto Moses, saying,

11 Go in, speak unto Pharaoh king of Egypt, that he let the children of Israel go out of his land.

12 And Moses spake before the LORD, saying, Behold, the children of Israel have ᵐ not hearkened unto me; how then shall Pharaoh hear me, who *am* of ⁿ uncircumcised lips?

13 And the Lord spake unto Moses and unto Aaron, and

---

l ch. 5: 21.   m Ver. 9.   n Ver. 30; Le . 26: 41; Je. 9: 26; Ac. 7: 51.

---

when they were only *a family.* Now, since their development in Egypt from a *family* to a *Nation,* God will formally establish His covenant relation to them in this new light. See Deut. 29: 13. The formal adoption of Israel as a nation took place at Sinai (ch. 19: 5.) There He will make Himself known to them as *Jehovah, your* (covenant) *God, which bringeth you out,* etc.—Exod. 30: 2.

8. He will also bring them into Canaan—*which I have lifted up my hand to give it,* etc,—the gesture of an oath, lifting the hand towards heaven. Deut. 32: 40. Comp. Gen. 14; 22. ¶ *I the Lord (Jehovah)* will do it.

LESSONS.—(1) God will have His people see what He can do. (2) God reveals Himself as Redeemer by His gracious redemptive works. In daily Providence He shows Himself to us as the God of grace. (3) To the mere reason God shows Himself as Creator. But there is a time when to each of His own people He makes Himself known as Redeemer, Saviour. (4) God's glory is to reveal Himself to us in grace as our covenant Jehovah. (5) God claims that He is ours, and we are His—and blessed are they who see and rejoice in this relation. (6) God remembers His covenant with the fathers, and blessed are they who honor and prize the household covenant and seals. (7) It is a high privilege to be the believing children of pious parents. It is a great disgrace to disown or deny our fathers' God.

§ 12. MOSES' DISCOURAGEMENT. — GOD'S COMMAND.—THEIR GENEALOGIES.—Ch. VI, 9–30.

9. *For anguish,* (Heb.) *for shortness of breath, or straitness of spirit*—depression. The severity of their bondage crushed their hope and did not allow any confidence. The different condition of the people led to a different reception from that in ch. 4: 31.

10-12. Again Jehovah bids Moses go in unto Pharaoh and make his demand. Moses objects that already he has failed to impress the people of Israel, and *how then shall Pharaoh hear me, who* (am) *of uncircumcised lips,* (Chald.) *of heavy speech.* (Gr.) $\alpha\lambda o\gamma o\varsigma$ *without speech,* the lips covered with a foreskin hindering the words, is the first idea—hesitating speech —without fluency. So here. See v. 30. (Then the lips *unrenewed*—as circumcision was a token of renewal of nature.) (Syr.) *Mine is a stammering tongue.* See ch. 4: 10. See also v. 30. There the objection is more fully answered. No natural defect is meant.

13. This repeated objection is

gave them a ° charge unto the children of Israel, and unto Pharaoh king of Egypt, to bring the children of Israel out of the land of Egypt.

14 These *be* the heads of their fathers' houses: P the sons of Reuben, the first-born of Israel; Hanoch, and Pallu, Hezron, and Carmi: these *be* the families of Reuben.

15 And q the sons of Simeon; Jemuel, and Jamin, and Ohad, and Jachin, and Zohar, and Shaul, the son of a Canaanitish woman: these *are* the families of Simeon.

16 And these *are* the names of the sons of r Levi, according to their generations: Gershon, and Kohath, and Merari. And the years of the life of Levi *were* an hundred thirty and seven years.

17 The sons of Gershon; Libni and Shimi, according to their families.

18 And the sons of Kohath; s Amram, and Izhar, and Hebron, and Uzziel. And the years of the life of Kohath *were* an hundred thirty and three years.

---

o Nu. 27: 19, 23; De. 31: 14. p Ge. 46: 9, &c.; 1Ch. 5: 3.   q 1Ch. 4: 24.   r Nu. 3: 17; 1 Ch. 6: 1.

---

met by a repeated charge to go forward to the work of deliverance. Before proceeding further in the narrative, the record is here given in brief of the genealogy of Moses and Aaron. For these men stand in special relation to the family and nation of Israel, just as the deliverance which they are charged to effect stands as the first great historical type of the redemption by Christ Jesus, under a Personal Lawgiver, Mediator, Prophet, and Leader, MOSES. Properly enough, therefore, the historian would here give their genealogy in connection with this eminent work to which they are called.

14–17. *These are the heads of their fathers' houses.* A question is raised here whether these are the genealogies of three tribes, or even of the tribe of Levi for four generations, or only a genealogy of the heads of Israelite families and of a few names conspicuous in the history. It is plainly the latter. According to the methods of genealogy in Israel there were subdivisions into tribes, thence into the families—*mishpachoth*—and these into the larger divisions, the *fathers' houses*. The names are given of such of Reuben's and Simeon's sons as were the founders of families, and then Levi and his three sons are given as he was the tribefather of Moses and Aaron. Amram, the son of Kohath, was not the same Amram as the father of Moses, and an indefinitely long list of generations has been omitted between the former and his descendant of the same name. *Colenso* claims that we have the entire list here, and that there is only an increase of one thousand in 38 years, whereas it should have been an increase of some 26,000, according to the rates of English increase. All this inference from English increase is arbitrary and the *assumption* that the whole list is given is the false ground of his objection to this part of the history. Besides, Colenso claims that the Exodus was in the *fourth descent,* or that of grandsons, grandsons of the Patriarchs, which is sheer mistake. This question is treated at length by *Birks* on *the*

CHAPTER VI. 65

19 And the sons of Merari; Mahali, and Mushi; these *are* the families of Levi, according to their generations.

20 And Amram took him Jochebed, his father's sister, to wife; and she bare him Aaron and Moses. And the years of the life of Amram *were* an hundred and thirty and seven years.

21 And the sons of Izhar; ᵗ Korah, and Nepheg, and Zichri.

22 And the sons of Uzziel; ᵘ Mishael, and Elzaphan, and Zithri.

23 And Aaron took him Elisheba, daughter of ᵛ Amminadab, sister of Naashon, to wife; and she bare him ʷ Nadab, and Abihu, Eleazar, and Ithamar.

24 And the sons of Korah; Assir, and Elkanah, Abiasaph; these *are* the families of the Korhites.

25 And Eleazar, Aaron's son, took him *one* of the daughters of Putiel to wife: and she bare him Phinehas; ˣ these *are* the heads of the fathers of the Levites, according to their families.

26 These *are* that Aaron and Moses, to whom the LORD said, Bring out the children of Israel from the land of Egypt according to their armies.

27 These *are* they which spake to ʸ Pharaoh king of Egypt,

---

s Nu. 26: 57. t Nu. 16: 1. u Le. 10: 4. v Ru. 4: 19. w 1Ch. 6: 3; 24: 1. x Jos. 24: 33.

Exodus of Israel. See also *Delitzsch* and *Murphy*.

20. We are brought down in the list to the parentage of Moses and Aaron. Amram married his aunt, as was allowed at that day, though afterwards forbidden, (Lev. 18). See ch 2: 1. It is not to be supposed that these were the only children of Amram. He was, probably, about a hundred years old at Moses' birth, and it is not likely that these were all his children—Moses, Aaron and Miriam—both the latter elder than Moses. (Numb. 26: 59.) The list is given so far as any names of interest in the after history are concerned, Korah (Num. 16.) Uzziel's sons (Lev. 10: 4.) The genealogy traces the descent of the leading priestly families. Aaron's and Eleazar's wives are given.

23. *Elisheba.* (Gr.) Ελισαβετ—*Elizabeth.* She was the fifth in descent from *Judah*, while Aaron was only the fourth from Levi by his father's side and the third by his mother's. This shows the disparity in the number of generations in different lines. Aaron's sons occur in the history hereafter. None of the sons of Moses are mentioned in this list, because his dignity did not descend in any line as Aaron's.

24. *The sons of Korah.* See Num. 26: 11.

25. *Phinehas*—the sixth [inclusive] from Levi and the seventh from Judah.

Plainly these fragments from the genealogical tables are inserted here with an object to make clear the position of these ambassadors in their relation to the covenant family and nation.

26, 27. *These are that Aaron and Moses.* These are the men, and this is their lineage. Aaron's name is here given first, as the elder and the representative of the

to bring out the children of Israel ᶻ from Egypt; these *are* that Moses and Aaron.

28 And it came to pass on the day *when* the LORD spake unto Moses in the land of Egypt,

29 That the LORD spake unto Moses, saying, I *am* the LORD; speak thou unto Pharaoh king of Egypt all ᵃ that I say unto thee.

30 And Moses said before the LORD, Behold, I *am* of ᵇ uncircumcised lips, and how shall Pharaoh hearken unto me?

CHAPTER VII.

AND the LORD said unto Moses, See, I have made thee a god ᵃ to Pharaoh; and Aaron thy brother shall be thy prophet.

2 Thou shalt speak all ᵇ that I command thee; and Aaron thy brother shall speak unto Pharaoh, that he send the children of Israel out of his land.

---

z ch. 33: 1; Ps. 77: 20; Mi. 6: 4.   a Je. 1; 7, 8, 17; 23: 28; 26: 2; Eze. 2: 6, 7; 3: 11; Ma. 28: 20.   b Ver. 12.   a Ps. 82: 6; Jno. 10: 35.   b ch. 6: 29.

---

line of Levi. But in v. 27, where the connection is with the subsequent history, the order is reversed,:*These, are that Moses and Aaron,*' as Moses was to take the leading part.

28. Here the history of the deliverance is resumed from v. 12.

29. I AM JEHOVAH. Thus He is making Himself known by His name *Jehovah*—Covenant God and Redeemer. This is the ample warrant for Moses to go forward, not fearing the face of man.

30. Moses repeats his objection from personal infirmity, as already noticed, and God will most fully meet it now.

CHAPTER VII.

§ 13. MIRACLE ACCREDITING THEIR MISSION. Ch. VII: 1-13.

It is commonly admitted that the deliverance of Israel must have resulted not from an uprising of the dependent and powerless people, nor from a foreign invasion, but from heavy calamities forcing at length a surrender which the government could no longer refuse or prevent. *Stanley* says that, "In all outward appearance, as the chief of the Tribe of Levi, as the head of the family of Amram, as the spokesman and interpreter, as the first who spake to the people and to Pharaoh all the words which the Lord had spoken to Moses and who did the signs in the sight of the people, as the permanent inheritor of the sacred staff or rod, the emblem of rule and power, Aaron, not Moses, must have been the representative and leader of Israel. But Moses was the inspiring, informing soul within and behind—and Moses the dumb, backward, disinterested prophet continues for all ages the foremost leader of the chosen People, the witness that something more is needed for man's guidance than the high, hereditary office, or the gift of fluent speech."—*Jewish Hist.* p. 127.

1, 2. *See, I have made thee a god to Pharaoh.* He was appointed, constituted God's representative in dealing with Pharaoh, armed with Divine judgments, etc. In ch. 4: 16, Moses was to be a god to Aaron, and Aaron is here to be his prophet to announce to Pharaoh the Divine

CHAPTER VII.

3 And I will ^c harden Pharaoh's heart, and multiply my signs and my wonders in the land of Egypt.

4 But Pharaoh shall not hearken unto you, that I may lay my hand upon Egypt, and bring forth mine armies, *and* my people the children of Israel, out of the land of Egypt by great judgments.

5 And the Egyptians shall know that I *am* the ^d LORD, when I stretch forth mine hand upon Egypt, and bring out the children of Israel from among them.

6 And Moses and Aaron did as the Lord commanded them, so did they.

7 And Moses *was* fourscore years old, and Aaron fourscore and three years old, when they spake unto Pharaoh.

8 And the Lord spake unto Moses and unto Aaron, saying,

9 When Pharaoh shall speak unto you, saying, Shew a miracle ^e for you; then thou shalt say unto Aaron, Take thy rod, and cast *it* before Pharaoh, *and* it shall become a serpent.

---

c ch. 11: 9.   d ch. 14: 4, 18; Ps. 9: 16.   e Matt. 12: 39; Jno. 2: 18.

---

revelations given to Moses. Their respective work is here laid down—what part each of them is to act in the great mission—*that he send.* Rather—*And so he will send.*

3. Here the part of God in the matter is revealed beforehand in that awful process of heart-hardening. Here the word means "I will *indurate*"—*make obstinate.* God's agency to this effect, as we have seen, was no severity, but only the natural working of the Divine dealing upon a depraved heart, whereas the effect would have been the very opposite upon a virtuous nature. God however, has his plans, and no Pharaoh can baffle them. He proposes in the same great programme, to *multiply His signs and His wonders* in the land of Egypt. These ought to have broken down his opposition and enlightened his mind in the knowledge of God. But they were the means of making him harder, not the cause of the hardening.

4. *But Pharaoh shall not hearken.,* lit., *will not hear.* There is nothing imperative here. *That I may lay,* etc., lit., *and I will lay my hand,* etc. The nation of Egypt was to be scourged for the sin of the king, because they were represented by him and sympathized with him, and were held righteously answerable. *My hosts, my armies.* This refers to them as going forth in military array.—ch. 13: 18; 12: 51. Comp. Num. 1, 6.

5. The effect upon the Egyptians is here stated. *They shall know that I am Jehovah.* Not merely to deliver Israel would He work these miracles, but to destroy in Egypt the system of their idolatry.

6. The venerable age of these brother messengers is now given as eighty and eighty-three—every way calculated to command respect and attention. This was their prime —and not more than *forty* now, in proportion to the average lifetime.

8, 9. Direction is now given for satisfying Pharaoh's demand for evidence of their Divine commissions. *Shew a miracle for you,* Heb. *Give a miracle* (omen) *for you.* This was in the tone of challenge—not pledging himself to be convinced—but rather defying them to do anything supernatural. A miracle was recognized as the sufficient attestation of a Divine commission. It belongs to the very idea of God to infer

10 And Moses and Aaron went in unto Pharaoh, and they did so as the LORD had commanded; and Aaron cast down his rod before Pharaoh, and before his servants, and it became a serpent.

11 Then Pharaoh also called the wise men and † the sorcerers; now the magicians of Egypt, they also did in like manner with their enchantments.

---

† Da. 2: 2; 2Ti. 3: 8.

---

that He will not put His Divine impress upon any imposture. Moses was to give direction from God to Aaron, and Aaron was to work the supernatural sign. Aaron was to cast down his rod (of power) before Pharaoh and it would become a serpent. Here the term is *Tannin*. It is rendered a *dragon*, as in Malachi. So the *Sept.*—a general term for the *snake*. It may have been the *asp* or *basilisk*, which was the emblem of royalty in Egypt. It is applied also to the *crocodile*, as a symbol of Egypt. Aaron's rod was the same as Moses' (ch. 4: 2–4). Comp. vs. 15, 17 with 19 and 20. This sign was chosen because the art of snake-charming was so prevalent in Egypt. These charmers boasted that they could turn a stick to a snake, and snakes into sticks. Moses was to awe them by performing the reality. They were skilled in making the snake to appear stiff and lifeless as a stick, and then they recovered it again. *Bush* thinks it was a *crocodile* (Ps. 74: 13). In v. 15 and in ch. 4: 3 the animal is called *nahhash*, a different kind of snake or serpent as better suited to the people of Israel before whom the miracle was first performed.

11. The contest opens now between the gods of Egypt and the God of the Hebrews. Pharaoh now summons *the magicians*. They were not the adroit and supple conjurers and tricksters, like Simon Magus at Samaria, whose profession was by secret arts and incantations to do wonders. But they were the *wise men*, educated in Divine wisdom, and of the priestly caste. The question whether they really wrought miracles involves the question how far God may allow to Satanic agencies any supernatural work for a purpose. The theory of Arnold and others, that a miracle can be wrought by Satan, and that you must first learn whether the miracle before you is wrought in the interest of good or evil, before you can decide what it attests, is fallacious, for precisely what we want to know by the miracle is whether the cause that is served by it, is good or evil. *Paul* refers to these magicians and names two of them, *Jannes and Jambres* (2 Tim. 3: 8). And as these professional magicians — *magi—Chartummim—* were of the priestly caste, the power of their gods was represented in their machinations. And their defeat by the messengers of Jehovah, was a defeat of Egypt's gods (ch. 12: 12). *They did in like manner with their enchantments—also they*—so; means 1st they did this thing after a fashion, *with their enchantments*, making it to appear by their skilful arts *in like manner*—as if it had been done. So in ch. 8: 18 it is recorded "And the magicians did so with their enchantments to bring forth lice, *but they could not.*"

12. *For they cast down every man his rod, and they became serpents. Bush* thinks it should be rendered —*that they might become serpents.* But there is no objection to the received reading. They became serpents, after a fashion—it is not said whether by natural or preternatural means, only that from the whole narrative we infer that it

12 For they cast down every man his rod, and they became serpents; but Aaron's rod swallowed up their rods.

13 And he hardened Pharaoh's heart, that he hearkened not unto them; as the ᵍ Lord had said.

14 And the Lord said unto Moses, Pharaoh's heart *is* hardened, ʰ he refuseth ⁱ to let the people go.

---

g Ver. 4.   h ch. 8: 15; 10: 1, 27.   i Je. 8: 5; Ho. 12: 25.

was a mere illusion and sham, according to their occult science. *But Aaron's rod*, etc. This is the great fact that settles the question between them. The Divine power is triumphant. The magicians' rods were *rods* still, and not serpents, and Aaron's had life to swallow up the rods of the magicians. Pharaoh had summoned these magicians to try their skill in the same direction so as to confound these messengers who boasted a Divine commission, and so as to show the gods of Egypt to be equal to those of the Hebrews. These magicians were counted *holy* among the Egyptians, and so the wonder-working stood connected with their religious faith and their system of idolatry. Many, such as Augustine, Calvin, Delitzsch, Hengstenberg, Trench, etc., think that the magicians in Egypt stood in relation to a spiritual kingdom as really as did Moses and Aaron, and that their feats were not indeed miracles in the sense of $\sigma\eta\mu\epsilon\iota\alpha\ \delta\nu\nu\alpha\mu\epsilon\iota\varsigma$, yet they were of the style of $\tau\epsilon\rho\alpha\tau\alpha$, prodigies—lying wonders (2 Thess. 2: 9) intended to support a Pantheism, a religion of nature which rendered homage to evil spirits, serpent-worship being a principal part of the system. And their power over serpents was that by which these Magi principally supported the dignity of their order as a guild. An assault upon this, therefore, properly enough, opened the religious contest. And when Aaron's rod swallowed up theirs, the symbol of their office was gone, and the *baton* of their power was missing. *Pharaoh*, however, was fain to believe that their power was of the same sort with that of the Divine messengers, and so his heart was hardend.

13. *And he hardened*, etc. This is the same phrase as in v. 22, and should be read the same—"*And Pharaoh's heart was hardened*—lit. *—became firm, strong, unyielding.*" The result was according as Jehovah had said. The cause was the heart-hardening of Pharaoh.

§ 14. The First Plague. Ch. VII: 14–25.

14. Jehovah now makes distinct announcement to Moses of the fact in regard to Pharaoh's stupid insensibility and refusal. The term used here is not the same as in the previous verse, but it is the verb meaning *to be heavy*. *Pharaoh's heart is heavy, insensible, stupid.* He vainly concluded that the Divine messengers were sufficiently matched by the magicians, or else perhaps the signal defeat of these latter vexed him, so as to provoke him to a sterner refusal. God does not interfere to compel Pharaoh's compliance. He will work by means, and leave the responsibility with the creature. *Murphy* calculates that this was about *Jan.* 20.

The plagues are *ten* in number—and this is the number denoting perfection. The last, however, was the extra and crowning one, which may be separated from the rest leaving nine, which may be ranged into threes. In the first of each three the warning is given to Pharaoh in the morning (7: 15; 8: 20; 9: 13). In the first and second of each three the plague is announced beforehand (8: 1; 9: 1; 10: 1). In the third not

70   EXODUS.

15 Get thee unto Pharaoh in the morning; lo, he goeth out unto the water; and thou shalt stand by the river's brink against he come; and the rod which was turned to a serpent ʲ shalt thou take in thine hand.

16 And thou shalt say unto him, The LORD God of the ᵏ Hebrews hath sent me unto thee, saying, Let my people go, ˡ that they may serve me in the wilderness, and, behold, hitherto thou wouldest not hear.

17 Thus saith the LORD, In this thou shalt know that I *am* ᵐ the LORD: behold, I will smite with the rod that *is* in mine hand upon the waters which *are* in the river, and they shall be turned ⁿ to blood.

---

j Ver. 10. k ch. 3: 18. l ch. 8: 1, &c. m Ver. 5; 1Sa. 17: 46; 1Ki. 20: 28; 2Ki. 19: 19; Eze. 29: 9; 30: 8; 38: 23. n Ps. 78: 44; 105: 29.

(8: 16; 9: 8; 10: 21). At the third the magicians of Pharaoh acknowledge the finger of God (8: 19). At the sixth they cannot stand before Moses (9: 11). And at the ninth Pharaoh refuses to see the face of Moses any more (10: 28). In the first three Aaron uses the rod. In the second three it is not mentioned. In the last three Moses uses it, though in the last one of these only his hand is mentioned. All these marks of order lie on the face of the narrative, and they point to a deeper order of nature and of reason out of which they spring. See *Murphy.* "In the first three signs the superior power of the God of Israel made itself sufficiently known to any one who did not studiously seek a support for his unbelief and rebellion." *Hengstenberg,* "The contest was first intentionally carried on in a sphere in which the Egyptian magicians, as we certainly know with reference to the first sign, had hitherto shown their principal power. After they had there been vanquished, the scene was changed to a sphere in which they could not at all further contend, and the doom which, in this way, came upon them fell through them upon their gods." "The gradation in the severity of the strokes is also obvious. In the first three no distinction is made between the inhabitants of the land. In the remaining seven the Israelites are shielded, and the Egyptians are exposed to the stroke. In these seven which are peculiar to the Egyptians, the order of the work of creation is reversed. Three refer to the animal and three to the vegetable world—the support of animal life. The last of these six is darkness the opposite of light (the product of the first day) and the seventh is death. The first three strike at the health and comfort. The next three strike away the staff of life. Then comes death itself—and so the destruction is complete."—*Murphy.*

15. *Lo! he goeth out,* etc. Doubtless it was to pay his daily homage to the sacred river, which the Egyptians regarded as their supreme Deity (ch. 2: 5). It was to the land the source of almost every blessing, for drink, for bathing, for irrigation, for planting of the bottom lands, over which it spread in its rise, by dropping the seed in the soft soil as it subsided.

16. Pharaoh is to be met on the bank of the sacred stream, and reminded of Moses' commission and of his refusal hitherto. *The Lord* —lit. *Jehovah.*

17. Pharaoh is now notified of the awful proof which Jehovah will give of Himself. *The rod* in Moses' hand was that which had been already used as an instrument

18 And the fish that *is* in the river shall die, and the river shall stink; and the Egyptians shall loath to drink of the water of the river.

19 And the LORD spake unto Moses, Say unto Aaron, Take thy rod, and stretch out thine hand upon the waters of Egypt, upon their streams, upon their rivers, and upon their ponds, and upon all their pools of water, that they may become blood; and *that* there may be blood throughout all the land of Egypt, both in *vessels of* wood, and in *vessels of* stone.

---

of Divine power. Now the effects of smiting the river with it are notified beforehand that the King might see the intelligent will and plan of Jehovah in it all. It is supposed by some that this was on the occasion of a public religious ceremony—probably after harvest at the annual rise of the river called the Red Nile, in June, when certain rites were performed in presence of the King to the River-God *Nu* or *Noah*—and a wooden statue of the River-God was carried through the villages on these occasions. But it is more probable that the miracle was wrought at a different season—in February. The Nile Divinity is known in the Inscriptions as "the Life-Giving father of all existences." *Blood.* It is remarkable that when the Nile rises, the water is very red in color, as if from deposits of red earth brought down by the swollen streams. *Ehrenberg* has found it, on analysis, owing to cryptogamic plants and infusoria. This phenomenon therefore was now wrought in a way to be miraculous and most severe. For the *red water* is most drinkable and delicious to the people. But this *blood-red* water becomes now offensive and death dealing! This would show how superior Jehovah must be to the *River-God* whom they worshipped.

19. Aaron was now, at Moses' direction, to use the rod for these threatened results. There was but one River in the land. But it had *streams,* or *arms*—branches—in the Delta where it runs into the sea.

Their rivers—the canals by which they watered the fields—*ponds*—large masses of standing water after the subsidence of the river—a marshy lake like *Mœris*—and *all their pools* of water—either other lakes or any artificial reservoirs for such as were distant—were turned to blood. The blood, into which the water was thus miraculously converted, was throughout all the land—*in wood and in stone* (vessels) as reservoirs for catching the overflow, or wherever it was kept for daily use of the people. This may also include the earthen conduits and hydrants for public use. There were also vessels of wood and stone for filtering the water. The phenomenon was taken out of the sphere of natural events by the notice given, and the immediate result following upon this use of the rod and the disastrous effect as threatened. Some suppose the blood was meant to symbolize the destruction of the enemies of Israel, and to remind Pharaoh of his bloody deeds. The Nile commonly begins to rise about the end of June, and attains to its height at the close of September. The miracle was wholly different from the annual reddening of the waters, however it may have seemed in the color to wear the aspect of blessing, in the result it was full of curse. *Murphy* instances thus— (1) It occurred at a different season of the year. (2) The water was not merely reddened, it was turned into blood. (3) The fish died as was not the case otherwise. (4) The river became offensive, quite opposite to

20 And Moses and Aaron did so, as the LORD commanded; and he lifted up the rod, and smote ᵒ the waters that *were* in the river, in the sight of Pharaoh, and in the sight of his servants; and all the waters that *were* in the river were turned to blood.

21 And the fish that *was* in the river died; and the river stank, and the Egyptians could not drink ᵖ of the water of the river; and there was blood throughout all the land of Egypt.

22 And the magicians of Egypt did ᑫ *so* with their enchantments; and Pharaoh's heart was hardened, neither did he hearken unto them; as the Lord had said.

23 And Pharaoh turned and went into his house, neither did he set his ʳ heart to this also.

---

o ch. 17: 5; Nu. 20: 11. p Ver. 18. q 2 Ti. 3: 8. r Is. 26: 11; Je. 5: 3; 36: 24; Hag. 1: 5.

---

the case in the ordinary reddening. (5) The miracle lasted seven days, whereas the common reddening lasted some three weeks. No one can imagine how awful this blow was in its disappointing and death-dealing effects. There was an object in working within the sphere of the natural phenomena, yet in a supernatural way, to show that God is the author of both the natural and the supernatural. There is no intimation here given of an overflow of the river, as if it were anywise connected with the annual phenomenon of reddening. Pharaoh walks to the river, brink and the people dig around the river for water. The water becomes putrid, which is indicative of no overflow. *Hengstenberg* thinks that this occurred at the time of the annual overflow and reddening, and that through the whole cycle of nine months God wrought, in connection with the ordinarily recurring circle of natural phenomena. *Kurtz* and others, however, reckoning from what is known of the dates, infer that not more than *nine weeks* were occupied in the whole list of plagues. *Vol. II*, p. 269. See ch. 9: 13. *Note.*

22–23. *The magicians—chartummim*—that is, the *sacred scribes.* Two of these are named in the New Testament, *Jannes* and *Jambres*—2 Tim. 3:8. These names mean *scribes* of divers sorts. They were masters of occult arts. When the kingdom of light is to be advanced, the kingdom of darkness always rallies its forces to resist it. In the 11th verse other terms are used meaning *wise men—magi.* Observe, *they did so*, not the very thing, but *like* it, with their *enchantments.* The *magicians* strove to imitate this wonder-working so as to sustain their idolatrous system, and not succumb to the Hebrew God Jehovah. There was little pure water to practise upon; but enough for the experiment, it would seem, and it was the Nile water, and not that in wells, that was spoiled; and, so far, the power which they were allowed to wield was in punishment, for it only added to the plague by spoiling more water, though it was a sham of theirs. Easily enough some coloring matter, or blood itself, might convert a small portion into the semblance of blood, like the liquefaction of St. Januarius' blood by the monks at Naples. Why did not they convert the bloody water into a pure, refreshing drink, such as the people needed? It was when *the magicians did so with their enchantments that Pharaoh's heart was hardened. He turned and went into his house,* chagrined, but unyielding. If he had been well dis-

24 And all the Egyptians digged round about the river for water to drink; for they could not drink of the water of the river.

25 And seven days were fulfilled, after that the Lord had smitten the river.

CHAPTER VIII.

AND the Lord spake unto Moses, Go unto Pharaoh, and say unto him, Thus saith the Lord, Let my people go, that they may serve me.

---

posed these poor cheats would have been detected. *To this also. Neither did he set his heart even to this*—to heed this, or be moved by this sign—though so much more fearful and damaging than the previous sign.

24. Pharaoh worshipped nature, in forms of base idolatry to natural laws. What desperate resorts men will make to relieve themselves, if possible, from God's judgments, rather than believe, or bow to the stroke. *Digged round about*, etc., so as to get some water from springs, or through the filtering of the sand.

25. The plague lasted a whole week. *Keil* and *Delitzsch* think it probable that this first plague occurred in September or October, and that the plague of hail, the seventh plague, was in February.

Stanley says: "It is impossible, as we read the description of the plagues, not to feel how much of force is added to it by a knowledge of the peculiar customs and character of the country in which they occurred. It is not an ordinary river that is turned into blood. It is the sacred, beneficent, solitary Nile, the very life of the State and of the people, in its streams and canals, and tanks, and vessels of wood and vessels of stone, then, as now, used for the filtration of the water from the sediment of the river bed. It is not an ordinary nation that is struck by the mass of putrefying vermin lying in heaps in the houses, the villages, and the fields, or multiplying out of the dust of the desert sands on each side of the Nile valley. It is the cleanliest of all the ancient nations, clothed in white linen, anticipating in their fastidious delicacy and ceremonial purity the habits of modern and northern Europe. It is not the ordinary cattle that died in the field, or ordinary fish that died in the river, or ordinary reptiles that were overcome by the rod of Aaron. It is the sacred goat of Mendes—the ram of Ammon—the calf of Heliopolis—the Bull Apis—the crocodile of Ombos—the carp of Latopolis. It is not an ordinary land of which the flax and the barley, and every green thing in the trees, and every herb of the field are smitten by the two great calamities of storm and locusts. It is the garden of the ancient Eastern world—the long line of green meadow and cornfield, and groves of palm and sycamore and fig-tree, from the Cataracts to the Delta; doubly refreshing from the desert which it intersects, doubly marvellous from the river whence it springs. If these signs were calamities anywhere, they were truly 'signs and wonders'—speaking signs and oracular wonders—in such a land as 'the land of Ham.'"—*Hist. of Jewish Ch.*, p. 131.

CHAPTER VIII.

§ 15. The Second Plague—Frogs. Ch. VIII: 1-15.

1-3. Moses is bidden to repeat his formal demand upon Pharaoh for the release of His people in or-

2 And if thou refuse to let *them* go, behold, I will smite all thy borders with frogs:

3 And the river shall bring forth frogs abundantly, which shall go up and come into thine house, and into thy bed-chamber, and upon thy bed, and into the house of thy servants, and upon thy people, and into thine ovens, and into thy kneading-troughs;

4 And the frogs shall come up, both on thee and upon thy people, and upon all thy servants.

5 And the LORD spake unto Moses, Say unto Aaron, Stretch forth thine hand with thy rod over the streams, over the rivers, and over the ponds, and cause frogs to come up upon the land of Egypt.

6 And Aaron stretched out his hand over the waters of Egypt: and the frogs a came up, and covered the land of Egypt.

7 And the magicians did so with their enchantments, and brought up frogs upon the land of Egypt.

---

a Ps. 78: 45; 105: 30.

---

der to a special religious service. He is moreover fairly notified what will be the penalty of refusal. This was announced to the King in his Palace, not at the River as before. The Plague now threatened is that of *Frogs*. These were familiar as belonging to the river Nile. But the miracle consisted in their immense and sudden multiplication, so as to swarm from the river at the lifting of the rod in Aaron's hand—*all thy borders*—the whole land—*behold I am smiting*—just ready to smite,—as a penal infliction—with these frogs. *And the river shall bring forth frogs abundantly—shall swarm with frogs.* (See Gen. 1: 20, where the verb used is the same.) They were to come up into the King's *bed-chamber*, and *upon his bed*. The *chambers* were often on the ground-floor, and the *bed* was a mat on the floor, or a *divan* raised a short distance above it. The *Ovens* were either a hole dug in the ground, and plastered round with mortar, or, an earthen pot, with a hole in the bottom for letting out the ashes. The fire is placed inside, and the dough laid on the outer surface, or on the inner surface after the fire was removed. Thus they infested all quarters, interfering with all domestic and personal comfort. These leaping, loathsome creatures everywhere. Yet the frog was one of the sacred animals of the Egyptians, and thus their idolatry was punished. *Kneading troughs*. These were bowls or troughs of wood or wicker-work. And according to the size they used the hands or the feet in working the dough. But the frogs even found their way hither, where they wished to put the flour for their bread.

4. The Plague should spare none from highest to lowest.

5, 6. What answer, if any, Pharaoh made to this demand is not recorded. He gave no satisfaction and the Plague was brought upon him as was threatened. The miracle consisted in their swarming so abundantly without any natural cause, but by the supernatural power represented by the uplifted rod, and in its coming to pass promptly in obedience to the signal, as could be by Divine power only.

7. *The magicians did so with their enchantments*—imitating the

CHAPTER VIII.

8 Then Pharaoh called for Moses and Aaron, and said, ^b Intreat the Lord, that he may take away the frogs from me, and from my people; and I will let the people go, that they may do sacrifice unto the Lord.

9 And Moses said unto Pharaoh, Glory over me: when shall I entreat for thee, and for thy servants, and for thy people, to destroy the frogs from thee and thy houses, *that* they may remain in the river only?

10 And he said, To-morrow. And he said, *Be it* according to thy word; that thou mayest know that ^c *there is* none like unto the Lord our God.

11 And the frogs shall depart from thee, and from thy houses, and from thy servants, and from thy people; they shall remain in the river only.

12 And Moses and Aaron went out from Pharaoh: and Moses ^d cried unto the Lord because of the frogs which he had brought against Pharaoh.

13 And the Lord did ^e according to the word of Moses; and the frogs died out of the houses, out of the villages, and out of the fields.

14 And they gathered them together upon heaps; and the land stank.

---

b ch. 9: 28; 10: 17; Nu. 21: 7; 1Ki. 13: 6; Ac. 8: 24.   c De. 32: 31; 33: 26.   d Ja. 5: 16, 18.   e De. 34: 10-12.

---

miracle—*and brought up frogs upon the land of Egypt.* As the creatures were swarming already they manipulated so as to seem to bring them up themselves—or perhaps even succeeded, in bringing them up from the river bed to particular spots. They could only aggravate the curse—not mitigate it. They could not remove the Plague.

8. *Pharaoh* suffers so under this terrible scourge that he begs Moses and Aaron to entreat Jehovah for his relief, and promises on this condition to grant the people's release. He thus admits that not the magicians, but Jehovah, had it in control.

9. *Glory over me.* Either —*Have the honor over me (of saying) when I shall entreat for thee*—or, *you are welcome to my services as intercessor for you.* The sense is, Command me as to the time—Name your own time. It would seem that Moses was most ready to meet Pharaoh with terms at the first moment of his yielding. The frogs were to be remanded to their natural place, in the river, where they would be harmless.

10. The day was fixed—and it was the nearest day—and Moses was ready to make this a proof to Pharaoh of God's almightiness against all the gods of the heathen.

11-14. It was done according to the time set by Pharaoh. The frog was held sacred and regarded with superstitious reverence as the symbol of human life in embryo. It is seen in the hieroglyphics sitting on a ring, and from its back rises a palm-branch, the symbol of the mouth, or of time. *Phtah* the creative or formative principle appears under the form of a god with a frog's head. Pharaoh now must see that this reptile is at the command of the god of Moses, to kill or

15 But when Pharaoh saw that there was respite, he f hardened his heart, and hearkened not unto them: as the LORD had said. g

16 And the LORD said unto Moses, Say unto Aaron, Stretch out thy rod, and smite the dust of the land, that it may become lice throughout all the land of Egypt.

17 And they did so: for Aaron stretched out his hand with his rod, and smote the dust of the earth, and it became ʰlice in man and in beast; all the dust of the land became lice throughout all the land of Egypt.

18 And the magicians did so with their enchantments to bring forth lice, but they could not: ⁱ so there were lice upon man, and upon beast.

---

f Ec. 8: 11. g ch. 7: 4. h Ps. 105: 31. i Ge. 41: 8; Is. 19: 12; 47: 12; Da. 2: 10.

---

to make alive. *Upon heaps.* The word is from the term meaning *omer*, or bushel measure—*by bushels.*

15. Pharaoh's perverseness is here noted. When he saw "that there was *breathing-time*—relief from an overpowering pressure—literally, as soon as he got air," *he hardened his heart*—*made his heart heavy*, so that he did not hearken to Moses and Aaron. And this was *as the Lord had said,* for God knew his heart.

§ 16. THE THIRD PLAGUE—LICE. Ch. VIII : 16-19.

16. *The dust of the land* was now to be smitten so that it should become *lice.* Some make it *gnats.* The term does not mean common lice, but a tiny insect of this species, stinging painfully, and swarming so as to infest the entire population, as if the dust of the streets were all turned into these. As in the previous plagues, this was not an entirely new thing in the country. God used natural agencies, but wrought supernaturally with them. The miracle consisted, not in creating a new insect, but in causing them to multiply so immensely at the lifting of Aaron's rod, by His command. These tiny creatures, fine as the dust, find their way into the eyes, ears and nostrils, and poison by their bite, and become a torment. We can testify from experience that vermin yet abound in Egypt, and are a serious annoyance to travellers, both inside the dwelling and in the tents pitched in the field. On the way we bought a contrivance to protect our sleep against such molestation. It consisted of a sheet sewed up, excepting an opening large enough to admit the person through a bag of mosquito netting, which, when you are within, is fastened above the head, to the top of the tent, and gives fair breathing space. This served as an admirable protection from such vermin; but some of our company preferred risking the vermin to being sewed up, in that singular manner, for sleep. Herodotus tells us that the priests of Egypt shave their whole body that no lice or other impure thing may adhere to them in the service of the gods.

18. *The magicians did so with their enchantments—to bring forth lice*—they smote the dust for the purpose, *but they could not.* Their skill was utterly baffled; they could not in any instance bring lice out of the dust, after this fashion. They are forced to confess themselves overmatched, and to exclaim, "*This is the finger of God.*" This, however, must not be understood as any

CHAPTER VIII. 77

19 Then the magicians said unto Pharaoh, This *is* the ʲ finger of God: and Pharaoh's heart was hardened, and he hearkened not unto them; as the Lord had said.

20 And the Lord said unto Moses, Rise up early in the morning, and stand before Pharaoh; lo, he cometh forth to the water; and say unto him, Thus saith the LORD, Let my people go, that they may serve me:

21 Else, if thou wilt not let my people go, behold, I will send swarms *of flies* upon thee, and upon thy servants, and upon thy people, and into thy houses; and the houses of the Egyptians shall be full of swarms *of flies*, and also the ground whereon they *are*.

22 And I will sever ᵏ in that day the land of Goshen, in

---

j 1Sa. 6:3,9; Ps. 8:3; Mat. 12:28; Lu. 11:20. k ch. 9:4, &c.; 10:23; 11:6,7; 12:13.

---

devout acknowledgment of the God of the Hebrews (*Jehovah*), but only a confession that it was supernatural, and not the work of Moses and Aaron. So *Bochart*. *Kurtz* thinks they meant to ascribe it to their own divinities—all in one Elohim—and that they did not go beyond their own idolatrous system in this confession. This would imply, if so, that they regarded their defeat as an expression of their own god in favor of the demand for Israel's release. The use of the phrase as to the magicians' work shows that their "*doing so with their enchantments*" does not mean that they wrought actually miracles, only that they strove to imitate Moses and Aaron.

OBSERVE.—The narrative here throughout shows that it could have been written only by one who, like Moses, had a thorough knowledge of Egyptian affairs.

§ 17. SECOND TRIO OF PLAGUES. THE FOURTH PLAGUE—FLIES. Ch. VIII: 20-32.

In this second trio of plagues God works without the symbolic rod of His servants, and thus He would show that He is not tied to this or that method. Henceforth, also, a distinction is openly put between the Israelites and the Egyptians, to show that God will honor and defend his own covenant people, and that the plagues issued from his hand.

20, 21. This fourth plague is notified to Pharaoh at the river bank, as at first, and in the morning. The formal demand is again made, accompanied with this threatening. The term means a *mingling* or *mixture*, as if it were a collection or swarm of noxious insects. But it means a species of fly—*gadfly* or *dogfly*. Such flies are commonly one of the severest pests of Egypt, some of them very large and of grievous bite, alighting everywhere on the exposed flesh, and frequently infesting the moist parts of the eyelids and nostrils. They were to attack the people, and fill the houses, and cover the ground. No one can conceive how terrible such a scourge would be. The miracle consisted in their immense *multiplication* and terrible execution — at the divine bidding.

22. *I will sever, in that day*. Now, a new token was to be given of Jehovah's design in the matter, by the exemption of His own people from the plague. The land of Goshen should be spared from the plague. *I will distinguish in a miraculous manner, in that day*, etc. And this should be to them a manifest token of Jehovah's hand *in the*

which my people dwell, that no swarms *of flies* shall be there; to the end thou mayest know that I *am* the LORD in the midst of the earth.

23 And I will put a division between my people and thy people: to-morrow shall this sign be.

24 And the LORD did so: and there came a grievous swarm *of flies* into the house of Pharaoh, and *into* his servants' houses, and into all the land of Egypt; the land was corrupted by reason of the swarm *of flies*.

25 And Pharaoh called for Moses and for Aaron, and said, Go ye, sacrifice to your God in the land.

26 And Moses said, It is not meet so to do; for we shall sacrifice the abomination [1] of the Egyptians to the LORD our God: lo, shall we sacrifice the abomination of the Egyptians before their eyes, and will they not stone us?

27 We will go [m] three days' journey into the wilderness, and sacrifice to the LORD our God, as he shall [n] command us.

28 And Pharaoh said, I will let you go, that ye may sacri-

---

1 Ge. 43: 32; 46: 34; De. 7: 25; 12: 31; 1Ki. 11: 5-7; 2Ki. 23: 13. m ch. 3: 18. n ch. 34: 11; Le. 10: 1; Matt. 23: 20.

---

midst of the earth, including the land of Egypt.

23. *And I will put a division*—lit. *a deliverance.* He would thus show (1) His will and power to deliver His own people, and (2) that He possessed unlimited sway in the land of Egypt, as elsewhere. Thus He would make himself known as *Jehovah.* The day was set. God can say *to-morrow* for judgment, to give time for repentance. For grace he says to-day.

24. The plague was brought on directly by God without the rod of His servants. The land was *corrupted*—lit. *destroyed, devoured,* (Ps 78: 45) by reason of the swarming insects, poisoning the blood, disfiguring and tormenting the people, and destroying vegetation also. The Egyptians worshipped the *fly-beetle,* etc.

25, 26. Pharaoh is now ready to propose a compromise; he is willing that they shall sacrifice to their God *in the land of Egypt.* Moses declines this offer. "*It is not meet (appointed) so to do; for we shall sacrifice the abominations of the Egyptians.* Not that they would sacrifice animals regarded as sacred by the Egyptians—for the word would not be applied to the sacred animals—but (1) That they would sacrifice to Jehovah, their God, as they were bidden to do. (2) Because their sacrificing in the land would be an abomination to the Egyptians. (3) Because they would not observe the minute ritual ordinances of the Egyptians, as to omens and regulations; and hence they would be held as insulting their religion. *Doing thus before their eyes, will they not stone us?*

27. The demand was pressed, according to the first formal application. *We will go three days' journey into the wilderness, and sacrifice to Jehovah, our God, according as He shall command us.* In this last clause the manner and extent of the service was left open for the Divine command, and referred for the future to the Divine direction—to go further if so commanded.

28. Pharaoh now comes to terms reluctantly, and with a caution as to the distance—*only ye shall not go very far away.* He was jealous of

CHAPTER IX.

fice to the LORD your God in the wilderness; only ye shall not go very far away: º entreat for me.

29 And Moses said, Behold, I go out from thee, and I will entreat the LORD that the swarms *of flies* may depart from Pharaoh, from his servants, and from his people, to-morrow: but let not Pharaoh deal P deceitfully any more in not letting the people go to sacrifice to the LORD.

30 And Moses went out from Pharaoh, and entreated the LORD.

31 And the LORD did according to the word of Moses; and he removed the swarms *of flies* from Pharaoh, from his servants, and from his people: there remained not one.

32 And Pharaoh q hardened his heart at this time also, neither would he let the people go.

CHAPTER IX.

THEN the LORD said unto Moses, Go in unto Pharaoh, and tell him, thus saith the LORD God of the Hebrews, Let my people go, that they may serve me.

---

o V. 8; ch. 9: 28; 1K. 13: 6. p Ps. 78: 34–37; Je. 42: 20. q V. 15: ch. 4: 21; Ro. 2: 5.

---

his authority, and suspicious of them, as he was anxious not to lose their bond-service. Pharaoh pleaded for release from the bondage of the plague, as Moses pleaded for release of his people from Pharaoh's bondage. So the world pleads for conformity of the church, and against entire separation. The *border people* who do not go very far away are still in bondage.—2 Peter 2: 20, 21.

29. Moses assents—appoints tomorrow for the intercession with Jehovah for Pharaoh's relief—and adds a caution to Pharaoh against breaking faith again as he had already done.

30. Moses' plea was so efficacious that the immense swarms were gone —*there remained not one to molest.* Whether the insect was a *large fly* of poisonous sting, or a beetle or a cockroach, as Dr. Kirby (Bridgewater Treatise) suggests, the plague was fearful; and as this species of insects was worshipped by the Egyptians, and the *scarabeus* is a venerated symbol among them representing the sun, the miracle, as before, struck at the system of idolatrous worship, and put the gods of Egypt to shame.

32. The record is made again against Pharaoh that he *hardened his heart at this time also, neither would he let the people go,* adding every time falsity in the very face of Jehovah, so soon as the affliction was removed at his promise and prayer. Broken vows, in defiance of God, make up the history of heart-hardening; and the narrative shows the processes of mental and moral operation whereby the career of such an one waxes worse and worse, deceiving and being deceived.

CHAPTER IX.

§ 18. THE FIFTH PLAGUE—RINDERPEST. Ch. IX: 1-7.

1-7. The threatening in this case was of a *rinderpest* or cattle disease.

2 For if thou refuse to let *them* go, and wilt hold them still,

3 Behold, the hand of the Lord is upon thy cattle which *is* in the field, upon the horses, upon the asses, upon the camels, upon the oxen, and upon the sheep: *there shall be* a very grievous murrain.

4 And the Lord shall sever between the cattle of Israel and the cattle of Egypt: and there shall nothing die of all *that is* the children's of Israel.

5 And the Lord appointed a set time, saying, To-morrow the Lord shall do this thing in the land.

6 And the Lord did that thing on the morrow, and [a] all the cattle of Egypt died; but of the cattle of the children of Israel died not one.

7 And Pharaoh sent, and, behold, there was not one of the cattle of the Israelites dead. And the heart of Pharaoh was hardened, and he did not let the people go.

---

a Ps. 78: 50.

They had reason to know something of this calamity, as it was more or less of annual occurrence at the subsidence of the Nile waters. But so they could understand it, and would dread it. And here it is threatened, *at the hand of Jehovah*, as a direct infliction. In 1782, and more recently in 1842, '63 and '66, nearly all of the herds were destroyed by the cattle disease. How serious a trouble this is we can judge somewhat from the similar calamity in Europe and America. Beasts of burden, as well as all domestic animals, were smitten with the pest. The horses and camels in the desert were reached by it.—Jer. 12: 4.

2. *Wilt hold them still—strengthenest*, or, *holdest fast upon them—obstinately persisting in keeping them by force.*

3. *The hand of the Lord (Jehovah).* Not by the rod of Aaron—making it thus more a direct visitation of Jehovah. *A very grievous murrain.* Sept.—*A death vehemently great.* The term in general means pestilence or epidemic disease, and includes the typhus and epizooty or catarrhal distemper. And as something of the kind was known in Egypt, the threatening would be sufficiently understood to be dreaded. And the miracle consisted in its coming as foretold, and at a set time, and in greatly increased severity, and in its being confined for a purpose to the Egyptian cattle, as stated in v. 4.

5. *A set time*—appointed and named—*to-morrow*—so as to give opportunity to avoid it by their compliance, and so as to prove the divine power by the occurrence at the time proposed.

6. *All the cattle.* The destruction spared no sort mentioned (v. 3.) nor any district of the Egyptians; yet some were left. See v. 19. The distinction between Israel and Egypt was most marked, and could not fail to prove the Divine intervention.

7. *Pharaoh's* attention was directed to the astonishing difference, as had been threatened. And yet there was no good result. Whether he persuaded himself that it was all accident or fatality or mere natural law, we do not need to know. ¶ *Not one.* That is, not one of those named as *in the field* (v. 3). Some of the Egyptian cattle were in the stalls, and not *in the field.* (See Wilkinson's Ancient Egypt, vol. 1, p. 96.)

8 And the LORD said unto Moses and unto Aaron, Take to you handfuls of ashes of the furnace, and let Moses sprinkle it toward the heaven in the sight of Pharaoh.

9 And it shall become small dust in all the land of Egypt, and shall be a boil ᵇ breaking forth *with* blains upon man and upon beast, throughout all the land of Egypt.

10 And they took ashes of the furnace, and stood before Pharaoh; and Moses sprinkled it up toward heaven: and it became a boil breaking forth *with* blains upon man and upon beast.

11 And the magicians could not ᶜ stand before Moses because of the boils; for the boil was upon the magicians, and upon all the Egyptians.

---

b De. 28: 27; Job 2: 7; Re. 16: 2.   c Is. 47: 12, 14.

And hence some cattle were not victims to the pest (v. 19). *Pharaoh's heart was hardened*, instead of melted and subdued. "The greatness of man's corruption is seen in the fact that he will not desist from sin. The greatness of God is seen in the fact that the man is not able to desist from that form of sin in which it is madness to persevere."—*Heng. King. of God*, vol. 1, p. 271. It must be remembered that this plague had a special significance and design because the Egyptians worshiped the leading agricultural and domestic animals, the ox, the cow and the ram, and so the plague was aimed at their false religion and their idolatry.

§ 19. THE SIXTH PLAGUE—BOILS AND BLAINS. Ch. IX: 8–12.

8–12. *The sixth plague — boils.* Yet another blow is struck at the proud and insolent king. This is not forewarned, but is visited without formal notice. These signs are at the same time punishments of unbelief and obduracy. He who will not turn is led with open eyes towards the abyss of destruction. ¶ *Ashes of the furnace*—a brick-kiln —or a *furnace* for smelting metals. The Israelites had been laborers at these furnaces, in their oppressive task-work as builders of tombs and temples; and there was a meaning in making the ashes from these furnaces to become a source of suffering in the shape of boils or ulcers breaking out upon the bodies of their masters. Some suppose the ashes referred to an old Egyptian rite of human sacrifices in which the ashes were scattered abroad, as a charm for the protection of all upon whom they fell (see *Plutarch*), and that perhaps it was while driven to this human sacrifice, and while the priests were performing this part of the rite. (Doubtful.)

But the term *furnace* does not mean an altar of sacrifice, and human sacrifices were not practised in Egypt then. But the *brick-kiln* which was connected with the oppressions of the Israelites was now employed as a means of chastisement to the Egyptians, their tyrannical masters. Such *boils—ulcers-- breaking forth with blains or blisters*, on man and beast, was an intensifying of what they had known something of, in lighter forms of cutaneous eruption — the severest inflammation in blotches, like erysipelas or carbuncles or leprosy. Job's disease, elephantiasis, was of this species, making the feet swollen and stiff as an elephant's. But here the miracle consists in producing it by the ashes, and according to a specific order given to Moses. The

12 And the LORD hardened the heart of Pharaoh, and he hearkened ᵈ not unto them, as the LORD had spoken ᵉ unto Moses.

13 And the LORD said unto Moses, Rise up early in the morning, and stand before Pharaoh, and say unto him, Thus saith the LORD God of the Hebrews, Let my people go that they may serve me.

14 For I will at this time send all ᶠ my plagues upon thine heart, and upon thy servants, and upon thy people; that thou mayest know that *there is* none like me in all the earth.

15 For now I will stretch out my hand, that I may smite thee, and ᵍ thy people with pestilence; and thou shalt be cut off from the earth.

---

d Ps. 81: 11. e ch. 4: 21. f Le. 26; 18; De. 28: 15· 29: 20; 32: 39; 1Sa. 4:'8; Je. 19: 8; Ro. 18: 8; 22: 18. g Pr. 2: 22.

---

act of sprinkling the ashes toward the heavens had a meaning; as in sacrifices, of calling God to witness.

11. The effect upon the magicians was to disable them by the attack of the disease upon their own persons. This was a peculiarity of this plague. The Egyptian priests were most intent upon personal cleanliness, washing twice each day and twice each night, and avoiding all defilement. To them it was the more shocking to be smitten with this loathsome disease. *The Lord* (Jehovah) *hardened*, etc. So ch. 4: 21. The Lord wrought the miracle which thus resulted in his hardening; though, as often, Pharaoh is said to have hardened his own heart. This plague strikes deeper than any of the rest, and threatens the life, and the sacred animals are made loathsome with disease. What a blow to the obstinate king and people! The magicians *could not stand*, and seem to have given way before Moses.

§ 20. THE THIRD TRIO. THE SEVENTH PLAGUE, HAIL. Ch. IX., 13–35.

13. There seems to have been a longer interval between this plague and the former, and a new and formal demand is again made, with a more prolonged address to Pharaoh.

As the plagues are divided into triplets, so this one begins the last series; and the announcement is terrible. *I will at this time send all my plagues upon thine heart*, as if he was now to look out for these blows at the very core, and for a concentration of them all. *At this time*—in this last series. The first message was in April and May, after the early harvest, when they could gather stubble; the second message, when the plagues began, was probably towards the end of June, going on at intervals until the winter. This was in February. See v. 31. *About this time to-morrow* (v. 18), Murphy says, " Pharaoh might have learned by this time that the Lord is punctual to His time."

14. *Upon thine heart*—which is so hardened. This plague was to go to the very core, and not merely to strike the surface. *That thou mayest know*. God will be known and acknowledged by the kings of the earth. Alas for those who are trying to persuade themselves and others (on scientific grounds!) that there is no personal God—only " a *power*." But what power, if not a Personal power? Only *a law*. But " a law implies a lawgiver, and the more law the more proof of a lawgiver."—*Prof. Henry.*

15. "*For now indeed had I stretched forth my hand and smitten thee, and*

16 And in very deed for ʰ this *cause* have I raised thee up, for to shew *in* thee my power; and that my name may be declared throughout all the earth.

17 As yet exaltest thou thyself ⁱ against my people, that thou wilt not let them go?

18 Behold, to-morrow, ᵏ about this time, I will cause it to rain ˡ a very grievous hail, such as hath not been in Egypt since the foundation thereof even until now.

19 Send therefore now, *and* gather thy cattle, and all that thou hast in the field; *for upon* every man and beast which shall be found in the field, and shall not be brought home, the hail shall come ᵐ down upon them, and they shall die.

20 He that feared the word ⁿ of the LORD among the servants of Pharaoh made his servants and his cattle flee into the houses:

21 And he that regarded ᵒ not the word of the LORD left his servants and his cattle in the field.

h Pr. 16: 4; Ro. 9: 17; 1 Pe. 2: 8. i Job 9: 4; 15; 25, 26. k 1 K. 19 2; 20 26. l Ps. 83: 15. m V. 25. n Pr. 16: 16; 22: 23. o ch. 7: 23.

thy people with the pestilence, then hadst thou been cut off from the earth."—Speaker's Com. "I might have smitten thee and thy people with the pestilence as easily as I smote thy cattle."—*Murphy.*

16. It is here declared why God had not thus cut him off. He had a great purpose to accomplish in his case, by making him an example, as he has truly been in all history. *Raised thee up,* lit. *made thee stand*—caused thee to remain—permitted thee to live and hold thy place. *To shew* (*in*) *thee my power.* Rom. 9: 17. Literally, to show thee my power for a motive to repentance and faith, as against all false gods. God had shown to him his long-suffering patience and goodness. *That my name,* etc. God's name (that character by which He makes Himself known) would thus be declared, published abroad in all the earth, as it has been.

17. *As yet.* Still, notwithstanding all God's judgments, he is holding out, and stubbornly, haughtily setting himself against God.

18. Such storms of rain in winter were rare, but were known, and even as early as in March, in Lower Egypt. This was to be of very great severity, and such as had never been experienced there. It was to be altogether beyond the working of natural law, and thus miraculous.

19. Yet how gracious, in the midst of this just visitation now threatened, to give a timely warning, so that any who believed in God might avoid the calamity. In judgment God remembers mercy. He would show that His object is not to destroy men, but to draw sinners to himself. The cattle were not all destroyed by the former plague. (See v. 3.) Some are left. They were turned out to pasture in the open field commonly from January to April, and after that they were *gathered,* that is, *brought in under cover,* and fed in stalls. ¶ *Not be brought home.* The only condition of salvation for man or beast was to get home. This is fulfilled in the gospel. We find a home in Christ rest for the soul, and a mansion in the Father's house.

20. *He that feared the Lord.* There were some who feared Jeho-

EXODUS.

22 And the LORD said unto Moses: Stretch forth thine hand toward heaven, that there may be hail in all the land of Egypt, upon man, and upon beast, and upon every herb of the field, throughout the land of Egypt.

23 And Moses stretched forth his rod toward heaven; and the LORD sent thunder and ᵖ hail, and the fire ran along upon the ground: and the LORD rained hail upon the land of Egypt.

24 So there was hail, and fire mingled with the hail very grievous, such as there was none like it in all the land of Egypt since it became a nation.

25 And the hail smote throughout all the land of Egypt all that *was* in the field, both man and beast; and the hail smote every herb of the field, and brake every tree of the field.

26 Only in the land of Goshen, ᵠ where the children of Israel *were*, was there no hail.

27 And Pharaoh sent, and called for Moses and Aaron, and said unto them, I have sinned this time: the LORD *is* righteous, and I and my people *are* wicked.

28 Entreat the LORD (for ʳ *it is* enough) that there be no *more* mighty thunderings and hail; and I will let you go, and ye shall stay no longer.

---

p Jos. 10: 11; 1Sa. 12: 17, 18; Job 38: 22; Ps. 18: 13; 78: 47; 105: 32; Is. 30: 30; Eze. 38: 22; Re. 8: 7.   q ch. 8: 22, &c.; Is. 32: 18, 19.   r Ac. 8: 24.

---

vah, even amongst the Egyptians. God gives ample warning, and opportunity for all such to escape.

22. The plague came at the time appointed. Moses is the visible agent in these three plagues, hail, locusts and darkness (see ch. x: 12-21,) by stretching forth his hand with the rod (v. 23), which was the symbol of power, toward heaven.

23. There was all the threatened severity, *"thunder and hail, and the fire ran along the ground"*—lit. *stalked along the ground*—in vivid flashes of lightning. ¶ *Rained hail.* Poured down hail like rain—in torrents. *Fire mingled with the hail.* Bolts of lightning flashing along with the hail, most terrifically displaying the Divine power, God in nature, and above nature, using nature to do His will.

26. *Only in the land of Goshen.* The miracle was shown by confining the plague to the Egyptians and sparing the Israelites.

27. Pharaoh was moved to seek terms. He so far humbled himself as to send for Moses and Aaron, and make confession of sin. *I have sinned this time*—this once. It is a confession for the whole controversy, and makes a clean breast of it. But it was the third time he had so confessed to no purpose. He must have seen that God had power to crush him, and he is driven by his fears to seek conciliation. *Jehovah is righteous, and I and my people are wicked.* This was a confession like that of Judas. It is the substantial form of a true confession, but it does not carry his heart by love. He is *driven*, not *drawn*.

28. He asks the intercession of Moses and Aaron. Better that he had been brought to his knees. They who only go so far as to seek the mediation and intercession of saints, on earth or in heaven, show no true repentance. *No more mighty thunderings*, lit., *voices of God.*

CHAPTER IX.

29 And Moses said unto him, As soon as I am gone out of the city I will spread abroad my hands ˢ unto the LORD; *and* the thunder shall cease, neither shall there be any more hail; that thou mayest know how that the earth *is* the LORD's.ᵗ

30 But as for thee and thy servants, I know that ye will not yet ᵛ fear the LORD God.

31 And the flax and the barley was smitten; ʷ for the barley *was* in the ear, and the flax *was* bolled.

32 But the wheat and the rye were not smitten; for they *were* not grown up.

33 And Moses went out of the city from Pharaoh, and spread abroad his hands unto the LORD; and the thunders and hail ceased, and the rain was not poured upon the earth.

34 And when Pharaoh saw that the rain and hail and the thunders were ceased, he sinned yet ˣ more, and hardened his heart, he and his servants.

35 And the heart of Pharaoh was hardened, neither would he let the children of Israel go; as the LORD had spoken by Moses.

---

s 1Ki. 8: 38; Ps. 143: 6; Is. 1: 15. t Ps. 24: 1; 1Co. 10: 26. v Is. 26; 10. w Am. 4: 9; Ha. 3: 17. x 2Ch. 33: 23; 36: 13; Ro. 2: 4, 5.

---

29. Moses consents to the proposition of Pharaoh; and this he did to show that the earth is the Lord's. Such control over all the phenomena and laws of nature would surely prove that Jehovah was Lord of the natural world.

30. Moses, however, notifies Pharaoh that his wicked obstinacy is not yet overcome.

31, 32. God pleased to smite the flax upon which the people depended for their linen fabrics, and the barley with which they fed their cattle. But he spared the wheat and the rye for flour and food. ¶ *The flax was bolled*, in blossom or in the pod. The barley being now in the ear shows that the season must have been about the first of March. ¶ *Rye* was not such as is known to us, but a coarse food known as *doora* among the natives — here rendered *spelt*. Egypt was the great granary of the world at that time, and even the damaging of the crop would be a serious loss.

34. When the immediate ground of fear was removed Pharaoh's *heart was hardened* as before, and *he sinned yet more*. So vain is a repentance that springs from mere terror. Here the term for *hardened* is not the same as is commonly used in the narrative; it means here *he stupefied his heart*—made it *dull*, *obtuse*, lit., *made heavy his heart*. And in the next sentence is the old word, and the heart of Pharaoh *was hardened*, etc. And this occurred as Moses had forewarned Pharaoh (v. 30), showing to the haughty monarch, and to the world, that God knows the heart and searches through all the vain disguises of it.

OBSERVE — Nature is not God. Laws of nature cannot dispense with God—a Personal God. For the more we find evidence of laws in nature the more proof we find of God, for law implies a lawgiver.

Hengstenberg says: "A natural substratum is present in all the plagues, while in none is a natural explanation admissible. The miracles are taken from the most various departments. That which was a

CHAPTER X.

AND the Lord said unto Moses, Go in unto Pharaoh: for I have ^a hardened his heart, and the heart of his servants, that I might shew these my signs before him:

2 And that thou mayest tell in the ears of thy son, ^b and of thy son's son, what things I have wrought in Egypt, and my signs which I have done among them; that ye may know how ^c that I *am* the Lord.

---

a ch. 7: 13, 14.   b De. 4: 9; 6: 20; Ps. 44: 1; 71: 18; 78: 5; Joel 1: 3.   c Ps. 58: 11.

---

blessing to Egypt was converted into a curse. That which was already in existence as an evil is increased to a fearful extent. The smallest animals become a terrible army of God. In this way it was shown that every blessing, which ungrateful Egypt attributed to its idols, originated with Jehovah, and that it was He alone who checked the efficacy of that which was injurious. *Calvin* says of Pharaoh, "The image of human pride and rebellion is submitted to us here in the person of one reprobate." *Hengstenberg* adds, "In conformity with God's constant method in nature and history, the matter was so arranged that unbelief always retained some hook to which it could hang, for God always gives light enough even for weak faith, at the same time leaving so much darkness that unbelief may continue its night-life.

CHAPTER X.

§ 21. THE EIGHTH PLAGUE—LOCUSTS. Ch. X: 1-21.

1. There is yet another blow to be struck at Pharaoh's obdurate impenitence. God's messengers are sent with still another presentation of the same old message. Thus God sends His gospel servants, and the same message is repeated to men—to believe and accept the salvation, and live. ¶ *For I have hardened, made heavy*, the same term as in ch. 9: 34. It came to pass that the dealing which should have quickened his heart only stupefied it because of its own dullness and insensibility to the truth. *Speaker's Com.* suggests that this can be accounted for as an effect of God's goodness in sparing the corn, and that when Pharaoh saw that this dependence was not cut off he became insensible and careless as ever. ¶ Rather, it occurred as in the case of Isaiah, who was commanded by God to make the heart of the people fat, and their ears dull of hearing; that is he was to preach on though plainly that would be the result of his preaching, and so he is spoken of as doing to them what his preaching effected, making them gross and stupid under his ministry. ¶ *That I might show*, lit. *might set*, or *put before him*. We are not to understand by this that God hardened him to make him a public spectacle. Rather, as his hardening was the effect of that Divine dealing which ought to have brought about his repentance, so God's plan was *to show these my signs before him—to set forth these my* (miraculous) *works in the midst of him*, i. e. of his people, the Egyptians.

2. *And that thou* (i. e. Moses and all Israel) *mayest tell*, for the benefit of after generations, and to show the principles of the Divine administration for all time, and to prove the Unity and Personality of Jehovah, as against all false gods. God thus advertises to Moses the plan of His operations with Pharaoh, and

CHAPTER X.

3 And Moses and Aaron came in unto Pharaoh, and said unto him, Thus saith the LORD God of the Hebrews, How long wilt thou refuse to humble ᵈ thyself before me? Let my people go, that they may serve me.

4 Else, if thou refuse to let my people go, behold, to-morrow will I bring the locusts ᵉ into thy coast:

5 And they shall cover the face of the earth, that one cannot be able to see the earth: and they shall eat the ᶠ residue of that which is escaped, which remaineth unto you from the hail, and shall eat every tree which groweth for you out of the field:

6 And they shall fill thy houses, ᵍ and the houses of all thy servants, and the houses of all the Egyptians; which neither thy fathers, nor thy fathers' fathers have seen, since the day that they were upon the earth unto this day. And he turned himself, and went out from Pharaoh.

---

d 1Ki. 21: 29; 2Ch. 7: 14; 33: 12, 19; Job. 42: 6; Je. 13: 18; Ja. 4: 10.   e Pr. 30: 27; Re. 9: 3.   f ch. 9: 32.   g ver. 14, 15; ch. 8: 3.

---

thus strengthens his faith and courage. *I have wrought.* The term implies a work of bringing to shame and grief. *That ye may know.* This is God's clearly-announced object in these wondrous works—to promote the faith of His people—"to reveal the Creator in His true character to man. This is the lesson of nature, of providence and of grace, to those who read and understand."—*Murphy.*

3. God's object with Pharaoh in these miraculous judgments was to bring him down from his loftiness and proud defiance to a becoming humility. This is not any arbitrary pleasure in man's humiliations. It is for man's good, in bringing him to take his proper place. All Pharaoh's pretended humility was nothing, because it resulted in nothing but pretence, and so was a mockery most offensive to God.

4. *The locusts. Lo! I am bringing to-morrow the locusts.* The locust belongs to the parts of Africa south and west of Egypt, and also to Asia. The term here is from a word meaning to *multiply*, and refers to their numbers. The prophet *Joel* describes a penal visitation of locusts. Travellers speak of them in clouds darkening the sky and covering the ground. *Tischendorf* speaks of such a locust storm, in which they covered the whole country, in March. The people often used them for food—but they made havoc of every green thing. They are four or five inches long, and much like the grasshopper, in appearance.

5. Here the devastation which the locusts would make is described in fearful terms. Pharaoh had fair notice. What was left from the hail would be destroyed by these insects, and the whole land would be stripped of verdure (ch. 9: 32). *Eat every tree.* Not only the leaves but the bark, killing the tree.

6. Worse than all, they would come into the houses through the open lattices or doorways (see Joel 2: 9). *Neither thy fathers.* It should be worse than was ever known within the memory of man.

7. *Pharaoh's servants.* Now for the first time the monarch's household is aroused, as they are deeply interested and have a right to protest against the wicked obstinacy of the king. ¶ *A snare—a trap.* They find themselves involved in certain ruin by this course, and they see the only remedy. *Let the men go,* that is, the people—and not the men alone. *Speak. Com.* thinks they meant the

88 EXODUS.

7 And Pharaoh's servants said unto him, How long shall this man be [h] a snare unto us? Let the men go, that they may serve the LORD, their God: Knowest thou not yet that Egypt is destroyed?

8 And Moses and Aaron were brought again unto Pharaoh: and he said unto them, Go serve the LORD, your God: *but* who *are* they that shall go?

9 And Moses said: We will go with our young and with our old, with our sons and with our daughters; with our flocks and with our herds will we go: for we *must hold* a feast unto the LORD.

10 And he said unto them, Let the LORD be so with you as I will let you go, and your little ones: look *to it;* for evil *is* before you.

11 Not so: go now ye *that are* men, and serve the LORD; for that ye did desire. And they were driven out from Pharaoh's presence.

12 And the LORD said unto Moses, Stretch [i] out thine hand

---

h ch. 23: 33; Jos. 23: 13; 1 Sa. 18: 21; Pr. 29; 6; Ec. 7: 26.   i ch. 7: 19.

---

men only, as Pharaoh proposes. The object is reasonable and proper *that they may serve Jehovah their God*. And the point is pressed as they see and feel it. Egypt is ruined by Pharaoh's obstinate and blind refusal. The king knew very little how widespread and woful was the ruin of the land. At least they think it was fair so to suppose. *Knowest thou not yet!*

8. Here at length Pharaoh yields, so as to have Moses and Aaron brought before him, and so far to grant their request as to propose a compromise. The question now is *Who shall go?* He is ready to grant. But. "*Go—who and who that shall go?*" lit—*who are the going ones?*"

9. It is customary to go with the little ones to great festivals. We have seen the multitudes in a caravan—the children swung on the backs and sides of the horses and asses—going to the Easter festival in Palestine.

10. Pharaoh was indignant and replied, *Jehovah be with you when I shall release you and your little ones.* Or, may Jehovah be with you in the same way as I shall let you go. This was a bold defiance of the Almighty as well as of His servants. *See! for evil is before your face,* or in your mind and purpose. Or it may mean—*Look ye—for you will have trouble.* This, then would be a threat. And this is the more likely interpretation.

11. *Not so.* It is not allowed them to do as they wish in a body, altogether—but only *the men. Go now ye that are men*—if you please to accept this compromise. But not waiting for an answer, nor wishing for any—he drove them—*one drove them out from the face of Pharaoh.* The term here for your *little ones*—taph-kem, Payne Smith takes to mean—*your household clans.* Another effort at compromise! So the world proposes to keep the children as a pledge for the parents' service. But no! The parents released and gone away and the children left in Egypt! And yet how many christian families make this compromise?

12. Moses is now bidden to execute God's threats and bring on the plague, upon the defiant Pharaoh.

over the land of Egypt for the locusts, that they may come up upon the land of Egypt, and eat every herb of the land, *even* all that the hail hath left.

13 And Moses stretched forth his rod over the land of Egypt, and the LORD brought an east wind upon the land all that day, and all *that* night; *and* when it was morning, the j east wind brought the locusts.

14 And the locusts k went up over all the land of Egypt, and rested in all the coasts of Egypt; very grievous *were they;* before them there were no such locusts 1 as they, neither after them shall be such:

15 For they covered the face of the whole earth, so that the land was darkened; and they did eat every herb of the land, and all the fruit of the trees which the hail had left: and there remained not any green thing in the trees, or in the herbs of the field, through all the land of Egypt.

16 Then Pharaoh called for Moses and Aaron in haste, and he said, I have sinned against m the LORD your God, and against you.

17 Now, therefore, forgive, I pray thee, my sin only n this

---

j Ps. 78: 26; 107: 25; Mat. 8: 27.   k Ps. 78: 46; 105: 34.   l Joel 2: 2.   m C. 9: 27.
n 1Ki. 13: 6; Is. 26: 16.

---

for the locust, Delitzsch reads *with the locust—so that they may come up*—as an army.

13. Moses did as he was bidden, *and Jehovah brought an East wind.* The locust storm was commonly brought about by a wind. But Jehovah *brought the wind,* which brought the locusts—"Who rideth upon the wings of the wind." The natural phenomenon is superseded here by the preternatural and miraculous. The wind rose at the signal of Moses' rod—and that wind brought at once such a locust storm as was never known before. God works in nature, through nature, and above nature, as the Lawgiver of natural law. This course of the wind was unusual in Egypt. *Brought.* This word in the two clauses answers to different Heb. terms. The first means *directed*—the second means *bore along.* The locusts were swept over from Arabia.

14. They swarmed so as to cover the land and to settle down upon the whole country. *Brown,* in his travels in Africa, mentions such a visitation, in which nearly 2000 square miles were covered by them. *Went up.* Rising like a cloud.

15. *The land was darkened.* They lay so thick on the ground as to blacken it—besides that in their flight the sun was obscured. *Major Moore* speaks of a locust-storm such as to hide the sun like an eclipse, and to settle on the ground for 500 miles in extent. The result was as widespread and desolating as had been threatened. See Joel chs. 1, 2.

16. This judgment brought Pharaoh to terms. *Pliny* calls this plague *Deorum iræ pestis.* Pharaoh is brought to confession of sin and humiliation before God's servants. His words are those of penitence. What will be his acts? He said truly that he had sinned both against God and against His servants. *David* said—" Against thee —thee only have I sinned." Ps. 51: 1.

17. Pharaoh asks forgiveness of

once, and entreat the LORD your God, that he may take away from me this death only.

18 And he went out from Pharaoh, and entreated the LORD.

19 And the LORD turned a mighty strong west wind, which took away the locusts, and cast them º into the Red Sea; there remained not one locust in all the coasts of Egypt.

20 But the LORD hardened Pharaoh's heart, so that he would not let the children of Israel go.

21 And the LORD said unto Moses, Stretch out thine hand toward heaven, that there may be darkness ᵖ over the land of Egypt, even darkness *which* may be felt.

o Joel 2: 20.   p Ps. 35: 6; 105: 28; Pr. 4: 19; Ec. 2: 14; 6: 4; Is. 8: 22.

God's servants, not of God himself, and he seeks their prayers that he may be saved from the penalty of his sin. *Only this once.* This is his second time of confessing his sin, and the fourth time of entreating deliverance. But he never was in such severe extremity as now. He thinks if *only this once* he can be spared, all will be well. This is like the entreaties of many a death-bed repentance that is equally insincere with this.

This death only. Pharaoh recognized this as a deadly destructive plague, resulting, if unchecked, in the starvation and ruin of his people. So some in great trouble, plead for the sparing of a child, or the removal of a grievous burden, and for *this only*—as if they could ask nothing greater, and would wish nothing more, and as if to secure this they would willingly do anything. But how often the prayer proves to be insincere. When the trouble is gone the pious pledges are gone also. God's demand of the world's kingdom is, "*Let my people go!*"

18, 19. Moses besought the Lord —Jehovah—according to Pharaoh's entreaty. And God showed to the king His absolute control of natural laws and events by staying the calamity, and this through means of physical operations. As He raised an East wind to bring on the locusts, so He raised a West wind to carry them off. ¶ *Turned a very mighty west wind,* lit., *a wind of the sea.* It would be a N. West wind from Egypt, but W. from Palestine. And so it would blow from the Mediterranean across Egypt in the direction of the Red Sea. This was a merciful disposition to make of such masses as would have created a pestilence if they had been laid dead and putrefying on the soil. ¶ *Red Sea* Heb. *See of Suph.* This term is supposed to refer to the sea-weed that floats upon the surface—though others think it is from a town of that name supposed to have stood at the head of the sea. The extermination of the locusts was complete.

20. *The Lord (Jehovah) hardened.* Murphy says, "The very long suffering of the Lord only adds to the infatuation of his ingrate heart."

§ 22. THE NINTH PLAGUE.— DARKNESS. Ch IX: 21-29.

21. God's methods were not yet exhausted. Now the penal infliction was darkness—thick darkness —*which may be felt,* lit., *and one shall grasp darkness.* Here again a blow was struck at the Egyptian idolatries. They were worshippers of the *Sun-God.* The plague came suddenly and without notice. The

CHAPTER X.

22 And Moses stretched forth his hand toward heaven, and there was a thick darkness in all the land of Egypt three days.

23 They saw not one another, neither rose any from his place for three days: but all the children of Israel had q light in their dwellings.

24 And Pharaoh called unto Moses and said, Go ye, serve the LORD; only let your flocks and your herds be stayed: let your little ones also go with you.

25 And Moses said, Thou must give us also sacrifices and burnt-offerings that we may sacrifice unto the LORD our God.

26 Our cattle r also shall go with us; there shall not an hoof be left behind: for thereof must we take to serve the LORD our God; and we know not with what we must serve the LORD until we come thither.

27 But the LORD hardened s Pharaoh's heart, and he would not let them go.

---

q Is. 42: 16; Col. 1: 13; 1Pe. 2: 9. r Ho. 5: 6; Zec. 14: 20. s Ver. 1: 20; ch. 14: 4, 8.

Egyptians knew something of darkness in the *Simoom* that blows after the vernal equinox and sweeps the fine sand from the desert in thick clouds, obscuring the sun and filling the air so as to make artificial light of little use. But this came at a sign from Moses—came with the utmost severity, blackening as never before the face of nature, and yet not extending to the abodes of the Israelites. This showed it to be miraculous.

22. *A thick darkness.* (See Ps. 105: 28,) lit—*darkness of gloom*—the thickest darkness. (See Rev. 16: 10.) It was blackness of darkness—as a significant penalty—a judgment upon the blind and wicked monarch. *Three days.* The duration of it is exactly noted, whether with any special significance or not.

23. *But.* The contrast shows the supernatural origin of this plague. It was light to the Israelites at the same time that the thick darkness hung upon the Egyptians.

24. Pharaoh now again seems to relent and to grant their release. Yet there is a *"but"*— an exception made. He will have the flocks and herds left behind, while he concedes what he had denied before, the departure of the little ones. Pharaoh would have the flocks and herds as a security for the people's return.

25. Moses here insisted upon cattle being allowed to them for their sacrifice. Not that Pharaoh should give these to the Israelites, but that he should allow them to take these with them for sacrifices, according to their declared object.

26. So Moses insists that it is essential to their purpose to offer sacrifice to God, and because they could not know precisely and fully what would be required of them in this matter until they should reach the place. He would not be trammelled or held in bondage. The people and what belonged to them must be free.

27. Here again it is on record, that Pharaoh's heart-hardening prevented the people's release. And again this result is ascribed to Jehovah, because it was the result of His Providential dealing. A hardened heart will always find something to object to in God's most righteous demands. And God does

28 And Pharaoh said unto him, Get thee from me, take heed to thyself, see my face no more: ᵗ for in *that* day thou seest my face thou shalt die.

29 And Moses said, Thou hast spoken well, ᵘ I will see thy face again no more.

CHAPTER XI.

AND the Lord said unto Moses, Yet will I bring one plague *more* upon Pharaoh, and upon Egypt; afterwards he will let you go hence: when he shall let *you* go, he shall surely thrust you out hence ᵃ altogether.

---

t 2Ch. 16: 10; 25: 16; Am. 7: 13. u He. 11: 27. a. ch. 12: 31–39.

---

not compel the sinner's obedience against his will—and if the will is not constrained, the act even is no real obedience in God's sight. God will take the will for the deed, but never the deed for the will.

28. Pharaoh now becomes exasperated and speaks like a madman. Unbelief often thus grows insane. He madly dismisses God's ambassador from his presence, and makes it a capital crime to visit him again, though Pharaoh had sent for him, (v. 16.)

29. Moses accepts the situation. *Very well*, he says, *I will leave you forever*, if you so please. Felix was more polite with Paul. He said, "Go thy way for this time, when I have a convenient season I will call for thee." (Acts. 24: 25.) But the result was much the same.

CHAPTER XI.

§ 23. The Tenth Plague Threatened.—Death of the First born. Ch. XI : 1–10.

While these interviews with Pharaoh were going on, and these successive rebuffs, Moses was keeping up communication with his people, doubtless, as he had begun, ch. 4: 29, 31, etc. But the historian cannot narrate them both at the same time. Some read here, *And the Lord had said unto Moses*, thus going back in the history to take up the thread of conference with Israel, in all this extremity. So that v. 4 of this chapter continues the conversation with Pharaoh from ch. 10 ; 29—and leaves vs. 1–3 of this chapter as a parenthesis, and the closing sentence of v. 8 is the *finale.*

1. *Yet one plague.* There was to be one more—and this was to be final and decisive—the tenth—as ten is the number of completion—as many plagues as there were to be commandments. Meanwhile God assures Moses of the result, which this time should be their release and deliverance. ¶ *When he shall*, etc. *Sp. Com.* suggests the reading, *When he lets you go altogether, he will surely thrust you out hence.* When he at length lets you go with children, flocks and herds altogether, he will drive you out in haste. "In fact, on each occasion, when Pharaoh relented for a season, immediate orders would of course be issued by Moses to the heads of the people, who were thus repeatedly brought into a state of more or less complete organization for the final movement." *Sp. Com.*

2. This is God's order for the thorough equipment of the people for their wilderness journey. ¶ *Let every man borrow.* Moses was to give this direction to the people,

2 Speak now in the ears of the people, and let every man borrow of his neighbor, and every woman of her neighbor, jewels of silver and jewels of gold.

3 And the Lord gave the people b favor in the sight of the Egyptians. Moreover, the man Moses *was* very great c in the land of Egypt, in the sight of Pharaoh's servants and in the sight of the people.

4 And Moses said, Thus saith the Lord, About midnight d will I go out into the midst of Egypt:

---

b ch. 12: 36; Ps. 106: 46.　　c 2Sa. 7: 9; Est. 9: 4; Re. 3: 9.　　d Job 34: 20; Mi. 2: 10; Ze. 14: 3.

(See ch. 3 : 21, 22.) The term here rendered *borrow*, is the word to *ask*—to *demand*, and may mean to ask as a favor, or to demand as a right—and may include both. Though sometimes meaning to *borrow*, this is plainly not the sense here, as all the context shows. It would be no time to *borrow*, when they were on the eve of being driven out, as a riddance. It would be far more likely that, amidst such terrible horrors from their detention, the Egyptians would gladly give them whatever would close up such a series of judgments on their account. "Egypt was glad when they departed—for the fear of them fell upon them." (Ps. 105 : 38.)

3. Here it is explained—*Jehovah gave them favor*—and it was so ordered as that their request or demand (as it might be in any case) was granted, and thus God's promise to them was fulfilled. (Ps. 106 ; 46.) *Moreover*—as an additional hold which the Israelites had upon the Egyptians this personal fact is narrated by Moses, as directed by inspiration. And as *Kalisch* well remarks, "The historian, with historical faithfulness, makes these remarks about his own person. They are historical facts, and he relates them with the same objective impartiality with which *Xenophon* speaks of himself in the Anabasis, or *Cesar* in his Commentaries."

4. Thus *Moses said* to Pharaoh in continuation of the last chapter, and after he had said that this would be their last meeting—the first 3 verses here being a parenthesis. *Murphy* says that "Allowing a week for each of the previous plagues, and four days for this one, we are brought to the 21st of March and perhaps to the eve of that night on which the Paschal Lamb was eaten, and the first born of Egypt were slain." *About midnight*—The day is not named. And it may be there were some few days intervening for preparation. ¶ *Will I go out.* It is no longer a direction to Moses to lift up his rod—but God Himself *will come forth,* and be personally engaged in this last plague. *First born.* This was a blow at the top. Every family was to be smitten in its *first born.* The grief would thus be most bitter "as when one mourneth for his first born." (Zech. 12 : 10.) The *first born* is the flower and crown and strength and hope of the family, (Gen. 40 : 3,) holding the right of primogeniture—having the double position, and being priest of the household, according to the ancients. This was to begin with Pharaoh, who had commanded the slaughter of all the male children of the Israelites, and now must lose his own first born, and that of all his people. ¶ *Behind the mill.* The grinding of grain was commonly done in the household by female slaves—two of whom sitting over against each other, turned the millstone by a handle, each working it half way around. (Isa. 47 : 1, 2.) It

5 And all the first-born in the land of Egypt shall die, e from the first-born of Pharaoh that sitteth upon his throne, even unto the first-born of the maid-servant that is behind the mill; and all the first-born of beasts.

6 And there shall be a great cry f throughout all the land of Egypt, such as there was none like it, nor shall be like it any more.

7 But against any of the children of Israel shall not a dog move his g tongue against man or beast; that ye may know how that the LORD doth put a difference between the Egyptians and Israel.

8 And all these thy servants h shall come down unto me, and bow down themselves unto me, saying, get thee out, and all the people that follow thee: and after that I will go out. And he went out from Pharaoh in a great anger.

9 And the LORD said unto Moses, Pharaoh shall not hearken unto you; that my wonders g may be multiplied in the land of Egypt.

---

e Am. 4: 10.   f ch. 12: 30; Am. 5: 17.   g Jos. 10: 21.   h ch. 12: 31, 33.   i ch. 7: 3.

---

was a menial and drudging employment. (Matt. 24: 40.) The upper stone was turned and the lower one was fixed, and the grain being poured into a hole in the centre of the upper stone, was crushed.

6. The wailing should be so bitter and universal in Egypt—altogether without a parallel, even in the time of the slaughter of all the male children.

7. Here again is the designed and predicted contrast which marks the event as miraculous. *Not a dog.* Dogs abound in the cities of the East, and their howling at night especially, is most distressing to a stranger. But amidst the universal wail in Egypt, not a dog should move (point) his tongue against the Israelites. The expression became proverbial to denote the most entire quiet and immunity from danger, not a dog even stirring his tongue to give any alarm, or to bite. God's object is here declared in this discriminating dealing. It is to show what difference He puts between Israel and the Egyptians. (See ch. 9; 6; 10: 20.) The difference was essential—and would be more and more marked—between the Church and the world—between the righteous and the wicked—between God's friends and His foes. Therefore God demands that they be set free.

8. The results upon the people are here forewarned. They would relent and would beg for Israel's departure. Their pride and obstinacy would be thoroughly humbled —and they would entreat them to go, *that follow thee,* lit., *who are at thy feet.* ¶ *And after that*—when at last there should be such a yielding and such an entreaty to do what they had asked leave to do—to go out all of them from Egypt—*after that* he says—*I will go out.* ¶ *In a great anger,* lit. *In a heat of wrath.* Boiling over with anger, with a just and righteous indignation at the monarch's insincerity and cruelty, and leaving with Pharaoh a notice (10: 29,) that this was the last interview, as he had requested.

9. *The Lord said.* Rather *Jehovah had said.* Repeating the pre-warning of the Almighty, already given, and more than once. ¶ *That my wonders.* Pharaoh's obstinacy

CHAPTER XII. 95

10 And Moses and Aaron did all these wonders before Pharaoh: and the LORD hardened Pharaoh's heart, so that he would not let the children of Israel go out of his land.

CHAPTER XII.

AND the LORD spake unto Moses and Aaron in the land of Egypt, saying,

---

gave occasion to such display of miracles.

10. *Did all these wonders.* This is the general summing up at the close of the narrative, a final statement covering, in brief, the whole ground. The term "*wonders*" means *portents*, and is rendered in the Septuagint by two Greek terms meaning "*Signs and wonders*," the same terms which are used for miracles in the N. Testament.

There is nothing incredible in a miracle if we believe in a Divine Being. The denial of the Supernatural as altogether impossible, results logically in the denial of God as a Supernatural Being. If His existence be admitted, then a miracle is only what may naturally be expected from such a source, for Supernatural acts are natural to a Supernatural Being. It is a poor shift and utterly arbitrary to say that these records of the miraculous are only the embellishments which the narrative has received in a later age. This is the absurdity of a "later age" pronouncing upon what is proper to history.

With the summary statement in these two verses closes one chief section of the history.

BOOK II.

THE COVENANT CONSECRATION AND SEAL— WITH THE DELIVERANCE. Chs. XII–XVIII.

CHAPTER XII.

§ 24. THE INSTITUTION OF THE FEAST OF THE PASSOVER. Ch. XII: vs. 1-20.

The historian now goes back to record the communications of Moses with his own people. We may suppose this section to have been thrown in here in the history to show that the Passover was instituted before the Exodus, and in anticipation of it—just as the Lord's supper was instituted before the betrayal of our Lord, and thus became a prophecy of that event. If Moses in the preceding chapter has brought the narrative up to the 14th Nisan, he here goes back to the early part of the month, 8th or 9th, at least, where these preparatory notices belong. As early as the interval between the plague of hail and that of the locusts and darkness, we may suppose this preparatory notice to have been given. Thus the covenant people were kept advised of what was coming on, and encouraged by the Divine preparations on their behalf. *In the land of Egypt.* The historian wrote this narrative after he had left Egypt.

2. *This month.* The month *Abib*, but called in later time *Nisan*, derived it is thought from *Nisannu*,

EXODUS.

2 This ᵃ month *shall be* unto you the beginning of months: it *shall be* the first month of the year to you.

3 Speak ye unto all the congregation of Israel, saying, In the tenth *day* of this month they shall take to them every man a lamb, according to the house of *their* fathers, a lamb for an house:

4 And if the household be too little for the lamb, let him

---

a ch. 13: 4; 34: 18; De. 16: 1.

---

of the Syrians and Babylonians, with whom it was the first month of the year. It is now to begin the ecclesiastical year to mark their religious services, as the month *Tisri* had been the first month of their civil year, at the ingathering of harvest, (ch. xxiii : 16.) ¶ *The beginning of months*—lit., the *head* or *chief* of months. It answers to our middle of March or 1st of April, as *Tisri* answered to the middle of September, six months apart. *Abib* —"the ear-month"—because the corn was in the ear. *The first month*—the leading month and most important to you for its solemn and precious associations. Covenant transactions, in which God will seal to us His covenant promises, make eras and epochs in our history, and our lives may well date from them. OBSERVE. This reckoning of the year is a well known fact, continuing down to the Maccabees, and to this day. And how else is it to be accounted for? *Jamison* says "The establishment of this new calendar was worthy of the wisdom and goodness of God, as it was calculated to inspire sentiments of thankfulness to Him by the presentation of first fruits, and consequently to withdraw the minds of the people from the worship of the Egyptian deities, to which—especially the great luminaries—many of the Israelites had shown themselves exceedingly prone." The idea here to be noticed is that the entrance upon God's covenant and service is the real beginning of life.

3. *All the congregation.* Heb. *Kahal.* As an organized body under their own officers and leaders. *Keil* says, "the nation represented by its elders." (See v. 21.) The entire body of the people was divided into tribes, families and fathers' houses, having each their respective heads. The family might have in it several branches or divisions, called father's houses, or the households severally. *Kurtz*, however, understands *fathers' house* as equivalent to a *tribe*. In v. 21, the larger family term is used. ¶ *In the tenth day.* The lamb was to be chosen out of the flock on that day. We may suppose that the plague of darkness lasted from the tenth to the fourteenth. Four days before the slaying of the lamb it was to be selected to ensure due care in the preparation. ¶ *A lamb*, lit., *a young one*—of sheep or goats. *For an house*—for the household, that is, for each several household circle. God's covenant is an household covenant, and the seals are household seals. And it has been His gracious plan in all the ages to propagate His Church by means of a pious posterity. He has a heart for the children, and seats at His table for the little ones. Jesus was a child, to compass the children with His provisions of grace, and He said, "Suffer the little children to come unto ME, for of such is the kingdom of heaven." Though the whole race is lost by the fall, yet there is ample provision for the children in the covenant of grace. The gracious responsibility is here devolved upon the father. *Every man* a *lamb*.

4. *If*—*too little*, lit., *small (from,*

CHAPTER XII.

and his neighbor next unto his house take *it* according to the number of the souls: every man, according to his eating, shall make your count for the lamb.

5 Your lamb shall be ᵇ without blemish, a male of the first year; ye shall take *it* out from the sheep, or from the goats:

6 And ye shall keep it up until the ᶜ fourteenth day of the same month: and the whole assembly of the congregation of Israel shall kill ᵈ it in the evening.

---

b Le. 22: 19–21; De. 17: 1; Mal. 1: 8, 14; 1Pe. 1: 19.   c Le. 23: 5; Nu. 9: 3; 28: 16; De 16: 1, 6.   d ch. 16: 12.

---

or more than) *smaller than a lamb.* In case there was a very small household, then they were to join with a next neighbor. "*Let him and his nearest neighbor against his house take (a lamb) according to the reckoning of the (souls) persons. Every man according to the mouth* (measure of) *his eating, shall ye reckon for the lamb,* estimating that is, how much each might be fairly expected to eat. In later time it became customary to reckon *ten persons,* at least, for a lamb, and tradition has it that they were expected to eat as much in size as an olive. But it was the law that the lamb should be entirely consumed.

5. The strict and significant requirements are now announced. ¶ *Without blemish.* This was a requisite in the offering—and it was typical of Christ—"*Who did no sin,* etc." "Holy, harmless undefiled and separate from sinners." (Heb.) Any defect or deformity would spoil it for a sacrifice, but especially for this paschal offering (see Levit. 22: 20.) *A male.* This also represented Christ. And here the lamb was to be a substitute, in the typical transaction for the first born. The burnt offerings were to be males. (Lev. 1: 3, 11.) See Matt. 1: 14. *A year old,* lit., *the son of a year*—"because it was not till then that it reached the full, fresh vigor of its life." *Keil*—"at the age when its flesh was most tender and grateful," and because during that period it retains its lamb-like humbleness and simpli-city." *Bush*—"This rather refers to the condition of perfect innocence in the antitype—the Lamb of God." ¶ *From the sheep, or from the goats.* A kid was allowable, if no sheep was had. But the sheep was judged preferable. As typical of Christ, we understand this distinction.

6. *Keep it up*—i. e., shall keep it *in charge.* Heb. implies careful keeping, lit., *It shall be to you for preservation.* ¶ *Until the fourteenth day.* Some suppose that our Lord died on the day of the regular passover, thereby completing the antitypical transaction. But it is more commonly supposed that He ate the regular Passover with His disciples, and died the next day. ¶ *The whole assembly*—not that the whole body of the people should kill each lamb. But that all should at the same time, participate in the killing, by taking part some at one home and some at another, for every Israelite must keep the feast on pain of excommunication for neglect. *In the evening.* Heb. *between the two evenings.* Some understand this to be between 3 o'clock and sunset. Our Lord was slain at 3 o'clock—*the ninth hour. Keil* and others understand it to mean at sunset. (Num. 9: 3, 5, 11. Deut. 16: 5.) "In the evening as soon as the sun goes down." *Keil* says that although the Israelites reckoned the day of 24 hours from sunset to sunset, yet in numbering the days they followed the natural day, and numbered each day according to the

7 And they shall take of the blood, and strike *it* on the two side-posts and on the upper door-post of the houses wherein they shall eat it.

period between sunrise and sunset. And in proof of this he cites the fast prescribed for the day of Atonement, which fell upon the 10th day of the 7th month, and yet it was ordered to commence on the evening of the 9th day, from even to even. (See Vol. 2, Pent. p. 12.) This then, would go far to explain the difference about the time of the Passover and Crucifixion, as given by John. The term of the Paschal meal was limited in the ritual by the midnight and morning. Part of the Paschal ceremonies fell on the 14th and part on the 15th, and so the Evangelists may locate it on different days, from different points of view. Therefore, though the lamb was slain on Thursday evening, the Passover would not be eaten and concluded before the Friday morning, that is, during the night following Thursday. (And in addition to this it is maintained that the phrase to eat the Passover, includes the keeping of the festival throughout, and beyond the Paschal meal. (see v. 48). In ch. 12: 18, the command is that unleavened bread should be eaten from the 14th day of the month at even until the 21st at even—while in Levit. 23: 6, we read—"*from the fifteenth* ye are to eat unleavened bread *seven days.*" *Lange* suggests, that "since Christ desired to develop the Passover into the New Testament form of the Supper, it was quite significant that He so ordered the feast that the Passover itself took place before the beginning of the 15th Nisan, and only the Supper fell into the full feast. Therefore He came early into Jerusalem with the disciples and commanded the celebration before the turning point of the two days, that is, before 6 o'clock on the evening of the 14th Nisan. So early was it that the conclusion of the Paschal feast, or original *Agape,* was reached before six o'clock, or, at all events, just about that hour. *Sanday* says "the Paschal Supper was to be eaten before the morning time following the 14th Nisan, which would be our Friday—but really on the 15th Nisan, Jewish—but not Saturday. He thinks the confusion arises from confounding the Julian and Jewish day.—*Notes on John. Kurtz* says the lamb could not possibly have been slain before the sunset "as soon as the sun goes down." (This would be sunset of the 14th, but strictly the beginning of the 15th. The lamb was to be roasted and eaten before the morning of the 15th, and Jesus died at evening of the same day. But it happened in the rush and bustle of Christ's arraignment and trial, that some of the Jews, as late as early dawn, had not yet eaten the Passover. But they overrode all their customary rules on that occasion.) *Kurtz* adds: We learn from comparison of passages that agreeably to its natural character, the first evening (i. e., the time of evening twilight) could be regarded as either the termination of one day or the commencement of another."

7. *Take of the blood.* Blood is the standing symbol of expiation, in reference to the great bloodshedding of Christ. And it was ordained, "Without shedding of blood is no remission." *Strike it,* lit., *Put it—place it—on the two posts.* Some have thought that this referred to tents. But doorposts and lintel would rather refer to fixed dwellings, and these would be the places where the blood-marks would most conspicuously appear to all passers-by, and mark the house with this sign or token of the sacrifice. Right and left. and overhead, to all that entered in, the blood mark would appear. Only

8 And they shall eat the flesh in that night, roast with fire, and ᵉ unleavened bread, *and* with bitter *herbs* they shall eat it.

9 Eat not of it raw, nor sodden at all with water, but roast *with* fire; his head with his legs, and with the purtenance thereof.

10 And ye shall let nothing of it ᶠ remain until the morning; and that which remaineth of it until the morning ye shall burn with fire.

11 And thus shall ye eat it: *With* your loins girded, your shoes on your feet, and your staff in your hand; and ye shall eat it in haste: it *is* the LORD's passover.

---

e ch. 34: 25; De. 16: 3; 1Co. 5: 8.   f ch. 23: 18.

---

not on the threshold to be trampled under foot. It was an appointed covenant sign to Israel of deliverance from the destroyer.

8, 9. *In that night.* The night following the 14th day, and according to Jewish reckoning, the beginning of the 15th. As slaying the lamb was the substitutionary, sacrificial act which denoted the giving of a life instead of the offerer's own, so the sprinkling of the blood was the symbol of *applied atonement.* The offerer's own act indicated thus his acceptance of the pardon and redemption purchased by the blood of Christ—the antitype—and that for himself not only, but also for his household. "It was commonly reckoned from sunset to sunrise." *Roast with fire.* Fire was a symbol of the Holy Ghost, as a purifying agent. "He shall baptize you with the Holy Ghost and with fire." (Matt. 3: 11.) *Cloven tongues, like as of fire.*" (Acts 2: 3.) "He is like a refiner's fire." (Mal. 3: 2.) *And unleavened bread with* (on) *bitter herbs, shall they eat it.* OBSERVE.—It was to be roasted not because of the haste, but so as to retain its entireness and its strength and substance, thus showing forth the fulness and perfectness of the sacrifice and the salvation. Herein this differed from all the other sacrifices. None of it was to be eaten underdone, nor *raw nor sodden,* (seethed or boiled) in water whereby the substance would more or less be lost, and the mass dissolved. But in the entirety of the animal, head and legs, and thus a perfect whole, not at all mutilated. The whole *Christ* and the whole *Church* are denoted. Num. 9: 12, vs. 34: 20, 1 Cor. 5: 7, 10; 17. The *unleavened bread* denoted the absence of corruption, as leaven is the souring and corruption, or spoiling element of the mass. The *bitter herbs* pointed to the tribulations of the occasion. These herbs and bread were to be the basis of the meal.

10. *Until the morning.* The meal was to be eaten between the sunset and the daydawn. It was for this use alone, and for none other, in any part or atom of it. Therefore, any remnant of it, was to be burnt with fire, if it was not practicable to eat it all. The Passover was different from all other sacrifices—in this that it was to be for the people's consumption, first of all and chief of all—partaken as a whole by them, and wholly by them, and thus entering wholly into them for substance. (1) It was a social family meal. (2) It was eucharistic. (3) It was expiatory. The atonement and the salvation were to be held as *all-sufficient,* but with no *surplus,* to be thrown away or devoted to any other use.

11. *Thus.* Special directions are given as to the manner of eating and their equipment for the meals. *Loins girded,* for action, the long,

100 EXODUS.

12 For I will pass through the land of Egypt this night, and will smite all the first-born in the land of Egypt, both man and beast; and against all the gods of Egypt g I will execute judgment: I *am* the LORD.

13 And the blood shall be to you for a token upon the houses

---
g ch. 12: 36; Ps. 106: 46.
---

flowing robe tucked up and fastened about the loins by the girdle, so as to be fitted to march without any impediment of the clothing, and braced by the girdle. *Shoes*—sandals *on your feet*, so as to be shod for rough roads. *Staff*, such as they use on journeys for walking a distance. God would open the way for them; but they must do the marching, each for himself. Our agency is requisite in our salvation, and all Christ's finished work, free as its benefits are, is nothing if we do not apply it by sprinkling the blood upon our doorways, and if we do not march out of our bondage. ¶ *In haste, In anxious plight.*—Keil. These directions applied only to the original passover in Egypt, and not to after celebrations; but they have typical significance. Every believer must stand habitually in readiness for action. "That the man of God may be *perfect*." The term means *ready* (2 Tim 3: 17). In the attitude not of loiterers but of travellers and of workers, and of those who are expectants *of orders to move* at any moment. This is the attitude of the apostles—*Watching!* "The day of the Lord cometh!" "*Looking for and hasting*" the coming! They were not ignorant nor mistaken nor deceived by false expectations. They were waiting and ready for the orders from headquarters at any moment. In v. 3 they were notified to be ready. ☞ *The Lord's passover to Jehovah.* This declaration gives dignity and significance to the whole transaction. It is an ordinance of Jehovah, and the term by which it is called *passover* means not only to *pass over* in the way of *sparing* the people, but also as a bird with outstretched wings, *protecting* the people of Israel. In *Egyptian* the word means to spread the wings over for protection. Keil says, "As birds flying so will the Lord of hosts defend Jerusalem; defending, also He will deliver it, and passing over, He will preserve it." The term is explained in the next verses. *For I will pass through this night.* That is the same night on which they were to eat the passover. They who will find fault with the narrative, and call it unhistorical, demand that *this night* is to be understood as meaning the night on which Jehovah speaks. But in Hebrew the pronoun refers always to that which is already spoken of. And here it points to the night following the fourteenth of the month, at least a week after this was spoken. ¶ *Will smite*, etc. This was to be God's direct act, which made this plague the concentration of all the foregoing. It was God's redemption of His own first-born. *Against all the gods of Egypt.* Calvin explains this, "that it was most apparent then how little help was to be found in these false gods, and how fallacious was their worship." It may mean that in smiting the first-born of beasts God would smite the objects of Egyptian worship. The worship of animals was universal; the bull and cow and goat and ram and cat were worshipped throughout Egypt. The rabbins understood it that every temple and idol was destroyed by earthquake or lightning; but Moses' Egyptian learning is manifest in this record, which would not have occurred to a stranger in Egypt.

13. The blood-mark would surely be recognized as a sacramental sign to them—a pledge of mercy—

CHAPTER XII.

where ye *are:* and when I see the blood I will pass over you, and the plague shall not be upon you to destroy *you* when I smite the land of Egypt.

14 And this day shall be unto you for a memorial; and ye shall keep it a [h] feast to the Lord throughout your generations; ye shall keep it a feast by an ordinance for ever.

15 Seven days [i] shall ye eat unleavened bread; even the first

---

h Le. 33: 4, 5; 2Ki. 23: 21; 1Co. 5: 8.   i ch. 13: 6, &c.; Nu. 28: 17.

---

marking the house on which it was, for the sparing mercy of God. ¶ *When I see the blood.* Not when I see you, but when I see the blood, for the blood was the controlling sign, as it was the token of expiation, and all the merit lay in the sacrifice, and not in them. (2) Though it was at midnight that the destroying angel would pass through, He would see the blood-mark, however dim it was, and however dark the night might be. "He is faithful that promised." He overlooks nothing that His grace can find.

14. *This day.* The fourteenth—referred to—the Paschal day—though the feast was eaten at night following, yet the lamb was slain on the 14th. *For a memorial.* A day of commemorative ordinance in which their redemption was to be called to mind, while it was to be also for a reminder to God in this sacramental seal of His covenant. "*This do in remembrance of me.*" — εις την αναμνησιν εμου—for my reminding or remembrance. It was to be kept *throughout your* (Jewish) *generations forever*—that it was to be of perpetual obligation. It was *a feast,* also, not *a fast.* Some look upon the New Testament paschal feast as a gloomy, repulsive ordinance, and more like a fast. But *no,* we are banqueted there upon the provisions which He has purchased with His blood. We should come with *hosannas,* and feed upon Christ, and feel ourselves richly feasted.

"A wondrous feast His love prepares
Bought with His wounds and groans and tears."

Keil says "The Passover was a sacrifice which combined in itself the signification of the future sin-offerings and peace offerings." It was eucharistic as a social meal, and it was expiatory as a sin offering. We should therefore come with joy. The feast is spread for us, and entirely of His providing. "In the meal," says *Keil,* the *sacrificium,* became a *sacramentum,* the flesh of the sacrifice a means of grace by which the Lord adopted His spared and redeemed people, into the fellowship of His house, and gave them food for the refreshing of their souls." It is to be remarked here that this ordinance was most important to be established at that very time—as notifying Israel on their leaving Egypt to what they were called, that their deliverance was nothing little or insignificant in the eye of God—as its celebration was to be commemorated even to the most distant generations, the people must have seen in that an indication of the great destiny which the Lord had in view for them at that moment, and their gaze was elevated from the present to the future." *Havernick's Int.* 251. Further, the directions for eating the meal in the houses, show that it was at a time when as yet they had no sanctuary. And so every particular agrees with the circumstances and shows it to be historical.

§ 24. Institution of the Feast of Unleavened Bread. Ch. XII: 15-20.

15. *Seven days.* This was a feast

day ye shall put away leaven out of your houses: for whosoever eateth leavened bread from the first day until the seventh day,[k] that soul shall be cut off from Israel.

16 And in the first day *there-shall be* an holy [1] convocation, and in the seventh day there shall be an holy convocation to you; no manner of work shall be done in them, save *that* which every man must eat, that only may be done of you.

17 And ye shall observe *the feast of* unleavened bread; for in this self-same day have I brought your armies out of the land of Egypt: therefore shall ye observe this day in your generations by an ordinance for ever.

18 In the first *month*, on the fourteenth day of the month at

---

k Nu. 9: 13. l Nu. 29: 12.

---

connected with the Passover, beginning at the close of the Paschal supper. The seven days' time is accounted for by some as commemorating the haste in which they were moving, so that they would be obliged to eat without leaven till they crossed the Red Sea, one week. (v. 39.) But a better reason is a more sacred one and more pertaining to the ritual. It was in order that the feast should include a Sabbath and thus take in the whole cycle of the week, in accordance with the Sabbath feature of the ritual. Supposing the Sabbath to have been already instituted, as we believe, and known from the beginning, this is the better explanation. ¶ *Even (only) the first day* (that is *not later than the first day*,) (the 14th at even (v. 18) *Ye shall put away leaven,* etc. In the Corinthians Paul explains this feature and shows the symbolical meaning of it. (1 Cor. 5: 7. See also Luke 12: 1.) "Unleavened bread" is the type of holy fervor and pure, pious living, without the principle of corruption at work within. The new life was thus symbolized, as cleansed from the leaven of a sinful nature. "Therefore, (says Paul) let us keep the (paschal) feast, not with old leaven, neither with the leaven of malice and wickedness, but with the unleavened bread of sincerity and truth." ¶ *Whosoever.* The violation of this law was a capital offence. *That soul*—that person *shall be cut off*—excommunicated from the covenant membership, and the privileges of Israel.

16. *Holy convocation*—a sacred assembly for religious worship, in prayer and praise, and perhaps also reading of the scripture and remark, as it came to be afterwards in the synagogue. This public religious gathering and service were to be on the first day and the seventh, making the beginning and close of the festival Sabbatic. The preparation of necessary food was allowed, as it was not on the Sabbath, and the day of Atonement. (Exod. ch. 16: 23, 24.) There were seven such Sabbatic days in the year besides the seventh-day Sabbath—the first and last days of unleavened bread, and of the feast of Tabernacles, the day of Pentecost, the first day of the seventh month and the day of Atonement (see Levit. 23; Numb. 28, 29). The term for convocation is derived in Hebrew, as in Latin, from the verb to *call.* So is *ecclesia* in the Greek, but further meaning "*called* out from."

17. The reason for the observance is here given: *Have I brought.* That which had not yet come to pass is stated to be the ground for this religious observance, so that the transaction is prophetic and promissory. So also "the Lord's supper"

CHAPTER XII. 103

even, ye shall eat unleavened bread, until the one and twentieth day of the month at even.

19 Seven days shall there be no ᵐ leaven found in your houses; for whosoever eateth that which is leavened, even that soul shall be cut off from the congregation of Israel, whether he be a stranger, or born in the land.

20 Ye shall eat nothing leavened; in all your habitations shall ye eat unleavened bread.

21 Then Moses called for all the elders of Israel, and said unto them, Draw out and take you a lamb according to your families, and kill the ⁿ passover.

22 And ye shall take a bunch of hyssop, and dip *it* in the blood that *is* in the basin, and strike ᵒ the lintel and the two

---

m ch. 23: 15; 34: 18; De. 16: 3. n Jos. 5: 10; 2Ki. 23: 21; Ezr. 6: 20; Mat. 26: 18; Mar. 14: 12; Lu. 22: 7, &c. o Le. 14: 6, 7; Ps. 51: 7; He. 9: 19; 11: 28.

---

was instituted as a memorial of what had not yet come to pass, and was in so far prophetic.

18. A more precise statement of v. 15.

19. A restatement of v. 15, last clause. *A stranger.* These were afterwards distinguished as of two classes, proselytes of righteousness, circumcised, and proselytes of the gate, uncircumcised, but who acknowledged the God of Israel and the Noachic precepts. But no foreigner could eat of the passover unless he had been circumcised, and had thus the badge of membership. *Born in the land.* Native of the country, a native Israelite, descended from Isaac and Jacob, to whom birth in the land of Canaan, and property in the soil, were vital matters of God's covenant. "One 'born in the land,' therefore, was *indigenous*, belonging to the country by virtue of descent, that descent being reckoned from Abraham, to whom Canaan was promised as a perpetual inheritance."—*Sp. Com.* Not a Hebrew born in Egypt (as Jamieson thinks), as a stranger might be born in Egypt.

20. The prohibition of leaven is here again repeated. "To eat leavened bread at this feast would have been a denial of the divine act by which Israel was introduced into the new life of fellowship with Jehovah."—*Murphy. In all your habitations,* as well as in the public service of the sanctuary during the feast. We are bound to be pious and devout at home as well as in the house of God.

§ 25. JEHOVAH'S PASSOVER. Ch. XII: 21–30.

21. Moses, having now recited the Divine directions, records also the leading items in his instructions to the elders of the people. The elders were officers in the church, and have continued to be such. *Draw out.* Take out—separate from the fold and take, etc. It has been objected that there was not time for these orders to be duly published; but it is assumed erroneously that there were only twelve hours, as if these orders had been given on the last day. But as the lamb was to be taken from the fold on the tenth, these orders were published before that day, and hence four, five or more days would remain. *A lamb according to your families,* that is, a lamb for each family (as many lambs as families), *and kill the passover*—the *passover lamb* selected.

22. *Hyssop.* Here follows a direction for sprinkling the blood.

side-posts with the blood that *is* in the basin; and none of you shall go out at the door of his house until the morning.

23 For the LORD will pass through to smite the Egyptians; and when he seeth the blood p upon the lintel, and on the two side-posts, the LORD will pass over the door, and q will not suffer the destroyer to come in unto your houses to smite *you*.

p He. 12: 24. q 2Sa. 24: 16; Eze. 9: 4-6; Re. 7: 3; 9: 4.

There were different species of this plant, but well adapted for this use —*a bunch*—of several stalks. The process was to dip the hyssop in the blood (of the animal) which was in the basin, and then apply the blood as directed. It has been insisted that as baptism has a meaning from the root *bap* — to *dip* — therefore, the subject must be *dipped*. But throughout the ritual, the dipping is of the instrument by which the sprinkling or baptizing is done. *Baptise* is not to *dip*; but to *dippize*, or to apply the element to the person by the article dipped, not by dipping the person in the element. So we never read of immersing one in the Holy Ghost. Else we must make the immersion to be in the blood of Christ; and this is no longer the idea of Baptism, which refers not to justification, but to sanctification. This is the essential idea in sprinkling. When the soldiers filled a sponge with vinegar and put it upon hyssop and gave our crucified Lord to drink, they were unconsciously using the passover instrument here mentioned. (Lev. 14: 51; Numb. 19: 18.) The hyssop was used in ordinary purifications to sprinkle the blood. It had thus a symbolical significance. "Purge me with hyssop, and I shall be clean."—Ps. 51.

None of you. This was to prevent the Israelites being, in any way, mixed with the Egyptians, where the most entire separation was to be carried out, and also, to prevent any suspicion of their being agents in the terrible destruction; and further, as there was no safety to any one except behind a blood-stained door; and as the house was consecrated by the *blood-mark*, this was their great security. Hence they must abide in the place.

23. Moses here repeated the order given him by God. The paschal blood was the saving mark for those Israelites who would so use it. It must be understood that as it is Jehovah's Passover and altogether a plan of grace, so He has the sovereign right to prescribe the terms of the salvation. And these are in no wise *conditions*, in the sense of a bargain, but provisions for our acceptance—and only such as are natural and necessary in the case to carry out the objects, and so these constitute the condition of things in which the benefits are to be bestowed.

When He seeth the blood. The Redemption mark is the signal for deliverance. (1) It is not our blood but the blood of the slain Lamb. (2) It must be accepted by us for a token and so applied by us as to indicate our acceptance of all the provisions. (3) It must be openly and publicly put forward as the shield and refuge under which we live. (4) It must be posted on our dwellings, as for ourselves, and our households in all our living. (5) We are not to reason against the provisions for they are all of grace. (6) Our great business is to be sure that we embrace the gospel provisions, and our question must be not as to the merit of our frames and exercises, but as to the fact of Christ's blood-shedding and our open and avowed acceptance and application of it to our case in all our living.

CHAPTER XII.

24 And ye shall observe this thing for an ordinance to thee and to thy sons for ever.

25 And it shall come to pass, when ye be come to the land which the LORD will give you, according as he hath promised, that ye shall keep this service.

26 And it shall come to pass, when your children shall say unto you, ᵣ What mean ye by this service?

---

r ch. 13: 8–14; De. 32: 7; Jos. 4: 6; Ps. 78· 6.

The Destroyer. A personal agent is referred to. In v. 29 it is ascribed to *the Lord*—Jehovah. In Heb. 11: 28, it is the Destroyer of the first-born.

24. *To thee and to thy sons forever.* So God has always graciously included the children in the blessings of His covenant. The ordinances are household ordinances. The new birth is not of *bloods*—one or another—yet the provision includes the children of believers as specially contemplated and cared for in the covenant. Therefore the paschal lamb was to be taken and slain and eaten *by families.* Bless the Lord for His grace to children's children in all the ages. *This thing,* lit., *this word*—this command or ordinance—It shall be a permanent institution in the Jewish church.

25. The people were in training for permanent religious services in the Promised Land. Here it is directed that this ordinance is for their observance in Canaan, as it was to teach them the vital principles of their faith, founded on the idea of sin and salvation by a Redeemer. It is called a *service,* since it was to be done in obedience to God, and was part of the service which as His servants they owed to Him. Though it was a provision for their good, yet they were held obligated to the performance. For God has pleased to make it our highest duty to accept His salvation. "This is the work of God that ye believe on Him whom He hath sent" (John 6: 29).

26. *When your children,* etc. Family religion is here supposed.

The children were expected to be at the Paschal table, and to ask questions about the ordinance, and the parents were to answer as instructed of God. The ordinance was a household ordinance. It was a family meal—and a family seal. And it is in this way that the New Testament sacraments are to be taught to the children, that they may understandingly partake as is provided. Christian parents are solemnly obligated by the terms of the baptismal ordinance to instruct their children in the nature of the obligations belonging to them and to be assumed by them at discretionary years. And because so little of this is done, therefore so little result is attained. ¶ *Ye shall say.* The ordinance was to be explained *as the sacrifice of the Lord's Passover.* (1) Its sacrificial nature is declared. As a bloody sacrifice the Passover had in it the essential element of the sin-offering. And as a social meal, it was *eucharistic*—a thank-offering. And so it combined in itself the essence of the whole sacrificial system. It was the top and crown of the whole. Hengstenberg shows that it was the foundation and centre of all sin-offerings. And the Rationalists who avoid the significance of this contend that it was originally a festival of nature to which a religious element was afterwards added. But nature worship has rather sprung from the religious sentiment which is plainly most prominent in all the Hebrew festivals. Yet they all had a threefold reference and significance. (1) The Historical. (2) The Agricultural. (3) The Evangelical,

27 That ye shall say, It *is* the sacrifice of the Lord's passover, who passed over the houses of the children of Israel in Egypt, when he smote the Egyptians, and delivered our houses. And the people bowed the head and ˢ worshipped.

28 And the children of Israel went away, and did as the Lord had commanded Moses and Aaron: so did they.

29 And it came to pass that at midnight the Lord smote ᵗ

---

s Ch. 4: 31. t Nu 3; 13; 8: 17; 33: 4; Ps, 78: 51: 105: 36; 135: 8; 136: 10; He. 11: 28.

(1) The Passover had the Historical reference as commemorating the wonderful deliverance of the covenant people from Egyptian bondage. (2) The Agricultural reference. At the opening of the barley harvest, the first ripe stalks were to be presented and waved before God. (3) The Evangelical reference—embracing both the others in the antitype. (a) The Deliverance from the bondage of the world (b) the first fruits of the Resurrection, or harvest of the world (Christ the first fruits. (1 Cor. 15: 23). We have had the Christian Passover, in which the type has passed into the antitype.— There was a meal in the ancient Passover, a feast upon the sacrifice, which meal remains as the eucharistic thanksgiving feature of this social and family ordinance.

Of the Lord's Passover—the sacrifice of the Passover (or Paschal lamb) *to Jehovah*—the lamb offered to Jehovah as expressive of atonement, as appointed by His gracious provision. Or it may be understood The sacrifice of the Passover ordinance which is Jehovah's—whose provisions are His. As we call the corresponding New Testament ordinance—*The Lord's Supper*—of His providing, and spreading and consecrating. It is the Lamb of God— God's Lamb. The recital of the Paschal history as the occasion of the ordinance is touching and comprehensive, holding up the great Redemptive fact as to be impressed most deeply on the household. This is the gospel teaching which is due to christian children from believing parents. Our Redemption is to be put forth as a joyous fact, when He passes over us and our houses, and in this our children are bidden to rejoice with us, and to celebrate with us the paschal ordinance. It is not so much *a profession of religion*—that is—of having a notable measure of religion fit to be mentioned. It is rather a *confession of Christ*, and of the facts upon which our faith fixes and rests. *The people bowed the head and worshipped* in expression of their reverent and devout reception of these instructions and of their purpose to abide by them.

28. The people obeyed the directions and accepted the provisions. Alas! for those who claim that they can do without the Lord's Supper and do not need it for their religious living. "If I wash thee not thou hast no part with me." (John 13.) If any one declines what Christ pronounces needful, how can he expect to attain to the salvation which Christ alone can provide? And it is not a repulsive medicine. It is a feast. And when He who knows our need has spread it freely for us, why shall we not gladly partake? How can any accept the Gospel feast, and refuse the Lord's Supper? It is plain that children ought to ask about the Lord's Supper and Baptism—to know what they mean and what they have to do with them— for they are deeply concerned in both these sacred and precious ordinances of Christ's house.

§ 26. THE TENTH AND FINAL PLAGUE. Ch. XII: 29-36.

29. The dreadful night of horrors has now arrived. According to all

all the first-born in the land of Egypt, from the first-born of Pharaoh that sat on his throne, unto the first-born of the captive that *was* in the dungeon; and all the first-born of cattle.

30 And Pharaoh rose up in the night, he and all his servants, and all the Egyptians; and there was a great cry ᵛ in Egypt; for *there was* not a house where *there was* not one dead.

---

v Ch. 11: 6; Pr. 21: 13; Am. 5: 17; Matt. 25: 6; Ja. 2: 13.

---

that was threatened and provided for so *it came to pass. At midnight*—in the time of deep sleep and security—the blow came as it had been forewarned, (ch. 11 : 4). Pharaoh might have averted it and escaped the deluge of wrath, had his wicked heart relented. But he went madly on—defying God to do His worst. And as he had cruelly slain the children of the Israelites, so he suffers in kind. The Plague is here ascribed to Jehovah. It was not by the rod of Moses as before, but more directly and personally. Yet this does not forbid the agency of a *Destroyer* such as is implied in Hebrews (11 : 28). And natural causes may also be admitted. Only that a pestilence confining its ravages to the first-born implies the direct and intelligent agency of a Personal mind and will. Evidently this Plague is emphasized as having been wrought by Jehovah. And there is nothing inconsistent with the supposition that it was the Covenant Angel, the Second Person of the Godhead. ¶ *The captive that* (was) *in the dungeon*, lit., *in the house of the pit.* In ch. 11 : 5, it is the woman behind the mill that is mentioned In both cases it is the same idea—from the highest to the lowest of society—from the king to the lowest menial or slave. Such a judgment was invited by the acts of Pharaoh and the people in destroying the male children of the Israelites. And this cruelty they had begun more than eighty years before and had been practising since, to the horror and wo of the families of Israel. And now in one night there comes such a fitting recompense from God. (1) God often pays in kind. (2) God visits men's iniquities on them often already, in this life. (3) God is just as well as loving and good. (4) Many cannot or will not believe that God will punish sin in another world. But even in this world, He punishes often in such a way as to show His principles of administration. And there must be a time for universal settlement. Men will sometime get the reward of their deeds; except as they take refuge in Christ, repenting and believing in Him. *The first-born of cattle.* The beasts are sharers in the wo which the monarch's sin has brought upon the land. "The whole creation groaneth and travaileth in pain together until now." (Rom. 8) But the animal creation and all created things on our planet will share in the blessedness of Christ's Redemption. There is a glorious resting for the creature as the result of Christ's finished work. How the pride and strength of Egypt was smitten in one night! ¶ *Not a house*, that is, of the class described, in which first born were found, of the rising generation—not themselves parents. (1) Alas! for the children. How they must suffer for the misdeeds of their parents. (2) How important for the children to have pious fathers and mothers. (3) Children, and especially the eldest, suffer for the drunkenness and theft and murder in which their parents are brought to shame and disgrace the household. (4) What a motive to parents to be the Lord's when their best beloved children must so much rise or fall by their

EXODUS.

31 And he called ^w for Moses and Aaron by night, and said, Rise up, *and* get you forth from among my people, both ye and the children of Israel; and go, serve the Lord, as ye have said.

32 Also take your flocks and your herds, as ye have said, and be gone; and ^x bless me also.

33 And the Egyptians were ^y urgent upon the people, that they might send them out of the land in haste; for they said, We *be* all dead *men*.

34 And the people took their dough before it was leavened, their kneading-troughs being bound up in their clothes upon their shoulders.

35 And the children of Israel did according to the word of Moses; and they borrowed of the Egyptians jewels of silver and jewels of gold, and raiment:

---

w Ch. 11: 1.   x Ge. 27: 34.   y Ps. 105: 38.

---

conduct. God "visits the iniquities of the fathers upon the children unto the third and fourth generation of those that hate Him." And this is commonly by a natural process in which vice spreads disaster through the household. While He "shews mercy unto thousands (or families) of them that love Him and keep His commandments." The blessedness and security of being in a pious family cannot be exaggerated. "The stout hearted are spoiled" (Ps. 76: 5). Pharaoh's heart quakes. He and all his people are smitten with horror at midnight and are roused from sleep.

The first born of Pharaoh himself was struck dead (v. 29).

31, 32. So it occurred as Moses had foretold him. (ch. 11 : 8.) It is evident that the King's residence (at Tanis or Zoan) must have been near to where Moses was, at Rameses, (v. 37) as the message is promptly delivered. ¶ *Both ye and the children.* Pharaoh no longer seeks compromise, but entreats them to be gone altogether, with flocks and herds. He was now eager to grant them all that they had asked —*as ye have said.*—*And bless me also.* He asks to be on good terms with them—dreading any further curse, he bespeaks a blessing. How completely he is brought down. And yet how craven after his stubborn and cruel persistence against God and His servants. The worst men and most bitter opposers of christianity have quailed at the near prospect of death, and have cried for mercy.

33. *Urgent.* They were now eager and impatient to have them gone. They saw death and destruction staring them in the face. (Ps. 105 : 38.) *We be all dead men.* They made no demand for their return. God will have absolute and unconditional submission.

34. *Their dough* — unleavened, not raised—indicating their haste, (v. 39)—as the prohibition was not yet given. *Their kneading troughs.* These were bowls of wood or of wicker work, light and portable—and with the dough in them they could wrap them in their large loose mantle and swing them over the *shoulders.*

35. As Moses had directed them, so the Israelites *demanded* (not borrowed) *jewels of silver*, etc. They had need of supplies of valuables and raiment for their journey. They had a right to compensation for their long and laborious service. They make the demand—asking it as their right—and God by His Providence and Spirit disposed the Egyptians to grant this demand.

36. This might have been con-

CHAPTER XII.

36 And the Lord[z] gave the people favor in the sight of the Egyptians, so that they lent unto them *such things as they required;* and they spoiled the Egyptians.

37 And the children of Israel journeyed from [a] Rameses to

---

z Ge. 39: 21; ch. 3: 21: 11: 3.   a Nu. 1: 46; 11: 21.

---

tested and refused. But *the Lord* (Jehovah) *gave the people favor in the eyes of the Egyptians,* who were ready to give them anything they asked to get clear of the awful calamities which their detention involved. *They lent,* or, lit., *caused them to ask,* rather, *They gave them.* This is plain from all the connection of the narrative. Nothing was said about their return. The contrary is presumed (see 1 Sam.: 1 : 28). The direction to do this had been given prior to the last plague, and it was not all of a sudden, on the eve of their departure. ¶ *They spoiled*—despoiled—(ch. 3 : 21, 22; 11 : 2,) showing that it was no lending, but giving under the stress of the occasion—and so they took these treasures as *spoil* or booty (Gen. 15 : 14. Ezek. 39 : 10. Ps. 105 : 37). They came out of the land of bondage with great substance. "He brought them forth also with silver and gold." It was God's doing.

§ 27. The Exodus.—Ch. XII. 37-42.

37. *From Rameses.* This was probably the province or district—for no city would be a rendezvous for such a multitude. Yet the city of this name was probably the headquarters. Some, as Hengstenberg and Robinson, take this to have been Heroopolis, the chief city of Goshen, (So *Keil* and *Jamieson*) the modern *Abu Keishib,* near to Tanis or *Zoan,* the monarch's residence (Ps. 78 : 12). It is held to have been between the Pelusiac arm of the Nile and the N. W. extremity of the Bitter Lakes. *To Succoth.* The name means *booths,* probably a caravan station, well-known, about half way between Rameses and Etham, or the head of the Red Sea—the stations being about fifteen miles apart. That they went out so promptly is owing to the fact that they had received several days' notice, (ch. 11 : 2) and were in expectation of a release for sometime previous. Stanley (Hist. of Jewish Church) says: "How deeply that first resting-place was intended to be sunk into their remembrance may be gathered from the fact that this, rather than any other of the numerous halts in their later wanderings, was selected to be represented after their entrance into Palestine, as a memorial of their stay in the wilderness. The Feast of Tabernacles (Lev. 23 : 40) 43) or *Succoth*—was a feast, not of tents, but of huts woven together from the boughs of goodly trees, branches of palm trees, etc., that all their generations might know that the Lord made the children of Israel to dwell in booths when He brought them up out of the land of Egypt." *About six hundred thousand.* These were the marching men, and supposing them to include those above twelve or fourteen years of age (*Sp. Com.*: commonly reckoned above *twenty*) besides women and children, the whole people would easily amount to more than two millions. *Josephus* says "two hundred and forty myriads." It has been doubted by many whether there could have been such an increase of the Israelites during their sojourn in Egypt, whether that period be reckoned as four hundred years or two hundred and fifteen. But (1) this large multitude who went out of Egypt, though called Israelites, included with descendants of Jacob's family and of his household, the trained servants who went down with him, of whom Abraham had

Succoth, about ᵇ six hundred thousand on foot *that were* men, beside children.

38 And a mixed multitude ᶜ went up also with them, and flocks and herds, *even* very much cattle.

---

b Nu. 1: 46; 11: 21.   c Nu. 11: 4.

---

318 and Jacob, doubtless, had a large retinue. *Rawlinson* says: "It is not unlikely that the whole company which entered Egypt with Jacob amounted to above one thousand souls." (*Aids to Faith p.* 322.) All of these being circumcised, and perhaps born in the house, would be reckoned as Israelites. This supposition, however, is not necessary to account for the increase in Egypt. *Birks* makes the descent into Egypt to have been not of Jacob's family alone, but of a whole Hebrew tribe and so called Hebrews —including many more than Jacob's sons and grandsons, and probably not less than a thousand in all (pp. 139, 40). Doubtless a large retinue of household servants and attendants had been inherited by Jacob from Abraham and Isaac. *Keil,* however, declines to include these, and confines the reckoning to the seventy, who went in, as put in contrast with those who came out. Making all deductions from the 70, there remain forty-one grandsons who founded families, in addition to the Levites. Reckoning forty years as a generation (1 Chron. 7 : 20, etc.) the tenth generation of the 41 grandsons would be born about the year 400 of the sojourn in Egypt, and therefore would be over 20 years of age at the exodus. He calculates that there would be by ordinary reckoning 603,550 men who were more than 20 years old at the exodus. And this without any special Divine blessing for their extra increase. (2) But if their sojourn in Egypt was only 215 years, as we have supposed, then, taking seven descents or natural generations of 30 years, there is no impossibility in the numbers. But (3) there is to be considered God's special promise to the patriarchs of a very numerous seed. (4) The practice of polygamy would further need to be taken into the account, besides intermarriages with their household servants who were fellow-worshippers, and of their own domestic circle. Added to this their intermarriages with the Egyptians would need to be reckoned. It is capable of clearest proof, and it has been shown repeatedly and conclusively on various bases of calculation that these numbers are readily accounted for, even on the basis of 215 years sojourn in Egypt. (See *Payne Smith's Bampton Lectures,* 1869. III. p. 88.) The total here mentioned, 600,000, is admitted by *Ewald.* (See Gen. 12 : 2 ; 17 : 6 ; 22 : 17 ; 26 : 3 ; 46 : 3.) See also for the more direct number (Num. 2 : 32 ; 3 : 39). With 68 males for the first term—8 for the number of terms, and 4 for the common ratio, the last term, or the number of males at the exodus, would be 1,114,112.—*Murphy.*

38. *A mixed multitude.* A promiscuous crowd—many stragglers and hangers on, who were outsiders, however they may have formed the connection with the Israelites—fellow-workmen as captives in war perhaps—glad to escape with the released people, and impressed perhaps by the judgments wrought against Pharaoh and Egypt. ¶ *Very much cattle.* So it was provided that they should have means of sustenance in the wilderness. In illustration of this great Exodus a sudden retreat is recorded of 400,000 Tartars, a whole nomadic people, under cover of a single night (as late as the close of the last century), from the confines of Russia to their own wilds.— *Ewald.*

CHAPTER XII. 111

39 And they baked unleavened cakes of the dough which they brought forth out of Egypt, for it was not leavened; because they were thrust out of Egypt, and could not tarry, neither had they prepared for themselves any victual.

40 Now the sojourning of the children of Israel, who dwelt in Egypt, was ᵈ four hundred and thirty years.

41 And it came to pass at the end of the four hundred and

---

d Ge. 15: 13; Ac. 7: 6; Ga. 3: 17.

---

39. *Baked unleavened cakes.* The prohibition of leaven had not been made for the Passover night, and they had no time now, to procure leaven (v. 34). It is here accounted for from their haste in departing. Whatever notice of several days they had had, the excitement and the necessary preparations to go out, with all they had, would prevent many a comfort in the arrangement. ¶ *Any victual* —any provision for the journey.

40. *Now the sojourning,* etc. There has been much dispute as to the period passed in Egypt—and whether this term here named includes the sojourn in Canaan. The weight of modern opinion seems to be in favor of the longer chronology, making the 430 years to have been passed in Egypt. And some have adopted this view as better accounting for the large number of the people who came out of Egypt. But as we have seen, this is not necessary. And Paul in the Galatians (3: 17) states that the Law was given 430 years after the promise to Abraham. So Gen. 15: 13, 16, gives 400 years for the term of affliction and bondage of Abraham's seed in a strange land, and the "fourth generation" for the time of their return to Canaan. This seems to some inconsistent with the short chronology. But not necessarily so; yet if 430 years be the period from the call of Abraham, then 405 years would remain from the birth of Isaac to the year of the Exodus. *Keil* argues for the longer. So does *Havernich, Kurtz, Hengstenberg,* *Rawlinson,* etc.,—by supposing that some of the genealogical links are omitted. But this is conjecture. *Birks, MacDonald, Baumgarten, Murphy,* and others adopt the shorter. The Psalmist recognizes the fact that Canaan was to the patriarchs "a strange land," (Ps. 105). When they were but a few (men) in number, yea, very few, and *strangers in* it, (that is the land of Canaan, v. 11) and in this Psalm which refers to this so expressly, he recites their national history from Abraham's call, (v. 6) and traces them when they went from one nation to another, from one kingdom to another people (v. 13). Israel also came into Egypt and Jacob sojourned in the land of Ham." (v. 23.) Now, is it probable that the 400 years spoken of to Abraham would refer to a section of their sojournings and not to all, and that *the strange land* should not include the land of which it is here said they were strangers in it. Acts 7: 6. Gen. 15: 13. Gal. 3: 17. "By faith he sojourned in the land of promise as in a strange land." Heb. 11: 9. *Augustine* reckons from the 75th year of Abraham when he left Haran, then from Haran to Isaac 25 years, from Isaac to Jacob 60, Jacob to the entrance to Egypt 130, thence to the death of Joseph 71, to Moses 64, to Exodus 80, making in all 430 years.

41. *The self-same day.* God is exact in His time, and keeps His promises to the day and hour. "In the fulness (or fulfilling) of the times," as in smaller matters most

thirty years, even the self-same day it came to pass, that all the hosts of the LORD went out from the land of Egypt.

42 It *is* a night to be much ᶜ observed unto the LORD for bringing them out from the land of Egypt; this *is* that night of the LORD to be observed of all the children of Israel in their generations.

43 And the LORD said unto Moses and Aaron, This *is* the ordinance ᶠ of the passover: There shall no stranger eat thereof;

44 But every man's servant that is bought for money, when thou hast ᵍ circumcised him, then shall he eat thereof;

45 A ʰ foreigner and an hired servant shall not eat thereof.

---

e De. 16: 1-6.   f Nu. 9: 14.   g Ge. 17: 12.   h Le. 22: 10; Ep. 2: 12.

---

personal to us, He keeps His word punctually. It was fulfilled as spoken to, Abraham, Gen. 15:13-16. At the end of the four hundred and thirty years came the Exodus. ¶ *The hosts of Jehovah.* In ch. 7: 4, God calls the people of Israel His armies or hosts—and His title is the *Lord of hosts*—whether of starry hosts, or armies of people.

42. *A night, lit.*, a night of keepings—whether of preservation (*Keil*) or of observances (*Murphy* etc.) to be kept as a solemn observance *to* (in honor of) *Jehovah—this is that* (memorable) *night of Jehovah, to be observed*—(same phrase as before) *night of observances* (plur. of eminence) *to* (or *for*) *Jehovah—for all the children of Israel in their generations.* The repetition shows that this would be the leading festival and sacrament of their religion always.

A papyrus manuscript found in an Egyptian tomb has lately been translated by a scholar of Heidelberg. It is pronounced by the Heidelberger, says the *Jewish World*, to be an address of Rameses III. to all the nations of the earth, in which the King details minutely all the causes which led to the exodus of the Jews from the land of the Pharaohs.

§ 28. ORDINANCES OF THE PASSOVER. Ch. XII: 43-57.

43. *No stranger*—no one who was not of the commonwealth of Israel and who was a stranger to the covenants of promise—no alien, could be a partaker, or communicant.

44. *A servant* was to be circumcised and so admitted to partake—since circumcision was the badge of membership, and the personal seal of the covenant,—as Baptism now is, which takes its place. It was the duty of the householder to introduce his purchased servant into his church, as responsible for him. The proselytes who were circumcised were also baptised—to indicate their cleansing from ceremonial defilement as heathen. And when circumcision, which pointed to native depravity and to a miraculous generation, was discontinued by the coming of the *God-man,* then the baptism held over and was retained, as suited in all its ideas, to the extension of the church amongst the Gentiles.

45. *A foreigner,* lit., *a sojourner.* As the Passover was the sacrament of a covenant in which the Israelites were adopted as the people of God, it followed that a sojourner had no share, as not being of the people and having no fixed home, or permanent relation to a covenant household. *Hired servants*—having no permanent relation, but liable at any time to break their connection with Israel—were not admitted, as not of the covenant family. "A circumcised beggar, or slave, was nearer

CHAPTER XII.

46 In one house shall it be eaten; thou shalt not carry forth ought of the flesh abroad out of the house, neither shall ye break a bone [i] thereof.

47 All the congregation of Israel shall keep it.

48 And when a stranger shall sojourn with thee, and will keep the passover to the LORD, let all his males be circumcised, and then let him come near and keep it; and he shall be as one that *is* born in the land: for no uncircumcised person shall eat thereof.

49 One law [k] shall be to him that *is* home-born, and unto the stranger that sojourneth among you.

50 Thus did all the children of Israel; as the LORD commanded Moses and Aaron, so did they.

---

i Nu. 9: 12; Jno. 19: 33–36. k Nu. 9: 14; 15: 15, 16; Ga. 3: 28; Co. 3: 11.

---

to God than an uncircumcised king." "They that are in the flesh cannot please God" (Rom. 8 : 8). "Aliens from the commonwealth of Israel and strangers from the covenants of promise have no hope, and are without God in the world." But now, incorporated with the church, they are presumed to be one with Christ, and they so are, if they have living faith in Him, and as such they are no more strangers and foreigners, but fellow-citizens of the saints and of the household of God." (Ephes. 2 : 19, 20.)

46. *In one house.* Here is the unity of the church intimated. "One body and one spirit and one hope of our calling." The *Targum* renders it, *In one company.* The victim was to be consumed by the one company met for the passover, whether of the same family or not. ¶ *Neither break a bone.* Only this victim was to be kept entirely whole. A whole Saviour and not half, nor in parts—not as priest to atone, if not also as king to rule and as prophet to teach. John recognized the typical application of this to Christ Jesus (John 19 : 36).

47. *All the congregation*—or assembly. This is the oneness of the membership. "One body in Christ and every one members one of another (Rom. 12 : 5). It was as if all Israel were eating one Lamb. It was the communion of saints.

48. There was provision for a stranger, or sojourner, who settled with the covenant people—taking up his abode with them. The necessary condition of communion was the rite of circumcision as the covenant seal. *And will keep the Passover*, lit., *and he has made* (prepared) *a Passover* to *Jehovah, let every male be circumcised to him* — (he himself and all the male members of his house) and then he may draw near to Jehovah and keep it. Circumcision was the badge of membership.

49. Circumcision was the outward profession; and the door was open to the Gentiles on this sole condition admitting them to the church benefits. And so it was already made plain that the religion of the Jewish people was not exclusive, but was open to all, and was intended to include the Gentiles.

50. These requirements and instructions were faithfully observed by the people of Israel.

51. Here closes the narrative of the Paschal Deliverance. This verse properly belongs to the paragraph closing with v. 30. Yet it stands here as a connecting link with the next chapter. The Deliverance thus

51 And it came to pass, the¹ self-same day, *that* the LORD did bring the children of Israel out of the land of Egypt ᵐ by their armies.

---

1 Ver. 41.   m ch. 6: 26.

---

provided for was accomplished the self-same day as promised. For this all the warnings had been given to Pharaoh, and all the plagues had been wrought upon Egypt. The closing item of all earthly history will be like to this. Jehovah brought forth in that self-same day the covenant people (his own children) out of bondage to sin and death—*by their armies*, lit., *upon their hosts*. This does not refer to war, but to solid organized bands, tribes, etc., under their respective leaders—to show that it was done on the plan and basis of most orderly arrangement, and not at loose ends—not in straggling crowds. So the church of Christ is led forth from satanic bondage by individual churches The one communion is made up of distinct communions. The *Sept.* reads, *with their strength*. But the literal meaning is the better. They were led forth in orderly, well-arranged columns. (See ch. 13 : 18.) God is a God of order, and not of confusion. It is referred to in connection with our Lord's flight in infancy to Egypt and His return therefrom, to which this is likened as being the Deliverance of Israel, as the Son of Jehovah. For this Son is a complex Person, of which Christ is the Head and His people are the members. (1) This Deliverance of the church from Egypt was typical of the greater Deliverance of the church from the bondage of the world—of sin and death—by Jesus Christ. (2) It was, in the infancy of the church, the foreshadow of our Lord's return from Egypt in His infancy, and His Deliverance from persecutions which had driven Him there. (3) It was preparatory in the world's history for the Deliverance and salvation of the christian church then future.

OBSERVE, (1) Circumcision and the Passover denote Regeneration and Redemption. (2) Circumcision symbolizes the new birth without signifying its fruits. The Passover represents the effects of Redemption in the eating of the sacrifice—denoting the benefits received and enjoyed. (3) Circumcision referring to what is inward is personal and individual. The Passover referring to what is outside of ourselves is a social ordinance and exhibits the communion of saints. (4) In circumcision as in the new birth, the recipient is passive. In the Passover which implies a voluntary partaking of the sacrificial meal the recipient is active. (See *Murphy* ch. 12 : 11.)

OBSERVE, *further*. (1) It was *Jehovah's Passover*. (a) Provided by Him. (b) In honor of Him. (c) In celebration of His sparing mercy and redeeming grace. (2) The deliverance was by means of the *blood-mark*. Not by the blood-shedding, if the blood was not applied, for the public open acceptance and appropriation of the Paschal provision was requisite. (3) Leaven in the house would cut off from communion. But the blood-mark secured the salvation. Corruption spoils one's religious living and cuts off his fellowship. But it is not even the unleavened living that saves. It is still the blood. "When I see the blood" —not when I see the leaven all swept out. It is Christ's finished work for us—not the Spirit's finished work within us (alas! so unfinished) that is to be the basis of our hope, and which God looks upon for our salvation. (4) The leaven was put away by the covenant people because of their faith in the blood of expiation, and because of their being saved, not in order to be saved. And so faith works. It is not serv-

CHAPTER XIII.

AND the LORD spake unto Moses, saying,

2 Sanctify unto me all the ᵃ first-born, whatsoever openeth the womb among the children of Israel, *both* of man and of beast: it *is* mine.

3 And Moses said unto the people, Remember this ᵇ day, in which ye came out from Egypt, out of the house of bondage;

---

a Ver. 12; ch. 22: 29; 34: 19; Nu. 3: 13; De. 15: 19; Lu. 2: 23.   b ch. 12: 42.

---

ing God that we may gain Heaven. No! but because Heaven is gained for us by Christ, and we have it for nothing! (5) God from the first takes our side against our enemies, Satan, sin, the world, the flesh. They are His enemies also. He undertakes for us, and despoils them. Glory to God for our Redemption!

CHAPTER XIII.

§ 29. SANCTIFICATION OF THE FIRST-BORN. RULES FOR THE FEAST OF UNLEAVENED BREAD. Ch. XIII: 1–16.

God had acquired a special right to the first-born by His distinguishing grace in saving them when the first-born of Egypt were destroyed. Therefore He will have them solemnly set apart to Him and His service. This command was given therefore as a first requirement after the Deliverance and grounded upon it. *Keil* therefore pronounces it as in its proper place in the narrative, and as probably commanded at Succoth. The feast of unleavened bread had been already ordered by God to Moses. But Moses now gives the order to the people as required in ch. 12: 15, etc., —"Every first-born that is a male," (v. 12) *Sanctify.* The term means here *Set apart* as devoted.

2. It was not simply a right by creation but this special right by Redemption which is here insisted on. In this act and by this fact, God set them apart as His. The first-born of men as ministers—the first-born of beasts as victims. "*They are mine.*" (1) God claims the flower and strength of our redeemed households for His service. And Christian parents are specially bound to devote their first-born sons to God in the ministry. The Levites were afterwards set apart as a tribe in lieu of the first-born but on the basis of God's claim as here expressed, and then the first-born were to be redeemed from the claim. (2) This consideration is closely connected with the Passover. And hence, at every celebration of the Lord's Supper, the christian father and mother should recognize this right of God to their sons in the service of the ministry (Heb. 12: 23). It is eminently due to God in gratitude for His grace in sparing our households that we should consecrate our children to His special service.

3. The Passover was properly the opening of the feast of Unleavened Bread. *Remember this day.* As they were commanded to *remember* the Sabbath day, so they were commanded to remember this day of glorious Deliverance. It was the day that signalized God's covenant fidelity and love, and the day of the sacramental seal of that covenant. *The house of bondage,* lit., *the house of slaves,* where they had suffered such cruel treatment from which now they were exempt, and were become a nation emerged from thraldom. ¶ *By strength of hand.* By the display of Divine power, in

for by strength of hand the LORD brought you out from this *place:* there shall no leavened bread be eaten.

4 This day came ye out, c in the month *Abib.*

5 And it shall be, when the LORD shall bring thee into the land of the Canaanites, and the Hittites, and the Amorites, and the Hivites, and the Jebusites, which he d sware unto thy fathers to give thee, a land flowing with milk and honey, that thou shalt keep this service in this month.

6 Seven days e thou shalt eat unleavened bread, and in the seventh day *shall be* a feast to the LORD.

7 Unleavened bread shall be eaten seven days: and there shall f no leavened bread be seen with thee, neither shall there be leaven seen with thee in all thy quarters.

8 And thou shalt shew thy son g in that day, saying, *This is done* because of that *which* the LORD did unto me when I came forth out of Egypt.

---

c De. 16: 1–3. d Ge. 17: 8; 22: 16. e ch. 12: 15. f ch. 12: 19. g ch. 12: 26; ver. 14.

---

the judgments successively inflicted. All was due to God's mighty power. So recently in bondage and just now escaped, they were prepared to receive this charge. "With a strong hand, and with a stretched out arm" (Ps. 106: 12). ¶ *No leavened bread.* This prohibition is repeated and emphasized for its significance as to the putting away from them of pride and corruption.

4. The very day of the Exodus in the month *Abib* is to be borne in mind.

5. All the ritual observances were for their training to the great ideas of sin and salvation. Into their own land they were to be brought as a nation and there they were to be put under this ceremonial tutelage for the coming superior deliverance by Jesus Christ. Here they are charged that this feast is to be a permanent institution in the land of Canaan. During the wilderness wanderings they had little opportunity to keep the feast.

6. *A feast to the Lord Jehovah.* The seventh day of the feast of Mazzoth or unleavened bread was to be a feast to Jehovah by a holy convocation and suspension of work (12: 16). The first day was of course a feast of Jehovah. So that the Passover and the feast of unleavened bread occupied eight days. See Levit. ch 23. There is seen to be a significance in "the morning after the Sabbath," so much insisted on, and especially in the feast of tabernacles where it was the day for the waving of the first-fruits—and where thus there was an evident foresignifying of the New Testament Sabbath—as *the day after the Sabbath* when Christ the first-fruits was waved (passing up and down) before the Lord.

7. A still further repeating and insisting on the prohibition of leaven.

8. *Because of that,* lit., *Because of this that Jehovah did unto me—* that is—I observe this feast *because,* etc. (1) Instruction of the household was engrafted upon the whole service at this initial point, and it was held to be a fundamental duty, to teach and train the children for God. (2) The presence of the children at the solemn festival was taken for granted. Why should not the children of Christians take their places at the Lord's Supper? There are seats for the little ones at Christ's table.

9. The observance was to Is-

9 And it shall be for ʰ a sign unto thee upon thine hand, and for a memorial between thine eyes; that the LORD's law may be in thy mouth: for with a strong hand hath the LORD brought thee out of Egypt.

10 Thou shalt therefore keep this ordinance ⁱ in his season from year to year.

11 And it shall be, when the LORD shall bring thee into the land of the Canaanites, as he sware unto thee and to thy fathers, and shall give it thee,

12 That thou shalt set apart unto the LORD all that openeth the matrix, and every firstling that cometh of a beast which thou hast ; the males *shall be* the LORD's.

13 And every firstling of an ass thou shalt redeem with a lamb; and if thou wilt not redeem it, then thou shalt break his neck: and all the first born of man among thy children shalt thou redeem.

---

h Ver. 16; De. 6: 8; 11: 18; Pr. 1: 9; 6: 21; Ca. 8: 6.   i ch. 12: 14-24.

---

rael," *for a sign unto thee upon thine hand.*" It was to keep the events as constantly in view, as if it had been graven on the palms of their hands, or as if it had been worn as a jewel pendant between the eyes. *Murphy* thinks it refers to the ornamental bracelet which they wore about the wrist, and to the jewel on the forehead, called the frontlet, hanging between the eyes, and that the ordinance of the Passover and its accompanying solemnities were to serve as pleasing memorials in like manner as these personal ornaments often were, and he says " There is a beautiful consecration of personal ornament in this injunction." But the ordinance is to be our ornament and boast and joy— we are to wear it as a decoration and then to signalize our thankful and open glorying in the Lord and in His Covenant. All this for the express object—*that the law of the Lord may be in thy mouth*—as " it was by the reception of it into the heart and its continual fulfilment that it was to be placed in the mouth and talked of continually." —*Keil*, (See 2 : 16.)

10. *In his season.* Our version uses "*his,*" for "*its,*" *at its ap-* pointed time, *from days to days,* as often as the days returned (15th to 21st *Abib*).

11-16. Here again Moses gives to the people the directions for the permanent observance of this feast in Canaan. In regard to the first-born, it is here given to the Israelites, as God commanded Moses (vs. 1, 2).

13. *An ass.* In Egypt we found the donkey to be almost the only beast for travel, and these so domesticated as to be of great value for constant use. At Cairo, these animals, each having a boy to accompany him, were to be found in numbers at the door of the hotel for hire, and for hours the animal trots round the city, with the boy at his side, and the traveller on his back, the boy punching the animal with a sort of spike of iron to urge him on. *Every firstling* born of an ass was to be devoted to God and held as His property, and redeemed with a lamb, because the ass was unclean and could not be offered in sacrifice. It is thought to be probable that this was the only unclean animal domesticated among the Hebrews at the Exodus. If not redeemed with a lamb as a substitute

14 And it shall be, when thy son ʲ asketh thee in time to come, saying, What *is* this? that thou shalt say unto him, By strength of hand the Lord brought us out from Egypt, from the house of bondage:

15 And it came to pass, when Pharaoh would hardly let us go, that the Lord slew all the first born in the land of Egypt, both the first-born of man and the first-born of beast: therefore I sacrifice to the Lord all that openeth the matrix, being males; but all the first-born of my children I redeem.

16 And it shall be for a token upon thine hand and for frontlets between thine eyes: for by strength of hand ᵏ the Lord brought us forth out of Egypt.

17 And it came to pass, when Pharaoh had let the people go, that God led them not *through* the way of the land of the Philistines, although that *was* near; for God said, Lest peradventure the people ˡ repent when they see war, and they return ᵐ to Egypt:

18 But God ⁿ led the people about, *through* the way of the

---

j De. 6: 20; Jos. 4: 6, 21.   k De. 26: 8.   l ch. 14: 11, 12; Nu. 14: 1-4.   m De. 17: 16. n De. 32: 10.

---

to be offered in sacrifice, then it was to be slain. ¶ *First-born of man.* These of the Israelites were to be redeemed. This was positively required and no alternative was allowed. The redemption money was fixed in the law at five shekels of the sanctuary (Numb. 18: 16). The first-born males represented the entire offspring and succession.

14–16. Instructions for the household are here added. The reasons for the observance are to be carefully recited—the history is to be repeated. Our religion is not a theory, notion, or speculation. It is a religion of *facts*. The history is to be told over and over again to our children.

15. Lit. *When Pharaoh made hard to let us go.* Keil understands —made hard his heart. (ch. 7: 3.) *Germ.* Was hard to let us go. *Sept.*—*hardened* to send us away. The slaying of the Egyptian first-born was the great and awful fact which put in striking contrast the grace of the deliverance to Israel.

16. As in v. 9, the meaning is that the observance whose purport was supposed to be inquired about by the sons of the household, was to be *a sign*, as if graven on the palms of the hands, for a token and memorial, and a *confession*, as if hanging like a jewel pendant between the eyes. Here is implied—the idea of profession and practice. As if worn on the forehead — so openly and boldly confessed—and as if graven on the palms of the hands—so associated with all the doings. The Pharisaic custom that afterwards prevailed grew out of a mistaken view of this passage.

§ 30. The Exodus, continued.— Ch. XIII : 17–22.

17. It is here stated that when the people were released and had set out, God did not lead them by the shortest route to Canaan. Travellers now-a-days usually take this route from Cairo to Gaza—mentioned here as the way of the Philistines — and it occupies commonly about five days. The reason for avoiding this natural course is here given—that it would expose the

wilderness of the Red Sea: and the children of Israel went up harnessed out of the land of Egypt.

19 And Moses took the bones of Joseph with him: for he had straitly sworn the children of Israel, saying ᵒ God will surely visit you; and ye shall carry up my bones away hence with you.

20 And they took their journey ᵖ from Succoth, and encamped in Etham, in the edge of the wilderness.

o Ge. 50: 25; Jos. 24: 32; Ac. 7: 16.   p Nu. 33: 6.

Israelites to war. There was a standing quarrel between these two people (1 Chron. 7 : 21, 22) and at this outset such a conflict would have been likely to discourage them and to send them back to Egypt. It might be objected to this reasoning that God could control the case. But He works by natural means and leads His people by paths adapted to their condition—and so we pray "Lead us not into temptation" or trials of any severe kind. So God often deals with His people, leading them not by the way which is nearest, but the most roundabout, and always for sufficient reasons. ¶ *Led the people about.* He undertook their guidance. The way was not the most direct. We are impatient of any delay, and wish to reach the end most quickly. But God knows what is for us the best path, however circuitous, and so He leads us forward. ¶ *Through the way of the wilderness of the Red Sea.* God had His higher motives besides those already named for leading them by this route. The law was to be given them beyond the Sea, and the wonders of their deliverance were to be wrought in that bed of waters. This Sea is over eleven hundred miles long and one hundred and twenty miles wide—a gulf of the Indian Ocean, having two arms within which is included the peninsula of Arabia and the wilderness of Sinai. Some suppose it to have been originally a strait connecting the Mediterranean and Indian Oceans. (See the Map.)

OBSERVE. (1) The shortest way is not always the surest. (2) Jesus is the Alpha and Omega—the beginning and ending of our affairs. (3) Wait and trust, and not be discouraged, for however crooked now, the path will come to be straight at length and will lead home. ¶ *Went up harnessed.* This term is elsewhere rendered "*armed.*" And supposing this to be the meaning, it has been an objection to the narrative as unhistorical—that they could not have been *armed.* But they could have been armed after their fashion, and probably were. It is proper, however, to understand the word as meaning *orderly,* or *in columns,* probably on the basis of *five* abreast as the word would indicate, (as in the margin) or *five divisions.* Others read it *equipped.* Pharaoh plainly dreaded them as fighting men. And their numbers are given in the history here on the basis of ability to bear arms. This idea is conveyed. (See ch. 17 : 13.)

19. *Took the bones of Joseph.* The bones of Joseph had already been in their charge 140 years, and during all their troubles they were under a solemn covenant to take them up to the Holy Land, whenever they should go, as Joseph had faith that they would (Gen. 50 : 24, 25.) ¶ *Straitly sworn them.* Strictly bound them by oath. It was his faith in God's promise to give them possession of the land. They had, therefore, the constant reminder of Joseph's dying confidence, and this skeleton of Egypt's prime-minister, preserved in sacred keeping under such a charge, was doubtless

EXODUS.

21 And the LORD went before them ᑫ by day in a pillar of a cloud, to lead them the way, and by night in a pillar of fire, to give them light: to go by day and night.

22 He took not away the pillar of the cloud by day, nor the pillar of fire by night *from* before the people.

---

q Nu. 9: 15-23; 10: 34; 14: 14; De. 1: 33; Ne. 9: 12-19; Ps. 78: 14; 99: 7; 105: 39; Is. 4: 5;. 1Co. 10: 2; Re. 10: 1.

---

influential in keeping them encouraged during their deepest affliction.

20. After a kind of parenthesis from v. 17, the narrative is here resumed, showing the progress of their departure. At Succoth, doubtless, instructions were given and preparations were completed for the journey. ¶ *Etham* was their first camping ground after leaving Succoth—the booths. *Sp. Com.* understands *Etham* as the same with Pithom—the sanctuary of *Thum* (Sun God) and near Heroopolis the frontier city, at the edge of the Bitter Lakes. Others locate it between the Bitter Lakes and the head of the Arabian Gulf—though this interval may have been at that time covered with brackish water as now, or the two bodies of water may have been a connected whole. *Ajrud* is held to be the point called Etham, northwest of Suez and eastward from Succoth. So Tischendorf and others. It may be supposed to have been chosen with the purpose of going round the head of the gulf, and at the edge of the wilderness, a frontier point and near the border of the gulf, or Red Sea.

21, 22. *A Pillar of a cloud.* This column of cloud or misty, smoky vapor, would serve as a signal for so large a multitude, marking headquarters for the scattered companies pasturing their flocks, and serving, too, in its motion, as a sign for moving on. It was the protection also of the camp from the sun by day, and at night, as it was then luminous, it was a light for their journeyings. And altogether it was a sign of Jehovah's leadership. It is known that the Persians and Greeks used fire and smoke as signals in their marches. This was something far more. There was something significant in these tokens here — as afterwards in the Tabernacle and in the Temple the luminous cloud over the mercy-seat was the *Shekinah*, or visible presence of God, representing Jesus Christ. It was His Leadership, as the Angel of the Covenant, that was here set forth. (See ch. 14: 19.) This was something far superior to the common signals of Eastern armies, as caravan fires. There were not two pillars, but one only. *Kurtz* understands that the cloud represented the mercy of God and the fire the holiness of God. *He took not away the pillar of the cloud.* It did not disappear. It was a perfect reliance, always serving its purpose day and night with infinite adaptedness to their condition and wants. (See Neh. 9: 19.)

OBSERVE, (1) God's way is the best way for us, though it may not be the direct and immediate route that we would have chosen. (2) God's reasons are most sufficient and personal to us, and practical also, while He has higher reasons that He does not now reveal. (3) God is Himself the Leader of His church and people through the wilderness. (4) We march to the goodly land of Promise according to the faith of those long since departed. Their death is therefore precious to us, and we bear their remains in faithful and tender keeping as our sacred trust. (5) God indicates our route by plain signals and tokens of His truth and mercy in Jesus Christ. His visible presence is made manifest to us, with wonderful adaptedness to our case, in every condition

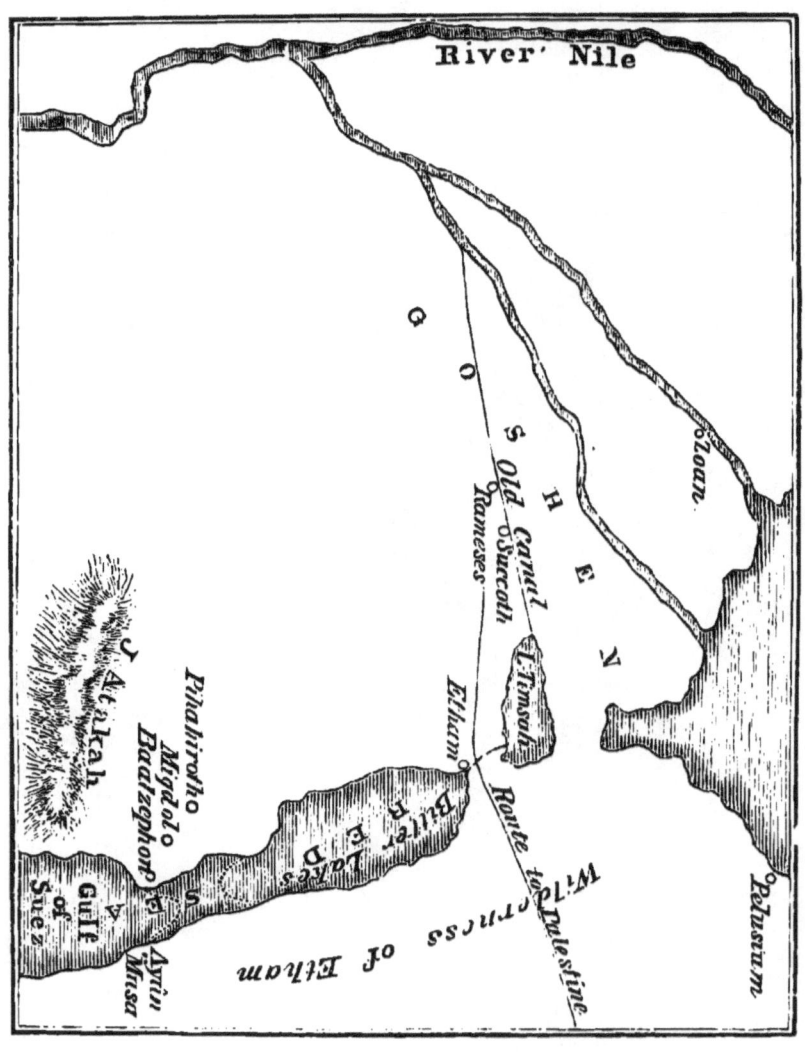

CHAPTER XIV.

AND the Lord spake unto Moses, saying,

2 Speak unto the children of Israel, that they turn and encamp before ^a Pi-hahiroth, between ^b Migdol and the sea, over against Baalzephon: before it shall ye encamp by the sea.

3 For Pharaoh will say of the children of Israel, ^c They *are* entangled in the land, the wilderness hath shut them in.

---

a Nu. 33: 7.   b Je. 44: 1.   c Ps. 3: 2; 71: 11; Je. 20: 10, 11.

---

and relation of life, day or night—at home and abroad—leading us to the better country, that is the heavenly. (6) Christ the Angel of the Covenant is as truly present with us and leading our way as if the pillar of cloud and fire were the visible signal. (7) The New Testament Passover is the commemoration of the death of Christ for us. The New Testament Sabbath is the commemoration of the Life of Christ for us, and of the Risen Christ as a Present Saviour. (8) Jesus Christ is with His ministers and with His Church alway, even unto the end of the world.

CHAPTER XIV.

§ 31. GOD'S MARCHING ORDERS, AND THE PURSUIT. Ch. XIV: 1-18.

1, 2. This is now the third day's march, and the orders come from the Divine Leader whose miraculous signal is displayed before them. They had come to Etham (ch. 13: 20) for encampment, and now, at the edge of the wilderness, was the critical step to be taken. They would naturally have gone forward towards the East, and into the desert with the Sea on their right. But thither Pharaoh might have pursued and overtaken them with his chariots. But God has for them a different plan. They are now ordered to march Southward by a short *turn* from the head of the Sea and down the Western shore, so that they turn aside from the direct route with all the disadvantage of having the Sea betwixt them and their destination. This would seem to the natural reason to be a 'blunder.' But the sequel will discover the Divine plan. *Before Pihahiroth.* The word means "*Mouth of the ravines*"—or (*Stanley*) *pastures,* or "*house of wells*" (*Sp. Com.*). This is supposed by *Sp. Com.* to be the same as *Ajrud*—four hours' journey to the N. W. of Suez, on the pilgrim route from Cairo to Mecca. This name seems to be Egyptian, meaning a *marshy place.* It is a fortress with a large well of water. *Migdol*—this name means a *tower*—and was two miles from Suez. Some take it to denote a lofty mountain peak of *Attakah.* A triangular plain of ten miles extent lay between this and the sea, bounded by this precipitous ridge which at the lower end shoots into the Sea, and thus shut them in. *Over against Baalzephon.* It was *by the sea.* It was at least six hours' journey from Etham. The camp would spread over many miles. *See Map.*

3. *For.* The reason is given here for this unexpected order, that Pharaoh would look upon the movement as affording him an excellent opportunity of successful pursuit (v. 4). *They are entangled in the land,* so that they cannot get out of Egypt. They are now hemmed in, and shut up, and cut off from escape by the sea. This was Pharaoh's thought. *The wilderness hath shut them in*—or rather, is closed to them. Or, the fear of per

EXODUS.

4 And I will harden ᵈ Pharaoh's heart, that he shall follow after them; and I will be honoured upon Pharaoh, and upon all his host; that the Egyptians may know that I *am* the LORD. And they did so.

5 And it was told the king of Egypt that the people fled: and the heart of Pharaoh and of his servants was turned ᵉ against the people, and they said, Why have we done this, that we have let Israel go from serving us?

6 And he made ready his chariot, and took his people with him:

7 And he took six hundred chosen chariots ᶠ and all the chariots of Egypt, and captains over every one of them.

---

d ch. 4: 21, &c.   e Ps. 105: 25.   f ch. 15: 4.

---

ishing in the wilderness has turned them aside. The Red Sea at that time, probably extended north to the Bitter Lakes, at least.

4. Pharaoh would thus be induced, freely in God's Providence and from his own judgment of the case, to pursue them. Thus God hardens his heart naturally and without compulsion by the working of his own sinful and rebellious principles. For sin is itself the natural and necessary punishment of sin. God will *be honored* also *upon Pharaoh* by the most signal displays of His power and glory before the Egyptian *hosts*. It would be to them a revelation of Himself as *Jehovah,* Redeemer of His people. *And they did so,* strictly obeying the Divine order.

5. *The people fled.* Pharaoh may, up to this time, have been uncertain whether they would return or not after keeping a feast, as was first spoken of. They may have had a route marked out to them by Pharaoh, so that this departure from it proved them to be in flight. How soon he could receive the intelligence from Etham is not certain. *Sp. Com.* thinks in less than a day—others suppose *two days*, and the preparation for pursuit as much more—*Keil* thinks that we have no ground for supposing such information being sent to Pharaoh of their change of route, but that his movement for the pursuit was prompted by his change of feeling and regret at letting them go. But v. 3 intimates that he was moved to the pursuit by their situation, and that this was on account of their new route by the Divine direction. Yet here the narrative is more that of the monarch's second thought after the people had actually gone out of their quarters. And if so, it may refer to Pharaoh's reflection on the day after their departure, so soon as the confusion and dismay of mourning their first-born had ceased. *Was turned.* Here is reconsideration, a regret at having yielded, the self-reproach at having let them go, and the determination to overtake them.

6, 7. *Made ready* (yoked) *his chariot—and took his people* (warriors) *with him—six hundred chosen chariots,* special and different from "the chariots of Egypt"—probably his own body-guard — containing the picked men of his army, and the best equipped—*all the chariots of Egypt,* which he could then muster in that quarter—*and captains,* commanders, royal guard, *over the whole of them* — (not charioteers). The chariots were drawn by two horses, and occupied by two men, one of whom was the driver and shield-bearer, and the other was armed with the bow, etc. These are shown on the monuments.

8 And the LORD hardened the heart of P'haraoh, king of Egypt, and he pursued after the children of Israel: and the children of Israel went out with an high ᵍ hand.

9 But the Egyptians pursued after them (all the horses *and* chariots of Pharaoh, and his horsemen, and his army) and overtook them encamping by the sea, beside Pi-hahiroth, before Baalzephon.

10 And when Pharaoh drew nigh, the children of Israel lifted up their eyes, and behold, the Egyptians marched after them; and they were sore ʰ afraid: and the children of Israel cried out unto the LORD.

11 And they said unto Moses, Because *there were* no graves

---

g Nu. 33: 3; De. 26: 8.   h Jos. 24: 7; Ne. 9: 9; Ps. 84: 17; 106: 44; 107: 6.

Sometimes besides the driver there were two warriors in the chariot. In other cases one drove and fought.

8, 9. *Hardened.* It occurred as God had said to Moses, v. 4. God's plans include the free actions of His creatures, whether good or bad. *With a high hand.* That is —of God—His power was engaged for their deliverance. The historian throws in this clause to show that, whatever the thought of Pharaoh, God had him under control, and used him as an instrument for His purpose, while at the same time the children of Israel were coming out of Egypt, with the outstretched hand of God engaged for them. *But*—notwithstanding the Divine engagement for them—*the Egyptians pursued after them. And his horsemen.* It has been doubted whether at this time there were horsemen, as cavalry, in the Egyptian service. But Diodorus Siculus states that Rameses II. had 24,000 cavalry. And Isaiah refers to horsemen of Egypt in distinction from chariots (ch. 31: 1). *Keil* remarks that God had decreed this hardening of Pharaoh to glorify Himself in the judgment and death of the proud king who would not honor Him in his life. *Overtook them.* The troops of Pharaoh would reach the encampment in much less time than the people of Israel—probably in a day and a half where the Israelites had taken three days.

10. When the Egyptian hosts came in sight, and the Israelites saw them marching upon them, no wonder they were *sore afraid.* To all human view they were most perilously situated. On the East was the Sea. On the West and South were the high mountains shutting them in, while their armed foes, who had oppressed them, were marching upon them from the North. And they so unprepared for war. Could they not remember God's marvellous working in bringing them out of Egypt? Could they not consider the tokens of the Divine Presence accompanying them—the pillar of cloud and fire? *They cried out unto the Lord*—though they so distrusted Him and evidently rather gave way to despair.

11. *Because there were no graves at all in Egypt, hast thou.* The language is strong and expressive, containing a double negative. *Sp. Com.* suggests that this taunt was probably suggested by the vast extent of cemeteries in Egypt, which might not improperly be called the land of tombs. *Hast thou fetched us to die in the desert?* "It was only when the oppression increased that they had hitherto complained of what Moses had

in Egypt, hast thou taken us away to die in the wilderness? Wherefore hast thou dealt with us, to carry us forth out of Egypt?

12 *Is* not this the word that we did tell thee in ⁱ Egypt, saying, Let us alone, that we may serve the Egyptians? For *it had been* better for us to serve the Egyptians, than that we should die in the wilderness.

13 And Moses said unto the people, Fear ye not, ʲ stand still, and see the salvation of the LORD, which he will shew to you to-day: for the Egyptians whom ye have seen to-day, ye shall see them again no more for ever.

14 The LORD shall fight ᵏ for you, and ye shall hold your peace.

15 And the LORD said unto Moses, Wherefore criest thou

---

i ch. 5: 21; 6: 9. j Nu. 14: 9; De. 20: 3; 2Ki. 6: 16; 2Ch. 20: 15–17; Ps. 27: 1, 2; 46: 1–3; Is. 41: 10–14. k De. 1: 30; 3: 22; 20: 4; Jos. 10: 14; 23: 3–10; 2Ch. 20: 29; Ne. 4: 20; Is. 30: 15.

---

done (ch. 5: 21), and afterwards they obeyed implicitly his directions." *Keil*. *Wherefore*. Thus they complain bitterly against Moses in their despair, as if he had wilfully brought them into this case.

12. This is the exaggerated aspect in which they put the matter. They refer now to their early shrinking and misgiving at the first trial, and are ready to say, "*We told you so.*" How perfectly natural, yet how grossly unfair! They evidently bring up this language as the suggestion of their present cowardice and distrust of God. *For better for us*, etc. This is now their clear conviction, begotten of their shameful unbelief.

13. Moses has faith for the exigency, and he rallies the despairing people. He had received such assurances from God as overcame his own natural distrust (v. 4). It was most essential that he, their appointed Leader, should not falter at the critical moment. Why should his faith fail? Had not his rod been Divinely successful to work wonders in all the realm of nature, and would he and his people who had been so delivered be deserted and destroyed now? *Fear ye not—stand still and see the salvation of Jehovah*. Deliverance was to come from without, and they were *to stand still and see*. Such sublime composure in such danger —the foe marching upon them, the people panic-stricken, and ready to lay all the blame upon him—is scarcely paralleled in history. What meekness under the injurious denunciations of the people. *Which He will shew to you to-day*. So assured was Moses that promptly as the crisis came so promptly should the deliverance follow. *For the Egyptians whom ye have seen to-day*, or, *for as ye have seen the Egyptians to-day*—ye shall never see them as ye have seen them to-day. He is sure, and so he assures them that their foes, however daring and confident, shall be utterly swept away. He may have had intimation of the way in which they should be destroyed.

14. *Jehovah shall fight for you*. The Almighty who had already so signally wrought for them would undertake the battle on their side, *and ye shall hold your peace*. That is ye shall have nothing to say, or do about it. It shall be wholly due to His Divine power and grace. Or, ye will be silent and cease your

unto me? Speak unto the children of Israel, that they go forward.

16 But lift thou up thy rod, and stretch out thy hand over the sea, and divide it: and the children of Israel shall go on dry *ground* through the midst of the sea.

17 And I, behold, I will harden the hearts of the Egyptians, and they shall follow them: and I will get me honour upon Pharaoh, and upon all his host, upon his chariots, and upon his horsemen.

18 And the Egyptians shall know that I *am* the LORD, when I have gotten me honour upon Pharaoh, upon his chariots, and upon his horsemen.

19 And the angel [1] of God which went before the camp of Israel, removed, and went behind them; and the pillar of the cloud went from before their face, and stood behind them:

20 And it came between the camp of the Egyptians and the camp of Israel; and it was a cloud and darkness *to them*, but it gave light by night *to these:* so that the one came not near the other all the night.

---

[1] Nu. 20: 16; Is. 63: 9.

---

complaining (Gen. 34 : 5). (*K & D.*)

15. Jehovah now replies to the cry of the people, and addressing Moses He asks: *Wherefore criest thou unto me?* from which it would appear that Moses was moved to cry to God, or, that he is spoken to as representative and head of the people. Yet, there is not necessarily any rebuke of his prayer, but only a call to action. Marching orders are put into his mouth. *That they go forward.* The word means *to break up*—as an encampment—*to set out*, (2 Kings 19 : 8) and it is used in v. 19 of the Angel of God *removing.*

16. Moses' rod was now again to come into use for the wonder-working power of God. He was ordered to *lift up his rod* and *stretch* his *hand* (with the rod) *over the sea and divide it* (the sea). Here the process was explained by which the deliverance should be effected. Moses was now plainly advertised of the way of escape. *Shall go on dry ground through the midst of the sea.* (See v. 21, notes).

17, 18. This is a repetition of the language in v. 4, somewhat more emphasized and at length.

§ 32. CROSSING THE RED SEA.— Ch. XIV : 19-31.

19. *The Angel of God.* He (Jehovah) who went before them in these miraculous tokens—the pillar of cloud and fire (See ch. 13 : 21)— *removed and went behind them. The pillar of the cloud* was here the Shekinah or visible manifestation of the Divine Presence as Angel of the Covenant. There was now to be a new purpose served by the miraculous pillar — discriminating between the Israelites and the Egyptians and effecting a separation and barrier between the two—dark to the Egyptians but light to Israel —and keeping them apart. " *And it was the cloud and the darkness* (to the Egyptians) *and lighted up the night* (to the Israelites).

21. *Caused the sea to go* (back) *by a strong East wind. Palmer* in his "Desert of the Exodus" says.

21 And Moses stretched out his hand over the sea; and the LORD caused the sea to go *back* by a strong east wind all that

"'Two hours' ride (south) from Suez brought us to *Ayun Musa*—or *Moses' wells*—a beautiful little oasis in the desert. To the north stretches a vast plain of sand, with a long chain of mountains bordering it on the East. And on the north-west the bold promontory of *Ras Atakah* overhangs the Gulf. Here tradition places the site of the passage of the Red Sea. And certain it is that within the range over which the eye can wander, the waters must have closed in upon Pharaoh's struggling hosts. From the narrative in Exod. 14, it would seem that the Egyptians came upon them before they had rounded the head of the Gulf, so as to compel them either to take to the water or to fall into their enemies' hands. But natural agencies miraculously accelerated are mentioned as the means employed by God in working out this signal deliverance, and we need not therefore suppose anything so contrary to the laws of nature as that the children of Israel crossed between two vertical walls of water in the midst of the deep sea, according to the popular mode of depicting the scene. (But see ch. 15 : 8. The floods stood upright as an heap). Some writers have imagined that a great change has taken place in the level of the sea since the time of the Exodus, but recent examination does not at all confirm this hypothesis, while there is abundant evidence that the N. end of the gulf of Suez has been silted up and that in consequence the shore line has steadily advanced further and further southwards. It follows from this that if, according to the view held by many modern authorities, the passage took place at the head of the Gulf, as it existed at the time of the Exodus, the Israelites must have crossed at a point several miles north of its present limits." *The Lord* (Jehovah) *caused the sea to go* (back — drove the sea—*by a strong east wind all that night and made the sea dry* (land) *and the waters were divided*. *Palmer* says, 'This is no sudden division of the waters, involving a suspension of physical laws, though to my mind it is much more wonderful as showing how those laws were subservient to the Divine purpose and will. A strong wind blowing from the East, at the moment of the setting in of the ebb tide, might so drive back the waters, that, towards the sea, they would be some feet higher than on the shore side. Such a phenomenon is frequently observed in lakes and inland seas, and if there were, as there would very likely be at the head of the Gulf, any inequality in the bed of the sea or any chain of sand-banks dividing the upper part of the Gulf into two basins, that portion might be blown dry and a path very soon be left with water on either side. As the parting of the sea was caused by an East wind, the sudden veering of this wind to the opposite quarter at the moment of the return tide would bring the waters back with unusual rapidity. This seems to have been actually the case, for we find that the waters returned, not with a sudden rush, overwhelming the Egyptians at once, but gradually and at first, as we might expect saturating the sand so that " it took off their chariot wheels that they drave them heavily." But (1) the sand bars run N. and S. And (2) this explanation does not suit the narrative (v. 22). *Keil* reads—*And the water split itself* (i. e., divided by flowing northward and southward, and the Israelites went *in the midst of the sea*) where the waters had been driven away by the wind) *on the dry ground*) *and the water was a wall* (i.e. a protection formed by the damming up of the water) *on the right and on the left*. The East is a general

CHAPTER XIV.

night, and made the sea ᵐ dry *land*, and the waters were divided.

22 And the children of Israel went into the midst ⁿ of the sea upon the dry *ground:* and the waters *were* a wall unto them on their right hand, and on their left.

---

m Jos. 3: 16; 4: 23; Ps. 66: 6.   n 1Co. 10: 1; He. 11: 29.

---

term including north-east and south-east, as the Hebrews had only four points of the compass. Whether the wind blew directly from the East or from the south-east or north-east, cannot be determined, as we do not know the exact spot where the passage was made. In any case the division of the water in both directions could have been effected only by an East wind. And although even now the ebb is strengthened by a north-east wind, as *Tischendorf* says, and the flood is driven so much to the south by a strong north-west wind that the Gulf can be ridden through and even forded on foot to the north of Suez, (and as a rule the rise and fall of the water in the Arabian Gulf is nowhere so dependent upon the wind as in Suez) yet the drying of the sea as here described, cannot be accounted for by an ebb strengthened by the east wind, because the water is all driven southward in the ebb, and not sent in the opposite direction. Such a division could only be produced by a wind sent by God, and working by Omnipotent force, in connection with which the natural force of the ebb may no doubt have exerted a subordinate influence. We can see the ground of the legend which arose among the people of that neighborhood and which was found even at Memphis, that the Israelites took advantage of a strong ebb to make the passage. See *Keil and note.* And it has been attempted thus to explain all the phenomena without anything supernatural. But the view of *Keil* is surely more accordant with the record, and with all the plain facts of the case as thus recited. The route is given in the annexed *Map,* showing the probable extent of the Red Sea north of its present bed, in the time of Moses. This is the finding of the most recent survey of Captains Wilson and Palmer, of the Royal Engineers. Thus the tongue of the Egyptian Sea has been dried up, as was predicted (Isa. 11: 15). *Dr. Olin,* who travelled over the route, disputes the Suez passage, as being too narrow for the Egyptian host, and too shallow to engulph them so suddenly. He decides for the extremity of *Mt. Attaka* where the sea is 10 or 12 miles wide, and where there is a wide triangular plain bounded by the sea and the mountain and the desert, and broad enough for the two armies.—*Olin's Travels.*

Doubtless quite beyond the utmost that could have occurred by a strong wind and the ebb of the tide, there was a supernatural agency using also the natural force supernaturally, and causing a mighty East wind to scoop out the waters so as to hollow out a passage, and make the waves recede on either side (N. and S.) as walls. This is the record. And we have no reason to evade the miraculous agency which so plainly appears. (Ps. 114: 3.) The sea stood as *heaps.* If the East wind only blew the water back, it would have swept over the camp. We must suppose a huge trough made in the sea exposing the dry bed, dry enough to *cross.* If the waters were only blown back to the South it must have been a North wind, and there could have been no heaping up on both sides.

22. *And the children of Israel went into the midst of the sea upon*

23 And the Egyptians pursued, and went in after them, to the midst of the sea, *even* all Pharaoh's horses, his chariots, and his horsemen.

24 And it came to pass that in the morning watch the Lord looked unto the host of the Egyptians through the pillar of fire and of the cloud, and troubled the host of the Egyptians,

25 And took off their chariot-wheels that they drave them

---

the dry (ground) *and the waters* (were) *a wall unto them on their right hand and on their left.* And this came from the miraculous division of the waters. It must continue long enough for this vast multitude of two and a half millions and their cattle to get across. *K. and D.* suppose that they might have entered upon the passage at nine in the evening and continued until the morning dawn, 4 or 5 o'clock (see v. 27). *Robinson* says, the result "was wrought by natural means supernaturally applied." But the effort has been made to minimize the supernatural so as virtually to dispense with it. But this is vain. God is displaying Himself to Pharaoh and to all men as above all the processes of nature. The laws of nature only prove a Lawgiver behind them and in them and in their operation.

23. *The Egyptians pursued.* They followed closely and were intercepted only by the miraculous pillar—and could not fully see ahead of them—but pressed on in the pursuit. They "were therefore in the midst of the Sea when the rear of the Israelites had reached the opposite shore." At the narrowest point above Suez the Sea is now only 3450 feet broad. The crossing must have been at a much broader point than it is—as it formerly was broader than this here no doubt, and is now broader opposite *Kolzum*. But to have the Sea engulph the Egyptian army of more than six hundred chariots and many horsemen, requires a greater breadth. The madness of the pursuit left no room for consideration, and the pillar of cloud gave them little opportunity to see whither they were rushing, except that they were following the foe. *Murphy* remarks "that at the base of *Jebel Attakah*, where the crossing probably occurred, the Sea is at least six or seven miles wide. If the dry ground were a quarter of a mile broad, the Israelites would form a column a quarter of a mile in rank and a mile in file. Such a body might cross a channel of six miles in six hours, and might easily decamp, set out, and reach the opposite bank in eight hours."

24. *In the morning watch.* They had two watches for the passage, or eight hours. About sunrise, which at this season of April was a little before six o'clock. *And Jehovah looked at the army of the Egyptians in* with *the pillar of cloud and fire.* This look of Jehovah may have been a lightning flash darting from the cloud—with a storm of thunder and rain—confounding the Egyptians and throwing them into dismay and panic. (See Ps. 77: 17, 18.) *Josephus* also describes the scene as full of terrible phenomena—lightning and thunder and rain, an elemental war. *And troubled the host.* Drove them into consternation.

25. *And took off the wheels of his* (the Egyptian's) *chariot*—made them give way. This would readily result from the panic, driving upon each other, and in the attempt to escape for life, sinking the wheels in the sea-bed so that they would break off, or *drive heavily—and caused that he drove with difficulty.*

CHAPTER XIV.

heavily: so that the Egyptians said, Let us flee from the face of Israel; for the Lord fighteth for them against the Egyptians.

26 And the Lord said unto Moses, Stretch out thine hand over the sea, that the waters may come again upon the Egyptians, upon their chariots, and upon their horsemen.

27 And Moses stretched forth his hand over the sea, and the sea returned to his strength when the morning appeared; and the Egyptians fled against it; and the Lord overthrew the Egyptians in the midst of the sea.

28 And the waters returned, and covered º the chariots, and the horsemen, *and* all the host of Pharaoh that came into the sea after them: there remained not so much as one of them.

---

o ch. 15: 10; Ps. 78: 53; 106: 11.

This sudden and awful reverse extorted from the bewildered host of Egypt the cry *Let us flee from the face of Israel, for Jehovah fighteth for them.* As Moses assured the Israelites it would be, so their enemies confess it has come to pass.

26. The covenant people are now safe. Their enemies who are in hot pursuit are now to be destroyed. God has planned the minutest result. The miracle is manifest here again (1) in that the rod of Moses, which had in itself no power, was the signal for the return of the waters, (2) in that these waters should flow back at the signal, just at the moment to accomplish the drowning of the Egyptians when they were in the midst of the sea. It is idle to attempt any such explanation of the record as will dispense with the miraculous in these phenomena, any more than in the former. To suppose here only "a sudden veering of the wind at the moment of the return tide," without any miracle, is to presume upon such a combination of circumstances as would imply a miracle, even if that would present all the necessary conditions of such a result as followed. Yet God pleased to use natural forces supernaturally and extraordinarily for this express purpose. *Foster* reads inscriptions on the Rocks at Sinai thus "Turned into dry land the Sea, the Hebrews flee through the Sea."

The record is plainly intended to convey the impression of the same miraculous power here as in all the plagues visited upon Egypt. The time for the continuance of the ebb tide would not have been long enough to effect the passage. But the miracle was in force all the night. The wind did its work promptly and made the passage at once, not by long blowing, so that they could begin the march at evening and continue it till morning. "Thou didst divide the Sea by thy strength" (Ps. 74: 13, 14).

27. *The Sea returned to his strength,* rather to *his permanent place, at the approach* (or *dawning*) *of the morning and the Egyptians were flying to meet it,* in the face of it, as it rushed upon them from the West, in their return. *And Jehovah shook out the Egyptians,* hurled them from their chariots, *in the midst of the Sea* (Ps. 136: 15).

28. The complete destruction by the over-rushing waters is here recorded. Some maintain that it is nowhere said that Pharaoh perished. But all perished who pursued the Israelites into the Sea. And in Egypt it was customary for the King to lead his armies in war. And it is said in the Psalm (136: 15) that Pharaoh was overthrown in the Sea along with his army, where the same verb is used as here. "*But shook out* Pharaoh and his host in

6*

29 But the children of Israel walked upon dry *land* in the midst of the sea; and the waters *were* a wall unto them on their right hand, and on their left.

30 Thus the LORD saved Israel that day out of the hand of the Egyptians: and Israel saw the Egyptians dead upon the sea-shore.

31 And Israel saw that great work which the LORD did upon the Egyptians: and the people feared the LORD, and believed p the LORD, and his servant Moses.

---

p ch. 19: 9; Jno. 2: 11; 11: 45.

---

the Red Sea." The blow was therefore most stunning to the Egyptians, and there was no recovery for them to continue the pursuit. *Not so much as one of them was left* (Ps. 106: 11).

29. The contrast in case of the Israelites was most miraculous. The walking on dry land across where their enemies were overtaken by the returning floods and drowned, and the waters serving them as walls right and left, north and south, for their safe passage—these items are repeated for emphasis. The facts are clearly historical, and are plainly befitting the whole record, and are every way appropriate to the case. We are to remember that God is supernatural, and to Him the supernatural is natural, however difficult it be to us to conceive.

30. *Thus.* This is the history of the salvation of Israel that day, says the historian. The effect upon Israel is recorded. They saw their enemies dead upon the sea-shore, their corpses swept upon the beach by the angry waters.

31. *And Israel saw the great work* (lit., *that* great hand) *which Jehovah did*—the great power which He displayed " with a strong hand, and with a stretched-out arm—*upon the Egyptians. And the people* (Israelites) *feared Jehovah and believed Jehovah and His servant Moses.* It was thus that, as Paul says, " they were all baptized unto Moses in the cloud and in the sea " (1 Cor. 10:2) that is—now at the very outstart and on the threshold of their wilderness journey they were, by this grand deliverance, as by a sacramental ordinance, solemnly consecrated and obligated to Moses in a public confession of him as a typical Mediator, and thus sworn to obedience as members of the church under the Mosaic economy. So also Jehovah as He had said, had gotten glory upon Pharaoh, who would not glorify Him by an obedient life and so must glorify Him by a penal and awful death. Moses must be believed in as Leader and Mediator for the people, and these results were well worthy of the miraculous demonstration.

LESSONS. (1) In the greatest straits we are to stand still and see the salvation of God. Our salvation does not come by our utmost action, but by our implicit trust in Christ's redemption. (2) Our enemies are Christ's enemies also, and He has undertaken to fight for us. (3) Where God bids us go forward, He will make a way for us through all obstacles. (4) All nature and its forces and elements are under the control of our Lord and Saviour, and He can make them subserve our interest and His design of grace. (5) By faith it is that we can cross any sea as on dry land, (Heb. 11 : 29.) and unbelievers and enemies of Christ madly attempting the same are *drowned* in destruction and perdition. (6) God puts Himself between His people and their enemies.

CHAPTER XV.

THEN sang ᵃ Moses and the children of Israel this song unto the LORD, and spake, saying, I will sing unto the LORD, for

a Ju. 5: 1; 2Sa. 22: 1; Ps. 106: 12.

The glorious Shekinah—a cloud indeed, but luminous with the Divine glory—must be gotten through by the enemy before we can be reached. And what foes can make their way through God Himself? (7) We pass "under the cloud" and "through the sea" to be baptized into our New Testament Moses—Leader, Lawgiver, Mediator, Teacher. But in every cloud let us see the Divine glory therein revealed—the Personal Shekinah. And through every sea, even the cold flood of death, we can go on dry land—and on foot — while the enemies of Christ—armed and driving in their chariots defying God and the church and the truth—are drowned! "*He turned* the sea into dry (land). They went through the flood on foot—there did we rejoice in Him (Ps. 66: 6). The conjunction of the cloud with the sea suggests that in these words there may be a literal reference to the spray which might fall upon the people from the over-canopying cloud, and from the liquid walls on their right hand and their left."

"Guide me, O Thou great Jehovah,
Pilgrim thro' this barren land!
I am weak, but Thou art mighty
Hold me with Thy powerful hand.
    Bread of Heaven,
Feed me till I want no more.

Open now the crystal fountain
Whence the healing streams do flow,
Let the fiery, cloudy pillar
Lead me all my journey through.
    Strong Deliverer,
Be Thou still my strength and shield."

CHAPTER XV.

§ 33. REVIEW—TRIUMPHAL SONG. Ch. XV. 1-21.

"The birthday of Israel — the birthday of the religion of the nation of Israel, was the passage of the Red Sea. No baser thoughts, no disturbing influences could mar the overwhelming sense of thankfulness with which, as if after a hard-won battle, the nation found its voice in the first Hebrew melody, in the first burst of national poetry, when Moses and the children of Israel met on the Arabian shore; met Miriam the Prophetess, the sister of Aaron the third member, the eldest born of that noble family, whose name now first appears in the history of the church, afterwards to become so renowned through its Grecian and European form of MARIA and MARY."—*Stanley.*

The sea safely crossed, the enemies drowned in the depths where they had passed safely through, what wonder that Moses and the people express themselves in song. This is the most ancient poem for singing. The sublimity of the sentiment, and the elevation and grandeur of the diction, have made it the admiration of the most cultivated minds. In all the circumstances it is impossible to account for it as from the unaided genius of Moses. It is the language of Divine inspiration—the word of God in the very words of man. Moses was prompted and enabled, on this grand occasion, to compose this song for the people's thanksgiving. And in the true spirit of devotion it extols no human power nor prowess, but *Jehovah* alone is exalted. The song of Moses, the servant of God, is to be sung along with the Song of the Lamb, when the triumphant Church of all the ages shall have crossed the sea of death, and all the enemies of God and His Christ shall have been destroyed. (Rev. 15 : 3.) Modern

he hath triumphed gloriously: the horse and his rider hath he thrown into the sea.

2 The LORD *is* my strength and *b* song, and he is become my salvation: he *is* my God, and I will prepare him an *c* habitation; my father's God, and I will exalt him.

3 The LORD *is* a man of *d* war: the LORD *is* his name.

---

b Ps. 18: 2; 27: 1; 62: 6; 118: 14; Is. 12: 2. c 1Ki. 8: 13-27. d Ps. 24: 8; 45: 3; Re. 19: 11.

---

criticism staggers at the prophetic passages in vs. 16, 17, simply on the assumption that prophecy is impossible. But on the same ground Moses' history and mission must be denied, and all the supernatural displays of God's power in Egypt must be set aside as unhistorical. "If ever there was a crisis calculated to elicit the spirit of prophecy, it was that of the Exodus. If ever a man was fitted to express that spirit it was Moses. Even objectors admit that Moses contemplated the invasion of Palestine; if so what more natural than that, after the great catastrophe, which they accept as an historical fact, he should anticipate the terror of the nations through whose territories the Israelites would pass, and whose destruction was an inevitable condition of their success? In every age this song gave the tone to the poetry of Israel, especially at great critical epochs of deliverance." *Sp. Com.* There are three sections of the song, each headed with an outburst of praise to God. (1) vs. 1-5. (2) 6-10. (3) 11-18.

1. *Then sang;* lit., *Then will sing Moses,* etc. *Sing will I to Jehovah, for gloriously glorious is He; horse, and his rider He hath cast into the sea.* The sense is, Most highly, supremely exalted above all potentates is He—all the pride and pomp of Egypt's greatness He hath hurled into the sea. The cavalry and charioteers are both included.

2. *My strength and song is* JAH, *and He is become my salvation.* Heb. He is to me for salvation. The name JAH is especially associated with victory by the Psalmist (Ps. 68: 4). It was doubtless chosen here by Moses to draw attention to the promise ratified by the name I AM. It is the abbreviation of *Jahveh* —*Jehovah,* and conveys the same idea. It is God's Redemptive name —as moving and manifesting Himself in the sphere of Redemption. This JAH is extolled as having been the strong resource of Israel, and as being the object of their joyous thanksgiving — as their Deliverer and Saviour. So Moses had bidden them "stand still and see the salvation of God." *He is my God,* lit., *This one,* or, *This* JAH *is my God, and I will prepare Him a habitation* —rather, *I will glorify Him,* as the word in this form means. The verb is so rendered in other versions, and our English is here at fault, representing Moses as having in mind to build a temple for God. *My father's God;* Abraham's, as father of the Jewish people, the covenant God, who had now signally fulfilled His promise. Gen. 15: 14; 46: 3, 4.

3. *Jehovah is a man of war.* So directly is all the honor ascribed to God as a great Conqueror, so proved in this victory which is not man's, but God's. (See Ps. 24: 8.) All warlike prowess is concentrated in Him, as one who knows how to battle and conquer. *Jehovah is His name.* So God displays Himself in His Redemptive capacity, and makes Himself known as *Jehovah,* beyond all previous manifestations of Himself in history. Let Him be adored.

4. *Pharaoh's chariots.* Here is the burden of the song. This is the glorious achievement: *And his host* (military host) *He hath hurled into*

CHAPTER XV.

4 Pharaoh's chariots and his host hath he cast into the sea: his chosen captains also are drowned in the Red Sea.

5 The depths have covered them: they sank into the bottom as a stone.

6 Thy right hand, ᵉ O LORD, is become glorious in power: thy right hand, O LORD, hath dashed in pieces the enemy.

7 And in the greatness of thine ᶠ excellency thou hast overthrown them that rose up against thee: thou sentest forth thy wrath, *which* consumed them ᵍ as stubble.

8 And with the blast of ʰ thy nostrils the waters were gathered together: the floods stood upright as an heap, *and* the depths were congealed in the heart of the sea.

---

e Ps. 118: 15-16. f De. 33: 26; Ps. 68: 33. g Ps. 59: 13; Is. 5: 24; 47: 14; Mat. 3: 12.
h 2Sa. 22: 16; Job 4: 9; 2Th. 2: 8.

---

the sea, and the chosen ones (the choice) *of his commanders* (see ch. 14: 7) *are drowned in the Red Sea.* The officers of highest rank—the royal guard, as body guard of Pharaoh—are drowned! *overwhelmed* in the rushing floods.

5. *The depths,* lit., *Floods covered them. They sank in the abysses like a stone*—dead weight—to the very bottom—and no recovery. As if millstones had been hung around their necks, they were drowned in the depths of the sea. *Handel's* great Oratorio of "Israel in Egypt" gives the grandest musical expression to this song. The writer can never forget the rendering of it by 5,000 performers in the Sydenham Palace at London, at the Handel festival, in 1865. Such impassioned passages as this verse 10th were expressed with overwhelming power. —The warriors were dressed with heavy coats of mail, plates of fine bronze reaching nearly to the elbows and the knees.

6. Here the outburst of praise begins another passage, the second triplet—*Thy right hand*—the "high hand" and strong hand of Jehovah all along referred to as the effective power in their deliverance—*is become glorious*—"glorified in power" (K. & D.)—gloriously equipped with power. The right hand of Jehovah has its most glorious exhibition of power in this overthrow of His enemies. *Thy right hand, O Jehovah, shall dash in pieces the enemy*—as here His ability is proved to demolish all His enemies in all the future.

7. *And in the greatness* (abundance) *of thy majesty* (glory) *thou shalt pull down thine opponents. Thou shalt send forth thy wrath—it shall devour them as stubble.* The force of the future tense in these passages is, that Jehovah has so abundantly proved His power over His foes as to make it certain for all the future. Reference may be here to the flash from the pillar (ch. 14: 24).

8. *And by the breath of thy nostrils,* lit., *with the wind of thy wrath.* The demolishing power is described as going forth from the very Presence of Jehovah. It was from the Shekinah, or visible manifestation of the Divine Presence in the pillar of cloud and fire. The reference is here in high poetic phrase to the *east wind* (ch. 14: 21). Ps. 18: 16 ; Job. 4: 9 ; 2 Thes. 2: 8. Anger inflating the nostrils, so that the same word has the meaning of *anger,* or *wrath,* and *nostril*—and the same other word meaning *breath* and *wind. The waters heaped themselves up,* or *were gathered up*—piled up as walls. *The floods stood upright as an heap.* K. & D. render—*The flowing ones* (floods) *stood up like a heap.*

9 The enemy said, I will pursue, I will overtake, I will divide the spoil; my lust shall be satisfied upon them; I will draw my sword, my hand shall destroy them.

10 Thou didst blow with thy ⁱ wind, the sea covered them; they sank as lead in the mighty waters.

11 Who *is* like ʲ unto thee, O LORD, among the gods? who *is* like thee, glorious in holiness, fearful *in* praises, doing wonders?

---

i ch. 14: 21; Ps. 147: 18.   j Is. 40: 18.

Great stress is laid upon this phenomenon, which constituted the miracle. The floods which would otherwise have had their natural flow were massed and stood upright as solid walls. It is idle to try and explain away the miraculous features, and make it a mere extraordinary ebbing of the tide by the means of a strong east wind. This could not explain the standing up and walling of the waters on the right hand and on the left for the passage across. *The depths were congealed* (stiffened and piled up as solid masses) *in the heart of the sea.* This expresses the phenomenon, quite another thing from a blowing back of the tide. Besides this, the effect of a strong east wind, if it did not drive the waters right and left, and scoop out a path on the bare sea-bed, must have been to drive the floods directly westward upon the camp of Israel as a huge tidal wave.

9. This abrupt and impassioned series of utterances gives a most vivid conception of the infuriated and maddened foe. "The haste, cupidity, and ferocity of the Egyptians, the reckless determination and headlong pursuit, are described in terms recognized by critics of all schools, as belonging to the highest order of poetry, and enable us to realize the feelings which induced Pharaoh and his host to pursue the Israelites."—*Sp. Com. My lust,* lit., *My soul shall be filled with them. I will draw my sword—my hand shall dispossess* (exterminate) *them—*or *repossess* them—bring them back to slavery.

10. So sudden and overwhelming was the blow—so awful was the reverse and the dismay. *Thou didst blow with thy wind*—thy breath—the blast of the breath of thy nostrils. "Whom the Lord shall consume with the breath of His mouth"—(2 Thess. 2 : 8). "One breath of God was sufficient to sink the proud foe in the waves of the sea." *The sea covered them*—so swift and sweeping and summary was the overthrow. It was done at the breath of God. *They sank like lead*—dead weight—powerless — irrecoverable. Their heavy metallic armor, which so constituted their pride and pomp of war, only made their drowning more sudden and helpless, and hopeless. *In the mighty waters* the adjective means *excellent*—surpassing—overwhelming.

11. Here the third strophe begins with an *ascription of praise* and passes to celebrate the glorious effect of this deliverance upon Israel and the world. *Who is like unto Thee, O Jehovah.* Acknowledging the pre-eminent glory of their covenant God above all false gods—pretended deities of the heathen. Their God had so proved Himself beyond all comparison of "mighty ones" of earth—human potentates, or false divinities for whom such attributes are claimed. It is absurd to find in this language any admission of the real existence of other gods, as if here was an acknowledgment that the heathen gods were veritable beings. The language is only a challenge of all pretended gods as being emptiness. As we

12 Thou stretchedst out thy right hand, the earth swallowed them.

13 Thou in thy mercy hast ᵏ led forth the people *which* thou hast redeemed: thou hast guided *them* in thy strength unto thy holy habitation.

14 The people shall hear, *and* be afraid: sorrow shall take hold on the inhabitants of Palestina.

---

k Is. 63: 13.

---

call the idols of the heathen their "*gods*" without any acknowledgment of their real being as deities. *Glorious in holiness.* The conflict with Egyptian powers was a rallying of the kingdom of light against the kingdom of darkness, as now it is Christ against Antichrist, and God is here pronounced so inimitable, *glorious*, or *glorified in holiness*, as shown in the deliverance and redemption of His people, and the overthrow of their wicked foes. "Be glad in Jehovah, ye righteous, and give thanks at the remembrance of His holiness." (Ps. 30 : 4.)

"Only the soul that feels His grace
Can triumph in His holiness."

Fearful in praises. Reverend, notable in His praiseworthy manifestations — *fearful in reference to praises*—to be feared in things calling for our praises. "Serve the Lord with fear and rejoice with trembling," Ps. 2. *Doing wonders*, τέρατα, a word used as one of the three meaning *miracles*—prodigies of supernatural power—(Job 5 : 9). "Who is a God like unto Thee that forgivest iniquity" etc.

12. *Thou stretchedst out Thy hand.* Here again the Divine power is extolled as effecting their deliverance. "This is the high hand and the stretched out arm" of the Almighty which is to be celebrated. *The earth swallowed them.* Some suppose that the song passes here to a more general view of God's wondrous dealings as wrapped up in this signal event, and that the reference is not here to the Egyptian overthrow. The verb is in the future.

The earth will swallow them—but this is the tense used in several of the clauses, rather to express the idea that it shall always be so, as has here been done (vs. 5, 6, 7). As regards the Egyptians, it may be said the earth swallowed them, whether as referred to the globe itself without distinction of land and sea—or as down in *the abysses*, swallowed up in the mire of the ocean beds (Jonah 2 : 6). And now the poet passes to notice that all this was for the salvation of Israel.

13. *Thou hast led, leddest* etc. God is here extolled as Leader of His people, who has delivered them from Egypt with a purpose to lead them to Canaan. *In Thy mercy*, or through Thy mercy. This deliverance was to be regarded, therefore, as a pledge of their entrance to the promised land. This is reiterated in the parallel clause, according to the Hebrew poetry. *Thou hast guided them* (gently leadest them) *through thy might*—no less than through thy mercy—the power and grace of God being pledged for the result — *to thy holy habitation*—which was Canaan (Ps. 78 : 54). "Thou leddest thy people like a flock by the hand of Moses and Aaron" (Ps. 77 : 20).

14. *Peoples hear — they are afraid.* The poet now passes in the transport of his inspired verse, to celebrate the effects of this event upon the inhabitants of Philistia—(Pelasheth). The very fame of the Deliverance shall inspire them with a salutary awe. It is objected by modern critics that so to understand the passage, would suppose Moses

136   EXODUS.

15 Then the dukes of Edom shall be amazed; the mighty men of Moab, trembling shall take hold upon them: all the inhabitants of Canaan shall melt ¹ away.

16 Fear and dread shall ᵐ fall upon them: by the greatness of thine arm they shall be *as* still ⁿ as a stone; till thy people pass over, O LORD, till the people pass over *which* ᵒ thou hast purchased.

17 Thou shalt bring them in, and ᵖ plant them in the mountain of thine inheritance, *in* the place, O LORD, *which* thou hast made for thee to dwell in; *in* the ᑫ sanctuary, O LORD, *which* thy hands have established.

---

l Jos. 5: 1. m De. 2: 25; 11: 25; Jos. 2: 9. n 1Sa. 25: 37. o Ps. 74: 2; Ac. 20: 28 p Ps. 44: 2. q Ps. 78: 54.

---

to have the gift of prophecy, which they assume to be impossible and hence they must construct another theory. But this was fulfilled, (See Josh. 2 : 9, 10 ; 5 : 9, 9). It is not the Canaanites, but the inhabitants of Pelasheth, or the *Philistines*, who are here named.

15. *The dukes, princes*, or heads, chiefs, or chieftains (rather than the kings) *of Edom are confounded— the mighty men of Moab, trembling shall take hold upon them.* The Moabites were of notable strength and stature (Jer. 48 : 29, 41). *All the inhabitants of Canaan melt away with fear.* This is true though Edom and Moab resisted their march (Numb. 20 : 18). It is plain from the mention of all these people on the same basis that the command to exterminate the Canaanites could not at this time have been given, as yet, and this agrees with the authorship of Moses and the time of the Exodus. The perfect tense here describes the future as if it had passed—the prophetic past.

16. *There shall fall upon them fear and dread*, through the *greatness of Thine arm they shall be dumb as a stone—petrified.* Here the future is used after the perfect—and thus intermingled, the sense is clearly anticipatory and prophetic —*till thy people pass over, O Jehovah.* The verb here would seem to refer to the passing over the wilderness or more particularly, the boundary line of the Holy Land. But it was most literally fulfilled in the passage over Jordan, which, however the poet could not have had in his view except so far as the original idea of the name *Hebrew* was "the *passers over*," those who passed over the Jordan, as the boundary line, and now they were again to be *passers* over, according to the idea of their original name. The allusion is to this rather than to the passage of the Red Sea just accomplished. *Which thou hast purchased.* Israel was claimed by God as a purchased possession—a peculiar people—that is, private property—peculiar, belonging to Him (Deut. 32 : 9 ; 1 Pet. 2 : 9 ; 2 Pet. 2 : 1).

17. Moses here distinctly contemplates and predicts their entrance into the Holy Land under the same Divine Leadership as had led them out of Egypt and through the Sea. The poet here clearly foresees and announces the establishment of the Divine worship in the mountain already designated by the words of Abraham at the sacrifice of Isaac— *Jehovah-jireh.* "In the mountain Jehovah shall be seen," and that God will lead His people thither and plant them there—as the vine of Egypt—setting up there His church and establishing there His worship. *In the place, O Jehovah, which Thou hast made for Thee to dwell in,* (in)

CHAPTER XV.

18 The LORD shall reign ʳ for ever and ever.

19 For the horse of Pharaoh went in with his chariots and with his horsemen into the sea, and the LORD brought again the waters of the sea upon them: but the children of Israel went on dry *land* in the midst of the sea.

20 And Miriam the prophetess, the sister of Aaron, ˢ took a timbrel in her hand, and all the women went out after her with timbrels and with dances.

---

r Ps. 146: 10; Da. 4: 3; 7: 27.   s Ju. 11: 34; 2Sa. 6: 5; Ps. 68: 25; 81: 2; 149: 3; 150: 4.

---

the Sanctuary, O Jehovah, which Thy hands have established. This is a most definite and unmistakable reference by the Spirit of prophecy to the event contemplated by the selection of Moriah for Isaac's sacrifice and the revelations there—the event to which the redemption from Egypt pointed forward as in the plan of God to place His people in His own land for their training in His worship and service, in preparation for Gospel times. Because of the distinct prediction here, objectors claim that the whole chapter is *unhistorical*, and that it could not have been written prior to the event, supposing it to refer to the establishment of God's worship in the Temple on Moriah. But surely this had been distinctly enough indicated in Abraham's history to form here the basis of Moses' song; and inspiration guides him to a clear expression of the idea to stand on record as the *pre-intimation* of what God would accomplish for His people.

18. *Jehovah shall reign for ever and ever.* This is the closing, crowning ascription of praise. And this is based upon the great fact, so signally come to pass—the drowning of Pharaoh's host and the deliverance of Israel in one grand and glorious event. Whether this verse belongs to the hymn or is a mere passage of transition to the narrative, the meaning is plain. Probably the previous verse closes the Song.

19. *For the horse of Pharaoh*—not his horsemen, but *his horse*, implying clearly that Pharaoh went into the sea, riding upon his horse at the head of his army, as was the custom, and this was a fact sufficiently important and notable to be mentioned here. *The Lord brought again.* Jehovah did it by the agency of Moses, and by means of the strong east wind, supernaturally operating. It was not the rod of Moses, nor the wind itself, but Jehovah in all. This verse recites in brief the eventful issue, for which Jehovah is to be praised as fit to be King for ever.

20. *Miriam.* Greek, *Mariam.* Latin, *Maria.* English, *Mary.* She is called the *prophetess*—not as Isaiah's wife is so called (Isa. 8:3) as being the wife of a prophet, but as Deborah, on account of being an organ of Divine communication, and perhaps, also, from her knowledge of sacred song—(1 Chron. 25:1). See Mic. 6:4, where she is spoken of as commissioned along with Moses and Aaron. The sense of *prophet* is not confined to prediction, but extends to proclaiming God's message, or uttering the truth as a messenger of God. *The sister of Aaron* she is called, though equally the sister of Moses, but ranking with Aaron rather than with Moses, who was chief and superior. *She took a timbrel in her hand.* This musical instrument seems to have been like our modern *tambourin*, a small drum-head, with tinkling plates or bells, and struck with the hand. Miriam was the leader of a train of women, all playing this instrument, and joining in a dance, expressive of their devout joy. It is not dancing itself that is necessarily wrong, but the spirit of

21 And Miriam answered them, Sing ye to the Lord, t for he hath triumphed gloriously; the horse and his rider hath he thrown into the sea.

22 So Moses brought Israel from the Red Sea; and they

t Ver. 1.

it and its accessories and effects, in the service of the world. Such dances as Miriam's, with songs of praise to God, would give quite a different aspect to the question, and would scarcely be accepted by its advocates as any valuable concession.

21. *Answered them* — responded to the men—(2 Sam. 6:14). The part which these players and dancers took was in responses to the male chorus, and here the refrain is given. To the words, " I will sing unto Jehovah," the response is, "*Sing ye to Jehovah*," then repeating the opening words of the song, verse 1.

LESSONS.—(1) God prefaces His commandments by reminding of His wondrous deliverance from the bondage, by which He claims to be Jehovah, the covenant God of his people, who has already achieved for them such signal deliverance, and now calls on them to obey Him in grateful, filial service. (2) God here points forward to a further deliverance as a fulfilment of this historico-prophetical act—the bringing of His Son out of Egypt. See Matt. 2:15.

" *Out of Egypt have I called my Son.*" He calls Israel His Son— (Hos. 11:1, and Exod. 4:22). Jesus, who is the head of the covenant and members, is His Son. All His people are one in Christ, as the body is one with the head. (3) And further, the deliverance from Egypt of the ancient Israel points forward to the greater deliverance from Satanic bondage already achieved for His people, by which He claims to be the God of each of us, and claims our devoted, free, and grateful obedience.

§ 34. THE BITTER WATERS SWEETENED. Ch. XV., 22–27.

22. The narrative now proceeds. From this scene of their triumphant praises on the further bank of the sea, Moses led the people onward *into the wilderness of Shur*. It is generally supposed that they came out of the sea at, or about, the spot called *Ayun Musa*—the fountains of Moses. These fountains are a group of seven springs, making an oasis in a desolate tract of desert, and the only spot thereabouts where water can now be had. It is about two miles from the shore, where also is a projecting point of land called Cape Moses, opposite to another cape on the western shore called *Ras Attaka*, or the *Cape of Deliverance.*" It is very remarkable that these names remain to give their traditional testimony to these sites, as connected with the historic events here recited. The name *Shur* bears also its testimony to the history. It means *a wall*, and would seem to be associated with the event here recorded, where the waters were massed as solid walls for the passage across. This desert or wilderness of Shur comprises the Western district of Arabia Petræa; indeed, extends from the northeast part of Egypt to Palestine. *Palmer*, in his Ordnance Survey, suggests another reference of the name, and says: " If we stand at *Ayun Musa*, and glance over the desert at the *Jebels er Rahah* and *et Tih*, which border the gleaming plain, we at once appreciate the fact that these long wall-like escarpments are the chief, if not the only, prominent characteristics of this portion of the wilderness, and we need not wonder

AYUN MOUSA, THE WELLS OF MOSES.

Exodus.

went out into the wilderness of ᵘ Shur: and they went three days in the wilderness and found no water.

ᵘ Ge. 16: 7.

that the Israelites should have named this memorable spot after its most salient feature—*the Wilderness of Shur*, or *the Wall*. To the southeast of *Ras Musa* there is the *Wady Sdur*, which is also the name (*Sdur*) of the coast northward. The camp of the Israelites must have stretched some distance. A little further down the coast is a frowning chalk cliff called Hamman Far'un, '*Pharaoh's Hot Bath*,' which the Arabs point out as the site of the miracle. Pharaoh's unquiet spirit is still supposed to haunt the deep, and to keep alive the boiling, sulphurous spring which started up at his last drowning gasp. The sea at this point is named *Birket Far'un* — Pharaoh's Lake."—*Palmer Survey*, p. 39. *Lepsius* takes *Far'un* for *Paran*. *Three days*. *Palmer* says: "From the *wells of Moses* we traversed an unvaried desert plain for three days, with the thought that, like the children of Israel, we had gone three days in the desert and had found no water. On the third day we reached *Ain Hawárah*, which most previous travellers have sought to identify with the *Marah* of Scripture. It is a solitary spring of bitter water, with a stunted palm tree growing near it, and affording a delicious shade. The name is rendered by Dr. Robinson, *Fount of Destruction*, but really signifies *a small pool*, the water of which sinks into the soil, little by little, leaving the rest unfit for drink—a description eminently fitted to the spring in question." *Palmer, Desert of the Exodus*, p. 40: " The spring, which is now sanded up, may have flowed more copiously at one time, when it was kept in better order."— *K. & Del.* They had probably taken a supply for the time, which had now run out. It is said that this fountain is about three feet deep, and contained in a basin of over ten feet in diameter and six feet in depth. *They could not drink*. *Wellsted*, a traveller, says that when he tasted the water, and muttered the word *Marah*, his Bedouin said, " You speak the word of truth. They are indeed *Marah*." The term *Huwara* is defined by *Freytag* as *ruin, destruction*, but the bitterness would suggest such a name as if it were *deadly*. The sites and route are differently given by Robinson and by Lepsius.

ROBINSON thus—

From Ayun Musa to Ain Hawareh, or *Marah*, three stations each of . . . 6 hours.
To Wady Gharundel, *Elim* 2 "
To the sea . . . . . . 8 "
To Wady Schellal — Wilderness of Sin . . . . 4 "
To Dophka and Alus—two stations to Firan, each . 7 "
To the plain of Raha—Rephidim and Sinai, two stations, each . . . . 8 "

LEPSIUS thus—

From Ayun Musa, three stations, to Wady Gharundel, or *Marah*, each, . 7 hours.
To the outlet of the valley near Abu Zelimeh — *Elim* . . . . 7 "
To Firan, by Dophka and Alus, to Rephidim at Sinai, three stations, each . . . . 6 "

Lepsius says: " It is easy to imagine why the latter stations are somewhat shorter than the first, on account of the greater difficulty of the road. According to Robinson the fourth station would be scarcely explicable. Why did the people murmur so near to the twelve springs of Elim ? How would precisely that strikingly long journey of more than eight hours, from Elim to the sea, not have been mentioned at all ? And how was it possible

23 And when they came to ᵛ Marah, they could not drink of the waters of Marah, for they *were* bitter: therefore the name of it was called Marah.

24 And the people murmured against Moses, saying, What shall we drink?

25 And he cried unto the LORD: and the LORD shewed him a tree, *which* when he had cast into ʷ the waters, the waters were made sweet: there he made for them a statute and an ordinance, and there he proved them,

---

v Nu. 33: 8.   w 2Ki. 2: 21; 4: 41.

---

that the days' marches should have constantly increased in length amid the lofty mountains and difficult ground?". These are forcible considerations.

23. Any one who has travelled in the hot countries of the Orient can understand how disappointing must be bitter water in the agony of thirst. We came to the Dead Sea after a hot and wearisome ride. The waters were clear and sparkling, just such as to promise the most satisfying draught. My horse eagerly put his mouth to the water's edge, when an Arab guide seized the bridle, and shouted that a sip of it would kill him, as it probably would. But here it was repulsive from its bitterness. *Osborne* gives the analysis of the water thus—

Sulphate of lime.....1.545
" magnesia 1.000
" soda..... .919
" potash... .281
Chloride of sodium...3.940
Chloride of sodium, with traces of bituminous matter and carbonic acid.......8.345 to the 1.000.

24. *Murmured.* So soon the people forget all that Moses had wrought, and all that God had done for them by his hand. They desire some provision for their thirst. "What shall we eat and what shall we drink?" is still the cry of the multitude, for answer to these natural demands. And Christ would have us trust in that covenant that guarantees to God's faithful people that their bread shall be given them and their water shall be sure. "Father Patterson," as he was called, a pioneer of the Church in Western Pennsylvania, said that when he was laboring amongst the Indians, he had for his common meal pounded corn and bears' grease, until he became sick of it. And he prayed one day that God would make good His promise and give him that day something he could relish for his dinner. And, said he, it was done. And what do you think I had? he added. I had pounded corn and bears' grease. *But I had an appetite.*

25. *A tree*, not necessarily a living tree, but *wood*—we know not of what sort, only that it was something which he could *cast into* the waters. Some have supposed it was a stick, which by piercing the bed of the spring, opened afresh the fountain. But it seems to have had a sweetening quality or power. God could have wrought the result without this natural agency. But He will show how He has the means always at command, and even a dead stick, like Moses' rod, He can make so effective. So His ministry is only Aaron's rod which budded. By this transaction *He made* here for Israel *a statute*. He took occasion, at this crisis, so early on their wilderness journey, to set forth the law of His providential administration for His people, turning the bitter into sweet—as at Cana He turned the water into wine. The gracious interposition, so promptly and freely

CHAPTER XV. 141

26 And said, If thou wilt diligently hearken to the voice of the LORD thy God, and wilt do that which is right in his sight, and wilt give ear to his commandments, and keep all his statutes, I will put none of these diseases upon thee, which I have brought upon the Egyptians: x for I *am* the LORD y that healeth thee.

---
x De 28; 27, 68.   y Ps: 41: 4; 103: 3.
---

rendered, invited trust for every exigency and every condition, and taught them that there is nothing that we come to sooner than the bitter waters of disappointment, sorrow, bereavement, and want. But that it is His prerogative to change the bitter into sweet by the commonest and simplest means and agencies, as by casting a stick into the bitter fountain. *And an ordinance.* Rather—*and a judgment,* or an *institute.* The term is sometimes used in the prophets for gospel institutes or decisions. There He took occasion to illustrate His grace, and to show the principles upon which He would administer His gracious covenant, in dealing with His needy people, in this wilderness world. *And there He proved them.* While thus He proved Himself and His grace, He proved them also. "I proved thee at the waters of Meribah"—waters of strife (Ps. 81: 7; Exod. 17: 6). *He proved them,* or *put them to the test.*

26. *And said.* Here is the definite principle which He sets forth, and by which He will have them tested. He lays it down as a fixed condition of the Divine favor, the confidence and obedience of the people, following the Divine directions. For how shall He conduct them to Canaan if they refuse to follow in the way He marks out? So the command in the Gospel is, "Follow me." To some this sounds like a harsh and inflexible order, while in truth it is a most gracious invitation. *Follow me!* I will lead you and carry you safely through! As this order was given by the Delivering Angel to Peter in the prison—his feet in the stocks and helpless—Follow me! It meant freedom from the chains—escape from the prison through the iron doors, and defiance of all his enemies. *Diligently hearken.* Heb., *If hearing thou wilt hear*—wilt hear to purpose, so as to obey. It is the same word in *Heb.* that means to *hear,* and to *obey.* And what can He possibly do for us if we refuse to hearken and obey His voice? *And will do that which is right in His sight.* This is not arbitrary. If God is to undertake for us we must do what He sees best, and not follow our own counsels, or be guided by other and false oracles. *And wilt give ear to His commandments.* For as He is Captain of our Salvation, it is only by giving ear to His orders that we can be saved. His commandments are life to us. His commandments are gracious commandments. He commands us to believe and be saved. To be saved by believing. It is our high, main duty to be saved, and so it becomes our high, main duty to believe. For it is to believe in the salvation which is freely and fully wrought out for us, that He has made to be our chief duty. *And keep* (inviolate) *all his statutes.* They are statutes of grace and salvation, and most worthy to be kept by us. "This is a faithful saying," etc. God cannot stipulate for a keeping in part or for a partial obedience. He must require a perfect obedience. There is no lower standard. Wherein we fail we have no recourse but to Christ and His perfect righteousness wrought out for us. *I will put,* etc. This hearty and full acceptance of His plan and rule of conduct is the condition of His grace and salvation. Not, however, as in a bargain. It is rather the necessary constitution of things in which He becomes every-

27 And they came to Elim, where *were* twelve wells of water, and threescore and ten palm-trees: and they encamped there by the waters.

---

thing to us. It is not so much the condition of the grace as the condition of things in which the grace operates—for to the unbelieving and the disobedient the grace is necessarily inoperative and of none effect. *I will put none of those diseases.* It is in the shape of a covenant to exempt them from the plagues that had fallen upon the Egyptians, if, by their trustful obedience, they would separate themselves from the conduct of the Egyptians that had brought upon them such signal destruction. Now, at the threshold of their wilderness journey under the escort of the Covenant Angel, this is the statute, and this is the judicial decision, not arbitrary, but gracious. And in this advertised ordinance lies their only salvation. *For I am Jehovah that healeth thee.* The Great Healer is He, here as in the New Testament—" all manner of sickness and all manner of diseases" among the people He heals. He only can work certain cures always, and, what is more, can even avert the diseases. By the awful example of the Egyptians, by all the plagues visited upon them—even to the death of their first-born and their destruction in the sea, in all their pride and defiance—He will have Israel learn to trust and obey Him that they may always find Him a Helper and a Healer—(Ps. 103 : 3). "And He healed them all."—(Matt. 12 : 18.) And as many as touched the hem of His garment were made whole (Matt. 14 : 36). "For He Himself took our infirmities and bare our sicknesses" (Matt. 8 : 17).

27. *Elim.* Only a short distance —a day at the most—from the bitter waters to the refreshing springs and shady palms. The word means *trees. Wells*—rather *springs. Ghurundel* is commonly taken to be *Elim*, though only two hours from Marah. It is a noted Arab watering place, and fulfils the conditions of the narrative thus: "Green tamarisks and feathery palms and a pleasant stream of running water." "It is clear," says *Palmer*, "that the site of Elim must lie somewhere in the immediate neighborhood." "The shade of one of these palm trees was measured and found to be 180 feet in circumference." Though only six miles from *Hawara*, or *Marah*, as *Robinson* supposes, yet encampments are chosen with reference to water supplies for the travellers and the cattle. By the other view it is a day's distance (Abu-Zenimeh on the sea being the Elim). Israel was here to learn how Jehovah, their covenant God, could make His people lie down by green pastures and by the still waters and that so soon after they had murmured at the bitter streams. Here they found most attractive camping grounds for the great multitude. And as regards the sites, there may easily be much uncertainty, as the camp would spread over a considerable distance. (See Map.)

LESSONS. (1) God leads His people like a flock by human agencies. And as He undertakes for them, He will not suffer them to fail. (2) He guarantees not wealth nor ease to His people, but their bread and their water shall be sure. (3) Harassing care and murmuring about what we shall eat and drink is wrong, as it is born of unbelief. (4) Jesus is Himself Bread of Life and Water of Life, which is better than the water of Jacob's wells. (5) We often come to Bitter Waters of pain and loss and trouble. But He can sweeten them by His grace, and in use of the commonest means. (6) God proves us in His Providence and urges upon us His requirement of faith and obedience as the condition in which we receive and enjoy His best blessings. (7) Elim is near to Marah in

CHAPTER XVI.

AND they took their journey from Elim; a and all the congregation of the children of Israel came unto the wilderness of b Sin, which *is* between Elim and Sinai, on the fifteenth day of the second month after their departing out of the land of Egypt.

---

a Nu. 33: 10.   b Eze. 30: 15.

the journey of the christian. "He maketh me to lie down in green pastures, He leadeth me beside the still waters" (Ps. 23 : 2).

CHAPTER XVI.

§ 35. THE BREAD FROM HEAVEN. Ch. XVI. 1–36.

1. The camp at Elim was so fitting for rest that they remained there a few days. Thence they took up their journey. The next point here mentioned gives the direction without noticing a halting place named in Numb. 33 : 10. *Keil* and others understand the *Debbet er Ramleh*—the Northern route—to be the *Wilderness of Sin*. *Robinson* understands that "they passed inside of Jebel Hammam to the head of Wady et Tabiyeh where the deep blue waters of the Red Sea would once again burst upon their view." *Stanley* says, "They once more saw their old enemy and friend and caught one more glimpse of Egypt dim in the distance in the shadowy hills beyond it." This spot is about eight hours' journey or sixteen miles distant, not too long a day's stretch for the host, considering their rest at Elim. The wilderness of Sin skirts the eastern shore of the sea—stretching from the *Tih* mountains from N. W. to S. E. to the Sinai range. This may explain the connection of the names Sin and Sinai. This desert, or wilderness, is a sandy table-land and in this they camped. Keil thinks possibly in Wady *Nasb*, where is a well of good water and within a day's march of Tabiyeh. The modern name of the desert is *Debbet er Ramleh*—the word *Debbet* in Arabic means the same as "*Sin*" in Heb.—"*a level broad plain.*" The Ordnance Survey, however, fixes upon a southern route. The first day's journey from *Ras Abu Zanimeh* southwards leads through a narrow slip of barren sand to the open plain of El Markha. A very even and tolerably wide tract of desert land extends through El Markha and at its southern extremity, by a sudden turn eastward, leads through the Wady Feiran. This tract is identified by the conductors of the Survey with the wilderness of Sin. (See *Appendix—from Desert of the Exodus*, also *see Map*). *Canon Cook* on the whole decides for the northern route, as also do *Keil and Murphy*. The last named gives his reasons for agreeing with *Robinson* and for preferring the *Debbet er Ramleh* route, the chief of which is that this is the more open and easy for a large body of men. There are some very difficult passes in the other route. Besides the *Delbet er Ramleh* agrees better with the description of the narrative — "between Elim and Sinai." Others mention that the route is most difficult on account of its narrow defiles. It is quite impossible to mark out the route with certainty.

On the fifteenth day. It was now one month since they left Egypt (see ch. 12 : 18) and here they first complain of lacking bread. But it is first water and then bread

2 And the whole congregation of the children of Israel c murmured against Moses and Aaron in the wilderness:

3 And the children of Israel said unto them, Would to God we had died by the hand of the Lord in the land of Egypt, when d we sat by the flesh pots, *and* when we did eat bread to the full! for ye have brought us forth into this wilderness, to kill this whole assembly with hunger.

4 Then said the Lord unto Moses, Behold, I will rain e bread from heaven for you; and the people shall go out and gather a certain rate every day, that I may f prove them, whether they will walk in my law or no.

---

c ch. 15: 24; Ps. 106: 25; 1Co. 10: 10.   d Nu. 11: 4–5.   e Ps. 78: 24; Jno. 6: 31–32.
f De. 8: 16.

---

that they lack. One thing or another. And forgetting the recent supply when they lacked water and complained, they now murmur as though nothing had been done for them. So the disciples "considered not the miracle of the loaves" (Mark 6:52). So we all forget and murmur when new trouble comes. They had travelled only about a hundred miles. They murmured against Moses and Aaron their leaders, but it was really a fault-finding with God. Their supply of corn was exhausted and there seemed no prospect of procuring any in that waste wilderness. To all human appearance they must starve in the desert. Could they not reason so far as to conclude that He who clave the sea for them to pass over had control of all agencies and elements for their salvation? They were almost as slow to understand as Pharaoh was. So we ought to reckon that God who spared not His Own Son, but delivered Him up for us all, cannot do otherwise than freely give us all things along with Him (Rom. 8:32).

3. *Died by the hand.* They would rather have died (they say) by the hand of Jehovah in the plague which smote the families of Egypt with death rather than die by starvation. *When we sat.* They had been fed in their bondage and they counted that a luxury that made slavery and death desirable in their present hunger and destitution. But they had their flocks and cattle and could not have starved—only they fret and murmur because all does not go well. New sorrows seem always the greatest we ever had and the most grievous to be borne. *To kill this whole assembly.* They charge them with such a base purpose. How shocking to these good men to be so scandalized. *This whole church* as the term is—for here is the church in the wilderness (Acts 7).

4. The long-suffering patience of God is here displayed. Instead of punishing them for their unbelief, He provided for their want and stops their murmuring mouths with food from Heaven. *Rain bread.* This announces the miraculous character of the supply. As He rained fire upon guilty Sodom, so He could rain bread upon His people's camp. God has undertaken for them and He will not suffer them to perish of want. *A certain rate every day.* They were to do something to have part in the work. Not to furnish the bread but to accept and apply it. This is what is asked of us in the Gospel provision—to receive the salvation and make it ours. So they were to go out and gather the daily portion. So we are to come to Christ and draw out of His fulness—bread of life—water of life—and be saved daily. *A certain rate*, lit., *The portion of a day in his day.* So we pray "Give us

CHAPTER XVI.

5 And it shall come to pass that on the sixth day they shall prepare *that* which they bring in; and it shall be twice g as much as they gather daily.

6 And Moses and Aaron said unto all the children of Israel, At even, then ye shall know that the LORD hath brought you out from the land of Egypt:

7 And in the morning, then ye shall see the glory h of the LORD; for that he heareth your murmurings against the LORD: and what *are* we, that ye murmur against us?

---

g Ver. 22.   h Ver. 10; ch. 40: 34; Nu. 14: 10.

---

this day our daily bread"—the day's portion—as if fresh from Heaven—direct from the hand of our Lord. *That I may prove them.* The whole Israel as one, or each man, literally *him.* This was the test to be applied whether they would believe and accept the provision and live upon God's gracious bounty. *Whether they will walk.* For this is the law of God's grace, and he who will not walk in this law, and come and gather his daily provision from God's heavenly supplies, must perish.

5. A special provision is now introduced, calling for their definite action. It is a positive injunction. No room for arguing the reason why. Only to obey. As with the washing of Peter's feet, it is no time for protesting on personal grounds (John 13). Where Christ appoints, the command is an invitation to benefits and blessings not to be had otherwise, and the compliance is the condition of the benefit. He who resists Christ's appointment resists his own salvation. "If I wash thee not" etc. *On the sixth day.* Here is recognized a specialty in the sixth day. It was a day of extra preparation. This was plainly because the following day was the Sabbath though not yet so announced at Sinai in the Law of Ten Commands, yet doubtless instituted from the beginning, on the basis of God's creative rest. So that when it came to be published at Sinai as one of the moral institutes the form of the Command was "*Remember* the Sabbath day" as something already established and observed. *They shall prepare.* This preparation pertains to the measuring according to the day's rate a double measure, and the making it ready for eating—by the pounding or grinding and cooking. Thus God would have them reverence the Sabbath and keep it holy, by doing this work of preparation on the previous day.

6. *At even,* lit., *between the evenings*—at twilight. What God has just assured to Moses and Aaron is now announced to the people by them—that before another day they should have proof of the same power on their behalf which had brought them out of Egypt. This came to pass as promised. (See v. 13.) The quails came that evening. It was a re-assurance to them of the Divine Power and grace manifested in their Deliverance that Jehovah had undertaken for them. So our present gracious deliverances are the proof of God's eternal love from the beginning and to the end.

7. *And in the morning.* This refers also to what should come to pass the next morning (see v. 16)—the *manna* should light upon the camp. They should thus behold the glory of the Lord, a visible manifestation of His Presence, as symbolized in the pillar of cloud and fire—all elements and agencies being enlisted on their behalf. *For that.* The ground of this action is here assigned—*for that He heareth*—*In His hearing*—*your murmurings against Jehovah*—though di-

8 And Moses said, *This shall be*, when the LORD shall give you in the evening flesh to eat, and in the morning bread to the full; for that the LORD heareth your murmurings which ye murmur against him: and what *are* we? your murmurings *are* not against us, ⁱ but against the LORD.

9 And Moses spake unto Aaron, Say unto all the congregation of the children of Israel, Come ʲ near before the LORD: for he hath heard your murmurings.

10 And it came to pass, As Aaron spake unto the whole congregation of the children of Israel, that they looked toward the wilderness, and behold, the glory of the LORD ᵏ appeared in the cloud.

11 And the LORD spake unto Moses, saying,

12 I have heard the ˡ murmurings of the children of Israel: speak unto them, saying, At even ye shall eat flesh, and in the morning ye shall be filled with bread; and ye shall know that I *am* the LORD your God.

---

i 1Sa. 8: 7; Matt. 10: 40; Lu. 10: 16.   j Nu. 16: 16.   k Nu. 14: 10; 1Ki. 8: 10.
l Ver. 7.

---

rected against Moses and Aaron—yet regarded by God and by His servants as against Himself. *What are we.* They were only God's ministers—so that their murmurings directed against them could not terminate upon them, but really extended to God Himself.

8. *And Moses said—when Jehovah shall give you.* He now explains what they had referred to in the 6th and 7th verses—as the knowledge and sight of God's glory. It should come to pass when these displays of His power and grace should take place and so soon—that evening and the next morning. *Not against us.* Really they are aimed at God, however they may name us.

9. *Come near.* This is a Gospel invitation. Notwithstanding their sinful murmurings, they are bidden to come near *before Jehovah*, and are not driven away in His wrath. So Jesus says to all sinners, "*Come unto me.*"

10. Before the provision should be miraculously supplied, Jehovah displayed Himself in the Shekinah —the miraculous pillar of cloud and fire—that they might know who supplied them. *Toward the wilderness*, namely, *of Sin*, to which they had come (v. 1). *And behold* the Shekinah, or *glory of Jehovah appeared in the cloud*—the same which had accompanied them, but which had lost in part its special significance. God here displayed Himself, manifesting His Personal Presence in flashes from the cloud, or in some way to be beheld, as their Glorious Deliverer, that so their faith might be revived by His gracious dealings.

11, 12. This is probably what had already been said to Moses (v. 17), given more in detail to show the source of Moses' announcement to the people. *Jehovah had said.—Flesh* and *bread*, refer here to the people's murmurings. He gives them quails as flesh and manna for bread. "He rained flesh also upon them as dust, and feathered fowl, like as the sand of the sea." Ps. 78 : 27.

13. The quail is a fowl resembling the partridge and is found in that region in large numbers. The miracle consisted in their being brought in such immense quantities

CHAPTER XVI. 147

13 And it came to pass that at even the quails ^m came up, and covered the camp; and in the morning the dew lay round about the host.

14 And when the dew that lay was gone up, behold, upon the face of the wilderness, *there lay* a small round thing, *as* small as the hoar-frost on the ground.

15 And when the children of Israel saw *it*, they said one to another, It *is* manna: ⁿ for they wist not what it *was*. And Moses said unto them, This *is* the bread which the LORD hath given you to eat.

16 This *is* the thing which the LORD hath commanded,

---

m Nu. 11: 31; Ps. 78: 27–31; 105: 40. n Ver. 31-33; Nu. 11: 7; De. 8: 3, 16; Jos. 5: 12; Ne. 9: 15; Ps. 78: 24; 105: 40; Jno. 6: 31, 49, 58; 1Co. 10: 3; He. 9: 4; Re. 2: 17.

---

and at the very time specified. It is said that they alight often quite exhausted with their flight, and are easily captured. But He who caused them to come up could secure them to the people. *The dew lay*, lit., *There was a layer of dew.*

14. *When the dew that lay* (around the camp) was gone up (had cleared away or evaporated)—*Keil*. But the verb is the same as in v. 13, and the reading is, *and the layer of the dew came up* (or made its appearance), *and behold*, etc. (See Numb. 11 : 9.) " And when the dew fell upon the camp in the night the manna fell upon it," that is, the manna fell with the dew, and upon it—*upon the face of the wilderness, fine, round, tiny, like the hoar-frost upon the ground.* It was in globules, moist with the dew. The article which may be called natural manna, such as is found in that country, does not lie upon the open plain, *the face of the wilderness*, but on fallen leaves, under the tamarisk tree, from the trunk and boughs of which it exudes.

15. *They said each man to his brother, Man hu.* This is commonly taken, as in *margin*, to mean, *What is this?* But that would be otherwise expressed in the Hebrew. And this is found to be the Egyptian name for manna, and known also to the Israelites — *Manhut.* meaning *white manna.* They give it the name of that which most resembled it, namely, the tamarisk gum, which, in small quantities, they knew of. The miracle consisted in (1) bringing it along with the dew, and in no connection with the tamarisk tree—(2) in the quantity—one day's measure being more than the whole annual product of the natural gum—and (3) in the fact that it was intermitted on Sabbath days. God pleased to feed His people with food which had a natural relation to that district rather than on food of other regions. (4) This manna was gathered, not in one season, as the other is in June, but daily, always excepting the Sabbath day, showing the Divine interposition in the whole matter. *For they wist not.* They gave it this name without knowing that it was an entirely new thing, and from a miraculous source. Moses explains and tells them—*This is the bread which Jehovah hath given you to eat.* This is that which was promised, and is now given by God Himself. Our Lord refers to this transaction : " Your fathers did eat manna in the wilderness and are dead," (John 6 : 21, 49) to show that that miraculous food had no power to give the people the Divine life as only He could have, whom that manna typified as " the Bread of Life." They carried about with them a specimen of this miraculous food as a type of the Promised Salvation (v. 33).

16. Moses now recites God's order in regard to the gathering. *Every*

Gather of it every man according to his eating; an omer for every man, *according to* the number of your persons: take ye every man for *them* which *are* in his tents.

17 And the children of Israel did so, and gathered, some more, some less.

18 And when they did mete *it* with an omer, o he that gathered much had nothing over, and he that gathered little had no lack: they gathered every man according to his eating.

19 And Moses said, Let no man p leave of it till the morning.

20 Notwithstanding they hearkened not unto Moses; but some of them left of it until the morning, and it bred worms, and stank; and Moses was wroth with them.

---

o 2Co. 8: 15.   p Matt. 6: 34.

---

man according to the mouth of his eating. Enough for his own daily consumption — *an omer for every man,* lit., *for a head.* This measure was about three quarts English — *for the number of your souls* (per-) *sons*) so as to meet the wants of each family. This is repeated — *Take ye every man for them which* (are) *in his tent.* It is not to be supposed that they all had tents; but this was the common phrase — as we say a *household.* Yet, in fact, they had booths — tents of boughs — and many being shepherds, brought their tents.

17. They gathered some more, etc., lit., *he that exceeded* and he that *fell short.* The people were thus put upon trial of their faith — to gather only enough for one day — and fully enough.

18. When they came to measure, here was a most remarkable interposition of God to equalize the portion. The one who exceeded his quota by grasping and greed *had nothing over,* and the one who, by timidity or ill success, fell short — *had no lack.* "A potent argument to teach them, if they would learn, that all men are equal in the sight of our Heavenly Father. He that distributed His bounty could equalize each single gathering as easily as the collected whole with the ration allotted to each." — *Murphy.*

Calvin thinks the mass was gathered in a heap and then measured out in the quantity that each required.

19. *Let no one* keep (any of) it over till the next day, either for fear of not getting the next day's portion or for any other reason, but each must conform to God's published plan of living by the day, and of daily habitual trust in Him as the Giver of our daily bread. "Give us this day our daily bread" is an item in the Lord's Prayer which is meant to put us upon God for daily supplies, and for our habitual dependence, knowing that He cares for us — and be the day long or short, dark or bright, He can and will adapt our supply to the day as it comes. We are ever prone to lay in a stock which shall keep us from this necessity of daily prayer and daily supply from God's direct bounty.

20. *Some of them,* notwithstanding this definite order, disobeyed, and left a portion of it until morning, sparing some from their measure so as not to be without any for the next day. *And it bred worms,* or *it swarmed worms, and stank.* The common manna lasted long without spoiling. But here was God's hand in the dispensation of this. So overgrown wealth that breeds a feeling of independence also breeds corruption.

21 And they gathered it every morning, every man according to his eating: and when the sun waxed hot, it melted.

22 And it came to pass, *that* on the sixth day they gathered twice as much bread, two omers for one *man:* and all the rulers of the congregation came and told Moses.

23 And he said unto them, This *is that* which the LORD hath said, To-morrow *is* the q rest of the holy sabbath unto the LORD: bake *that* which ye will bake *to-day*, and seethe that ye will seethe: and that which remaineth over lay up for you, to be kept until the morning.

24 And they laid it up till the morning, as Moses bade: and it did not r stink, neither was there any worm therein.

---

q Ge. 2: 3; ch, 20: 8; 31: 15; 35: 3; Le. 23: 3.   r Ver. 20.

---

21. *It melted.* The part of it that was not gathered was melted by the hot sun and disappeared.

22. *On the sixth day.* The Sabbath was thus specially provided for. They were thus reminded of it as a Divine institution and thus it came at Sinai to be incorporated into the Decalogue as the Lord's day to be remembered. But when the people, in obedience to the orders given gathered a double quantity on the sixth day *all the rulers of the congregation came and told Moses*—fearing it would seem lest this surplus might fare as did that noticed in v. 20. Moses had been advised of this arrangement of a double portion on the sixth day (v. 5). But he seems not to have so proclaimed to the people, only they were to find a double supply for the sixth, and none for the seventh day. Or possibly if the instructions were given to the people, as in v. 5 to Moses, they wished to know further how this was to be understood in consistency with the warning in v. 20. There is no ground here for inferring that they knew nothing of a Sabbath ordinance prior to this time. The order is given without explanation, as if presuming upon this knowledge of a Sabbath law. Or the Sabbath may have partially passed out of use in Egypt and it was now by this special appointment that God provided for its observance in connection with this gracious dispensation of heavenly food.

23. Moses now explains to them the Divine ordinance. *This is that.* This means the Sabbath observance. This is in accordance with what Jehovah hath said in appointing the Sabbath day. *To-morrow is a rest, a Sabbath holy to Jehovah.* "It is at once a statement and an injunction. They knew it as a Sabbath— they were to keep it as a festival." —*Sp. Com.* Or, rather, they are reminded of it as the Sabbath, and were required to observe it in this way, thus emphasizing the Sabbath ordinance, which else they might not have honored in this particular. *Bake,* etc. The ordinary manna of Tamarisk gum was of a totally different nature. It was used as honey. This had the quality of corn, to be baked, ground and boiled. The other is glutinous and oily. So that this supply is quite removed from the natural product in kind as well as in measure. *Lay up.* They were to keep the surplus for the Sabbath supply.

24. This that was thus laid up till the next day was exempt from the corruption that befel what was kept over from other days. (See v. 20.) God honors the Sabbath.

25, 26. The special order is repeated. They were now bidden to eat that portion which had been

150   EXODUS.

25 And Moses said, Eat that to-day, for to-day *is* a sabbath unto the Lord: to-day ye shall not find it in the field.

26 Six ˢ days ye shall gather it; but on the seventh day, *which is* the sabbath, in it there shall be none.

27 And it came to pass, *that* there went out *some* of the people on the seventh day for to gather, and they found none.

28 And the Lord said unto Moses, How long ᵗ refuse ye to keep my commandments and my laws?

---

s Ch. 20: 9-10. t Nu. 14: 11; 2Ki. 17: 14; Ps. 78; 10-22; 106: 13; Je. 9: 6: Eze. 5: 6.

---

laid over from the previous day, for it was not to be rained down upon them on that day. *For to-day is a Sabbath unto Jehovah.* Some have supposed that on this occasion the Sabbath was changed to the seventh day. It was originally the first day of the week, as it was the first day of Adam's life, and though the seventh day of God's creative week, it was the first day of man's week. But we are sure that there is no intimation given of the Sabbath being now first instituted, but quite otherwise. There was a Sabbath under the patriarchal dispensation and a Sabbath under the Levitical dispensation. So there is a Sabbath under the Christian dispensation—"there remaineth therefore a Sabbath-keeping for the people of God" which Jesus has instituted by His entering into His new-creative rest. And so there will be a glorious Sabbath-keeping in the heavenly dispensation. The Sabbath law was not newly formed at Sinai any more than the other commands of the Decalogue. They were the great fundamental principles of morality that were there grouped as of universal and perpetual obligation. And hence there could have been no abrogation of the Sabbath law by the change of dispensations, any more than the abrogation of any other of the Ten Commands. They were only such precepts as were binding everywhere and always which were there promulgated as God's moral code for mankind.

27. Some of the people not heeding these restrictions went out to gather on the Sabbath as on other days, and *they found none.* This was a gross disregard of God's directions and of His institutions—treating the Sabbath as any other day. But the result taught them a lesson of universal application—that they who turn the Sabbath into a week day for ordinary business and gain, *find nothing*—fail in their enterprises sooner or later in one way or another. God puts honor on His own day. And he whose delight is in the law of the Lord finds that whatever he doeth shall prosper (Ps. 1).

28. Jehovah here expostulates with the people to Moses. *How long,* etc. This violation of the Sabbath law was in God's sight a grievous wrong. This seems to imply that they had been guilty of this inattention to the Sabbath before this time. And it justifies the supposition that in their Egyptian bondage they had been prone to neglect the Sabbath. And now God will train His church in the wilderness to this fundamental observance. For it is universally true that the Sabbath observance is at the very foundation of social order and of public morality, no less than of private and personal virtue. Emphasis is therefore put upon it here at the outset of their journeyings. There is a plain reference to v. 4. There was a *proving* of the people in this command. The whole arrangement is now explained. *Abide ye every man in his place.* That is—go not out to gather manna—which was outside the camp on other days.

CHAPTER XVI.

29 See, for that the LORD hath given you the sabbath, therefore he giveth you on the sixth day the bread of two days: abide ye every man in his place; let no man go out of his place on the seventh day.

30 So the people rested on the seventh day.

31 And the house of Israel called the name thereof Manna: and it *was* like ᵘ coriander-seed, white; and the taste of it *was* like wafers *made* with honey.

32 And Moses said, This *is* the thing which the LORD com-

---
u Nu. 11: 7, 8.

The Sabbath was to be a day of cessation from ordinary business. *Rest* was the idea of it, and so the order was for every man to abide in his place — lit., *under himself* — with himself, in his own house. *Let no man go out of his place on the seventh day.* From this injunction it was inferred and held that no one should go farther on a Sabbath day than the distance from the extremity of the camp to the Tabernacle which was in the centre. The Rabbins made two thousand cubits to be a Sabbath day's journey, which was about three-fourths of a mile — a very short distance. And this regulation was enforced on the ground that, *the Lord* (Jehovah) *giveth you the Sabbath* as a free gift, and a gracious ordinance, and makes His other gifts in consistency with this, so as not to interfere with its observance. It may therefore be expected and it has everywhere been found that men who seek gain by breaking the Sabbath lose every way — body and soul, losing the benefits which God has provided in the Sabbath rest from worldly care and labors.

30. *So the people rested* — in obedience to the command, and in the spirit of the Sabbath. God rested on the seventh day from His creation work. The *resting* is not inconsistent with works of necessity, and mercy, and piety, which are of such a nature as not to violate the Sabbath spirit: neither is it meant that men shall simply rest their bodies by lounging and indolent case. They are to take rest in God — to find rest for the soul in Christ — to take the benefit of Christian trust in His covenant — and to embrace the provision which He freely gives — the heavenly manna — and the Personal Bread of Life, which is Christ. So they find Peace — His Peace — and the benediction of His courts, Grace, Mercy and Peace.

32. A special direction is here given for preserving a portion of this manna as a specimen to be carried about with them in their wilderness march, a treasure to be deposited along with the most sacred things in or before the Ark of the Testimony. No other miracle was so to be kept in remembrance. The reason is that this manna represented Christ, and so He Himself teaches in John 6. Most vital gospel truth was involved in it, as we there find. The Jews demanded of Jesus some such miracle as they ascribe to Moses in the manna. They believed that the Messiah was to reproduce the glories of the Mosaic theocracy, as well as of the Kingdom of David. But Jesus corrects their notion, and says, Moses gave you not that bread from heaven. Even the material, miraculous manna, did not come from Moses, but my Father gave it, as He now giveth you also what is so much more the true bread from Heaven (John 6).

¶ *That they may see the bread.* A sample was to be sacredly preserved to shew the future genera-

mandeth, Fill an omer of it to be kept for your generations; that they may see the bread wherewith I have fed you in the wilderness, when I brought you forth from the land of Egypt.

33 And Moses said unto Aaron, v Take a pot, and put an omer full of manna therein, and lay it up before the Lord, to be kept for your generations.

34 As the Lord commanded Moses, so Aaron laid it up w before the Testimony, to be kept.

35 And the children of Israel did eat manna x forty years, until they came to a land inhabited: they did eat manna, until they came unto the borders y of the land of Canaan.

36 Now an omer z is the tenth *part* of an ephah.

CHAPTER XVII.

AND all the congregation of the children of Israel journeyed from the wilderness of Sin, a after their journeys, according

---

v He. 9: 4. w ch. 25: 16; Nu. 1: 50; 17: 10; 1Ki. 8: 9. z Nu. 33: 8; De. 8: 2, 3; Ne. 9: 21; Jno. 6: 31-49. y Jos. 5: 12; Ne. 9: 15. z Ver. 16, 32, 33. a ch. 16: 1; Nu. 32: 12: 4.

---

tions of what sort this miraculous food had been. So there is provision in the gospel for the word of Christ to be set forth and Christ Himself to be exhibited as the Divine sustenance of the soul.

33. *Lay it up before the Lord. Before Jehovah.* It was to be deposited in the ark of the Testimony (Heb. 9: 4) though it was not found inside the ark in Solomon's time (I Kings 8: 9), but may then have been carried outside—hence some suppose that "before the Lord" means, before the ark. The ark was not yet made, but this direction was given beforehand, and was observed as we are here told, when the Tabernacle was built. See ch. 40: 20.

35. *Forty years.* So far as they had need; not however, eating manna alone, but all along their wilderness journey, they had the miraculous supply continued to them—to signify in the type, the permanency of Christ as the gospel provision. This was supplied to them until they reached the promised land, and until Moses died. This he testifies of, as the historical fact of which he was cognizant. It was no longer necessary after they had come *to a land inhabited* beyond the wilderness.

"Bread of Heaven
Feed me till I want no more."

36. Moses here defines the measure called an omer.

Lessons.—(1) The miracle here is a type and prophecy of Christ, the true manna—the Bread of Life. (2) He who provides for the soul also provides for the body. (3) This Bread of Life which Christ is, not only sustains life but gives life (John 6 :) (4) Christ gives His flesh for men—His broken body. We partake, by faith, the benefits of His atoning death. (5) His Personal Presence, also, is given to us as an Incarnate Saviour—for a living companion and friend. (6) Our spiritual supply for the Sabbath must depend upon what we gather during the week.

CHAPTER XVII.

§ 36. Murmuring for lack of Water. Horeb.—Ch. XVII. 1-7.

The journeying goes on under the same Divine guidance, and under the leadership of Moses.

CHAPTER XVII.

to the commandment of the LORD, and pitched in Rephidim: and *there was* no water for the people to drink.

2 Wherefore the people did chide ^b with Moses, and said, Give us water that we may drink. And Moses said unto them, Why chide ye with me? wherefore do ye tempt c the LORD?

3 And the people thirsted there for water; and the people murmured against Moses, and said, Wherefore *is* this *that* thou hast brought us up out of Egypt, to kill us and our children and our cattle with thirst?

4 And Moses cried unto the LORD, saying, What shall I do unto this people? they be almost ready ^d to stone me.

---

b Nu. 20: 3, 4. c De. 6: 16; Ps. 78: 18, 41; 95: 8, 9; Is. 7: 12; Mat. 4: 7; 1Co. 10: 9.
d 1Sa. 30: 6; Jno. 8: 59; 10: 31; Ac. 7: 59.

Having now lacked bread and obtained a miraculous supply, they soon lack water, and are thrown into a new distress and distrust of God. The occasion is found in our human want, to show the ample and varied resources that are heaped up in Christ as Bread of Life and Water of Life.

1. The main stations are given in this history, though from the fuller account in Numbers we find that some minor stations are omitted. These may be referred to, in the clause *"after their journeys."* In Numb. 33 the stations Dophkah and Alush are named as between the wilderness of Sin and Rephidim. *According to the commandment*—viz. —as indicated by the cloudy *pillar* marking the way. (See Numb. 9; 18, 19.) *Rephidim.* The members of the recent Ordnance Survey are not agreed as to this station. Captains Wilson and Palmer locate it in Wady Feiran under Mount Serbal. Mr. Holland understands that it was beyond the intersection of Wady Feiran with Wady Sheikh, at the pass of *Al Watiyeh*, where the conditions of the narrative as to the battle seem to be well fulfilled. *No water.* In that hot desert region, this was a most serious privation. Journeys are always made there in reference to the water-supplies, where the routes are familiar. Here Moses went under the Divine leading. OBSERVE. God throws us upon our own inability and destitution in order to provoke us to come and draw upon Him.

2. The people, as before in case of lacking bread, now complain and lay the responsibility upon Moses. The term here rendered *chide with* means to *strive, quarrel with*. They demand of him to give them water, as though he had it in his power, or as though he was obligated to furnish them with a supply. Moses replies that their chiding and reproof of him is unreasonable and wicked, that it is a *tempting* of Jehovah, laying the blame virtually upon Him, distrusting His care, despite His recent miraculous provision, and provoking Him to anger by their bad temper, and proud, defiant spirit, as if everything belonged to them, and forgetting their own sinful ill-desert.

3. *Thirsted.* The agony of thirst was that which wrung from Jesus the outcry on the cross '*I thirst*,' and it is expressive of all the most intense craving. *Wherefore.* They expostulate with Moses, as if he had purposely placed them in this fearful extremity, and had knowingly and wilfully subjected them to this new distress, which threatened their horrible death.

4. This led Moses to cry to Jehovah as before at Marah (ch. 15: 25). Only here, he seems to be in fear of his life, and begged of God to know what he should do unto them, how

7*

154　　　　　　　　EXODUS.

5 And the LORD said unto Moses, Go on before the people, and take with thee of the elders of Israel; and thy rod, wherewith thou smotest ᵉ the river, take in thine hand, and go:

6 Behold, I will stand before thee there upon the rock in Horeb; and thou shalt smite the rock, and there shall ᶠ come water out of it, that the people may drink. And Moses did so in the sight of the elders of Israel.

7 And he called the name of the place Massah and Meribah,

---

e ch. 7: 20; Nu. 20: 8-11.　　f Ps. 105: 41; 114: 8; 1Co. 10: 4.

---

he should deal with them, and treat them in their desperation. *Ready to stone me.* Their grievous raging, maddening thirst drove them to expressions perhaps purporting violence. Literally it reads *Yet a little and they will stone me.* How blessed in such a time of terror and trouble to have God for a friend and counsellor, as Moses had found.

5. He is directed not to smite the rebels but the rock. *Go on before the people—in advance of them—and take with thee of the elders of Israel,* some of them, as official witnesses representing the people, that there may be no doubt of the Divine intervention. *And thy rod*—the same rod with which he *smote the river* (Nile) when it was turned into blood —*take in thine hand and go.* For now it is quite as easy for God to bring water here out of a rock, as to have turned that Nile water into blood.

6. *I will stand before thee.* In the cloudy pillar. *The rock in Horeb.* This was just beyond Rephidim, but near. God promises to stand before him upon the rock. Rephidim lay in the plain at the foot of the mount. They had only to advance to the dry, rugged granite cliff overhanging the plain. *Horeb* means *dry,* and is the central group of the range of Sinai. If Rephidim is in the Wady et Sheikh, the smitten rock is probably to be found in *Jebel Musa.* This *Horeb* mount was the scene of the great miracle of the Burning Bush: which attested Moses' commission, and revealed the indestructibility of the Church, and these ideas were fit to be associated with this miracle of preserving the Church in a sore extremity like this of deadly thirst. *Smite the rock*—with his symbolical rod, or staff of power—*and there shall come water out of it.* Where the rock was smitten cannot now be ascertained. But the supply was abundant. Paul refers to it in 1 Cor. 10: 4, where he speaks as if the Rock followed them through the wilderness, by which we may suppose that the abundant supply is meant. "And they drank of that spiritual (symbolical) Rock which followed them. And that Rock was Christ." The miracle was typical and intended to represent here in the lower department of physical supply that greater, higher provision in the gospel which can be found in Christ alone. That smitten Rock was meant to set forth Christ as the foreshadowed and all sufficient resource, whose smitten body should pour out an immense fulness for His people's wants in all this wilderness. "And of His fulness have all we received and grace for grace" (John 1). *And Moses did so in the sight of the Elders of Israel,* before such competent official men, as witnesses.

7. *Massah* meaning *temptation*—referring to v. 2—where they were charged with tempting God. See Matt. 4: 7. *And Meribah:* meaning *strife* or *chiding*—See v. 2. This transaction is referred to in Heb. 3: 8, as a specimen of the people's obstinacy and bitter contention, and as a warning against

because of the chiding of the children of Israel, and because they tempted the LORD, saying, Is the LORD among us, or not?

8 Then came ᵍ Amalek, and fought with Israel in Rephidim.

9 And Moses said unto Joshua, Choose us out men, and go out, fight with Amalek: to-morrow I will stand on the top of the hill with the rod of God in mine hand.

---
g Ge. 36: 12; Nu. 24: 20.
---

their heart-hardening. "Harden not your hearts as in the provocation (*Meribah*) as in the day of temptation (*Massah*) in the wilderness—when your fathers tempted me (or put me to the test) proved me and (at the same time) saw my works." The point of their tempting God was the distrust of His Personal presence. In effect by their doubting and complaining at each new strait they said, *Is Jehovah among us, or not?* (*See Appendix C.*)

§ 37. DEFEAT OF AMALEK. Ch. XVII: 8-16.

8. *Then came Amalek.* "The attack upon the Israelites was made in circumstances at a time and place, fully explained by what is known of the Peninsula. It occurred about two months after the Exodus, towards the end of May, or early in June, when the Bedouins leave the lower plains to find pasture for their flocks on the cooler heights. The approach of the Israelites to Sinai would of course attract notice, and no cause of warfare is more common than a dispute for the right of pasturage. The Amalekites were at that time the most powerful race in the Peninsula, which from the earliest ages was peopled by fierce and warlike tribes with whom the Pharaohs, from the third dynasty downwards, were engaged in constant struggles"—*Sp. Com.* Amalek was chief of the heathen (Numb. 24: 20) the first of the heathen who attacked God's people, and were as such marked out for punishment, the more merited as they were descendants of the elder brother of Jacob, and therefore near kinsmen of the Israelites. They were descendants of Esau and held a bitter grudge against the birthright stock; fearing *that now their subjection was to be completed.* Their attack was a mean cowardly assault upon the rear and a wicked defiance of God. Deut. 25: 18. " In Amalek the heathen world commenced that conflict with the people of God, which, while it aims at their destruction, can be terminated only by the complete annihilation of the ungodly powers of the world. —*Keil.*

9. *Unto Joshua.* This great Captain of Israel's host here first appears in the history. He was now about 45 years old, and died about 65 years after this. His original name was Hosea, *Deliverance*, Salvation, and was changed by Moses to the fuller name that incorporates with it the name of Jehovah, and means *Salvation of Jehovah*, *Jehoshua*. It was the name Jesus in substance. And in Hebrews 4: 8, the Greek name is written Jesus and so rendered in our version. "For if Jesus (Joshua) had given them rest (in Canaan) etc." See also Acts 7: 45. *Keil* thinks this name was given to him at the time of his entering Moses' service either before or after the battle with Amalek (see Numb 13: 16). *Sp. Com.* thinks it was "given to him about forty years afterwards, as the name by which he was to be known to succeeding generations." *Choose us out men.* Moses had achieved his wonders heretofore simply by his rod of power. Now, however, he resorts to the arbitrament of war. Yet he will use his wonder-working rod. It was evidently a serious

10 So Joshua did as Moses had said to him, and fought with Amalek: and Moses, Aaron, and Hur, went up to the top of the hill.

11 And it came to pass, when Moses held up his hand, that Israel prevailed; and when he let down his hand, Amalek prevailed.

12 But Moses' hands *were* heavy; and they took a stone, and put *it* under him, and he sat thereon: and Aaron and Hur stayed up his hands, the one on the one side, and the other on the other side; and his hands were steady until the going down of the sun.

---

conflict, a rallying of the kingdom of darkness against the kingdom of light—involving the most serious consequences for the church and for the world. He will have in hand the same rod, to show that the Lord God who had wrought their deliverance from Pharaoh, could deliver them now, and He alone.

10. *Moses, Aaron and Hur.* Hur here first comes into view. He is said by tradition to have been the husband of Miriam, and thus the brother-in-law of the two leaders. He was the son of Caleb the fourth in descent from Judah (1 Chron. 2: 18–20). The hill on the top of which Moses stood, is involved in much doubt. Mr. Holland, of the Ordnance Survey locating Rephidim at *al Watiyeh*, finds all the conditions of the narrative satisfied, and at the foot of the conspicuous summit near, the Arabs point out a rock, which they call "the Seat of the Prophet Moses." Captains Wilson and Palmer locate it however in the Wady Feiran under Mount Serbal.

11. It was now observed that the battle seemed to turn upon the uplifting or falling of Moses' hands. Lifted up, the battle favored Israel —but, let fall the battle inclined to Aamlek. Both hands were elevated or lowered at intervals to show how dependent the issues were upon the symbolical power-rod. Most take the raising of the hands as the attitude of prayer. Some however understand it as the attitude of superintendence and command (*Kurtz*). But Moses lifted up his hands with this power-rod as the medium of God's manifestation, uplifted as an appeal to God in the spirit of believing prayer. It was not a sign to the Israelites, but a sign to God. This was a public confession of God. And it is put on record to teach the world the great lesson that the Church's battles can be won for her only by the uplifted hands of prayer and that her agencies of power (whatever wonder-working rod) must be referred to Him and must point upwards to Him in order to be effective for victory. Moses was the Mediator who foreshadowed Christ, interceding for the people. Christ "ever liveth to intercede for us."

12. *Were heavy.* Grew weary from being held in the same unnatural position for a long time. As the issues turned so upon their position, it became most important that his hands should not be lowered, but be held up continuously. An expedient was now used to ease his position, a stone for his seat and Aaron and Hur, one on either side to hold up his hands. So it was accomplished that "*his hands were steady* until the going down of the sun." This shows the severity of the conflict. The Israelites doubtless brought with them from Egypt such simple implements of warfare as were mostly in use, and it is suggested they may have gotten some of the arms of the Egyptians after their destruction in the Sea. It was

CHAPTER XVII.

13 And Joshua discomfited Amalek and his people with the edge of the sword.

14 And the LORD said unto Moses, Write this *for* a memorial in a book, and rehearse *it* in the ears of Joshua: for I will utterly put out the remembrance of Amalek ʰ from under heaven.

15 And Moses built an altar, and called the name of it JEHOVAH-nissi:

16 For he said, Because the LORD hath sworn *that* the LORD *will have* war with Amalek from generation to generation.

---

h Nu. 24: 20; De. 25: 19.

---

no mere raid of a depredating tribe. It was a fierce struggle of a powerful force, well trained by frequent battles with the Egyptians.

13. *The edge of the sword.* That is with great slaughter, without quarter (Gen 34: 26).

14. *Write this.* This is the first mention we have of this word *to write.* But writing was now familiar. This event was so important and signal as to be worthy of a permanent record. *In a book.* Rather— *In the book,* showing that there was such a book containing the records of God's dealings with Israel. We have in this history such a record as Moses might be supposed to have written at this command. The Pentateuch, or Book of the Law, is the Book to which similar reference is elsewhere made, and written by Moses (see Exod. 24: 4. 7; 34: 27; Numb. 33: 1, 2; 36: 13; Deut. 28: 61). *Rehearse it.* Joshua was to have recited to him and impressed upon him this order of God regarding Amalek, since Joshua was the chosen Captain who was now to lead Israel in their conflicts, and he was to be encouraged by this declared purpose of God against the enemies of the Church. *For I will.* This may rather read *That I will,* as the record to be written. This sentence was fulfilled under the reign of Hezekiah, when 500 of the tribe of Simeon "smote the rest of the Amalekites that were escaped," and retained possession of Mount Seir (1 Chron. 4: 43). In Deut. 25: 19 the Israelites were commanded to exterminate Amalek after coming to their rest in Canaan.

15. Moses makes devout recognition of this great typical event, the Deliverance of the Church from assailing enemies and the discomfiture of the foe. *He built an altar, and called the name of it Jehovah-nissi. Jehovah my banner.* The *banner* under which Moses professes to fight is the name of *Jehovah,* the redemptive name of God. This is the stand proper to be taken now in the presence of all Israel, and in their name, by their appointed Leader. It is a public confession of Jehovah as the Deliverer of His Church and people in every conflict with the enemy. And in this name *Jehovah,* the Church will conquer. Ps. 110: 1, " Jehovah said unto my Lord, Sit thou on my right hand until I make thine enemies thy footstool." This is the decree that has gone forth.

16. *For he said—Because* etc. lit., *The hand upon the throne of Jehovah.* It would seem to refer to the hand of prayer that is to lay hold upon God's throne, after the example of Moses, and as the rule for all ages and conflicts of the Church. But some understand it of Amalek's hand set against the throne of Jehovah, which also would be a clear idea (see *Murphy*). [Our version understands it of *swearing The hand* of Jehovah *upon the throne.* But Jehovah swears by Himself and not by His throne.] A reason may be understood to be given for the waging of an exterminating war upon

CHAPTER XVIII.

WHEN ªJethro, the priest of Midian, Moses' father-in-law, heard of all that God had done for Moses, and for Israel his people, *and* that the LORD had brought Israel out of Egypt,

2 Then Jethro, Moses' father-in-law, took Zipporah, Moses' wife, after he had sent her back,

---

a ch. 2: 16.

Amalek, that his hand is set upon the throne of Jehovah, to defeat His counsels for His Church and Kingdom.

LESSONS—(1) The Church of God may expect enemies, in this wilderness. (2) Besides providing for our hunger and thirst, our God can give victory over every foe. (3) Prayer is the force which, like a law in nature, controls the results in keeping with the Divine promises. (4) We may not only pray ourselves, but we may hold up the hands of others in prayer. Church members and officers may hold up the hands of their minister in prayer. (5) The gates of Hell shall not prevail against the Church. But the uplifted hands of believing prayer shall prevail against the gates of Hell. (6) God covenants to fight for His Church and people, because their foes are His foes also.

CHAPTER XVIII.

§ 38. VISIT OF JETHRO, MOSES' FATHER-IN-LAW. Ch. XVIII.

As in the conflict with Amalek there was figured forth the hostility of the world-kingdoms to the Church and kingdom of God, so here we have in the visit of the Midianite Jethro, the first fruits of the heathen in the future, seeking the living God, and entering into fellowship with the people of God. *Keil* further suggests that as both the Amalekites and the Midianites were descended from Abraham, and stood in blood relationship to Israel, we have here foreshadowed and typified the twofold attitude which the heathen world would assume towards the kingdom of God. Some suppose that this visit of Jethro must have occurred sometime after the departure from Sinai chiefly on account of the well organized condition in which the people are found, and also on account of seeming references to the giving of the law, as in offering sacrifices (v. 12, etc). But *Keil* contends that the narrative is quite in keeping with the context, and there is no need of supposing it interjected here, or out of proper order. So Canon Cook in *Sp. Com.* Since Moses, while tending the flocks of Jethro, had led them as far as "the Mount of God in Horeb," he is now in the neighborhood of Jethro's residence, who was "*the priest of Midian*" and *Moses' father-in-law.* Some think that Jethro was Moses' brother-in-law. *Sp. Com.*, see ch. 2: 18-21. When he *heard*—not necessarily the result of the battle with Amalek, though this is possible—but *of all that God had done for Moses and for Israel His people and that the Lord had brought Israel out of Egypt.* There was doubtless an understanding that Jethro should bring the wife and sons back to Moses when he should arrive at Horeb as God had promised, (ch. 3: 12). *After he had sent her back.* This clause is here thrown in to state the fact not elsewhere given that Moses had sent her back to her father's house. It is thought to have been at the circumcision of

CHAPTER XVIII.

3 And her two sons; of which the name of the one *was* Gershom; (for he said, I have been an alien in a strange land:)

4 And the name of the other *was* Eliezer; (for the God of my Father, *said he, was* my help, and delivered me from the sword of Pharaoh).

5 And Jethro, Moses' father-in-law, came with his sons and his wife unto Moses into the wilderness, where he encamped at the mount ᵇ of God:

6 And he said unto Moses, I thy father-in-law Jethro am come unto thee, and thy wife, and her two sons with her.

7 And Moses went out to meet his father-in-law, and did obeisance, ᶜ and kissed him: and they asked each other of *their* welfare; and they came into the tent.

8 And Moses told his father-in-law all that the LORD had done unto Pharaoh and to the Egyptians for Israel's sake, *and* all the travail that had come upon them by the way, and *how* the LORD ᵈ delivered them.

9 And Jethro rejoiced ᵉ for all the goodness which the LORD had done to Israel, whom he had delivered out of the hand of the Egyptians.

---

b ch. 3: 1-12.   c Ge. 29: 13; 33: 4.   d Ps. 106: 43; 107: 2.   e Ro. 12: 15.

---

the younger son, who perhaps was unable to proceed further at the time, (ch. 4: 16). Besides he may have thought that on such a mission as that to Pharaoh, the presence of his wife and children would be no help but a hindrance.

3, 4. *Gershom.* lit., *A Stranger there*—The name was given as a reminder of his constrained residence in Midian (see ch. 2: 22) which should also be a memorial to his son of his paternal history—when he was an alien—away from his home, for his love of his countrymen *and country. Eliezer*, meaning *My God a help*, supposed the same as ch. 4: 20-24. This is in memory of his deliverance from the punishment of Pharaoh when he slew the Egyptian,—though some regard it as prospective.

5. *Where he encamped. The Mount of God* may be *Horeb*, as in ch. 3: 1. Horeb is also a more general name of the district. But as Horeb bears this special designation there would seem to be no proof that he had already left Sinai, as *Murphy* and others suppose. It is *the Mount* of the God—the true God.

6. *He said*—It would seem, by a messenger. The Sept. Greek reads "And it was told to Moses," etc.

7. Moses receives Jethro with all the honors due to his rank and relationship, and in true Oriental style. *Did obeisance.* We have seen the sheikh of a village, or the head of an encampment make the most profound salutation of obeisance to one regarded as of higher rank, or to one of near kin. *Asked each other of (their) welfare,* or, more properly *bade each other peace,* the Oriental *salaam.* Came into the tent—the mark of friendly hospitality towards Jethro.

8 Moses now rehearsed to his father-in-law God's dealings towards him—their trials and deliverances —reciting the leading items in the wondrous history.

9, 10, 11. Jethro was full of joy at this narrative of the events. And he so expressed himself in the language of sacred praise. *Blessed*

10 And Jethro said, ᶠ Blessed *be* the LORD, who hath delivered you out of the hand of the Egyptians, and out of the hand of Pharaoh, who hath delivered the people from under the hand of the Egyptians.

11 Now I know that the LORD *is* greater than all ᵍ gods: for in the thing wherein they dealt proudly ʰ *he was* above them.

12 And Jethro, Moses' father-in-law, took a burnt-offering and sacrifices for God: and Aaron came, and all the elders of Israel, to eat bread with Moses' father-in-law ⁱ before God.

13 And it came to pass on the morrow, that Moses sat to judge the people: and the people stood by Moses from the morning unto the evening.

---

f 2Sa. 18: 28; Lu. 1: 68. g Ps. 95: 3; 97: 9. h Job. 40: 11; Da. 4: 37. i De. 12. 7; 1Ch. 29: 22; 1Co. 10: 21.

be Jehovah. He most distinctly acknowledges and confesses the God of the Hebrews as their mighty deliverer, in a conflict with Pharaoh and the Egyptians thus proving Himself to be superior to the idols of Egypt. *Now I know*—Not as if he was now for the first time convinced of this, for he was probably a priest of the true God, as Melchizedek was. *Greater than all gods.* This is no recognition of the Egyptian idols as being any real gods, however inferior, but as being claimed to be such. The Psalmist so expresses himself repeatedly, "For the Lord is a great God, and a great King above all gods," etc. Ps. 95: 3, 97: 9. And in Ps. 135: 5, this is the language with express reference to these dealings with Egypt, "For I know that the Lord is great and that our Lord is above all gods." *For in the thing* (lit) *wherein they dealt proudly against them*—that is, the Egyptians against the Israelites—God had proved His preëminence above all heathen idols and religions.

12. *A burnt-offering and bloody sacrifices.* The burnt-offering was expressive of entire consecration—the consuming of the victim signifying the fullest personal surrender to God. The bloody *sacrifices* expressed the sense of sin, and the idea of expiation by a substitutionary victim and sin-offerings—and they were also Eucharistic, making a social meal for thanksgiving to God. Jethro was thus a worshipper of the true God, and knew the meaning of sacrifice. And the communion with him by the Elders of Israel shows the substantial oneness of their religious faith. Melchizedek also was a priest of the Most High God. So that the worship of Jehovah was maintained among the people outside of the Jewish nation. (See Notes on Genesis, ch. 14: 18.) Communion with God and communion with one another are here celebrated in this thanksgiving meal. How appropriate was all this devout and public recognition of Jehovah's power and grace towards His Church in the wilderness. And that it should have been done by the agency of this Midianite priest of God, who was here publicly brought into communion and recognition before the Church, is most remarkable.

13. The administration of justice had been carried on in Egypt by the patriarchal rule of Elders. But this had become very much superseded by the Divine legation of Moses, investing him with personal office as a sovereign. Now,

CHAPTER XVIII. 161

14 And when Moses' father-in-law saw all that he did to the people, he said, What *is* this thing that thou doest to the people? why sittest thou thyself alone, and all the people stand by thee from morning unto even?

15 And Moses said unto his father-in-law, Because the people come unto j me to inquire of God:

16 When they have a matter, they come unto me; and I judge between one and another; and I do make *them* know the statutes of God, and his laws.

17 And Moses' father-in-law said unto him, The thing that thou doest *is* not good.

18 Thou wilt surely wear away, both thou, and this people

---

j Nu. 15: 34; 27: 5; De. 17: 8, 9.

---

however, the burden became too heavy in this disorganized condition in the wilderness. *Moses sat to judge.* In Oriental cities the head or chief sits in the open space at the gate to receive complaints and hear causes brought for decision. Here Moses occupied a public, conspicuous position, where the people might gather round him and state their cases, and have them adjudged. This was the first opportunity, probably, that had offered since the outstart of their march, at any rate since they left Elim, and it has been supposed that the battle with the Amalekites had furnished numerous cases for trial, as to dividing the spoils, or other questions, or various grievances. A whole day was given to the work—*from the morning unto the evening.* And it would be most exhausting to Moses. The judge *sat* —the people *stood*—that is, those whose cases were on trial.

14. Jethro, seeing this, expostulates with his son-in-law, at the needless task borne by him, thus alone.

15, 16. Moses now states his office-work, and its relations to the people in this matter of judicial decisions. *The people come unto me to inquire of God.* This is understood to be the Divine method for learning the Divine will. It is not to inquire of Moses as an individual—but of Moses as the organ and oracle of God. Magistrates are ordained of God. But Moses was Divinely commissioned as leader of the people, and Mediator between God and them. And in coming to him for the settlement of disputes between themselves they recognized him as God's mouth-piece and vicegerent, whose decisions were the decisions of God Himself (ch. 21: 6). *And I do make* (*them*) *know*—Moses declared to them the principles of the Divine administration, and expounded them to the people, with all the disadvantage, however, of having no written code. Here the necessity became most apparent for the publication of a Divine code as was so soon to be done at Sinai. God allows men thus to find out the necessity for the further revelations He is about to make.

17-20. The method practised by Moses was declared by Jethro to be *not good*—but burdensome and exhausting both to Moses and to the people, and therefore not suited to secure the ends of justice. Overwork—energies of mind and body overtaxed, must serve to cut short the valuable lives of God's servants, and therefore should be protested against as is here done by Jethro. Such a process as Moses', too, would often defeat justice by the necessary delays where all the

that *is* with thee: for this thing *is* too heavy ᵏ for thee; thou art not able to perform it thyself alone.

19 Hearken now unto my voice, I will give thee counsel: and God shall be with thee: be thou for the people ˡ to Godward, that thou mayest bring the causes unto God:

20 And thou shalt teach them ᵐ ordinances and laws, and shalt shew them the way wherein they must walk, and the work that they must do.

21 Moreover, thou shalt provide out of all the people able men, such as ⁿ fear God, men of truth, hating covetousness:

---

k De. 1: 9, 12. l ch. 20: 19; De. 5: 5. m De. 4: 1; 6: 1, 2; Ne. 9: 14. n De. 1: 15–17; 16: 18; 2Sa. 23: 3; Job 29: 16; 31: 13.

---

cases must wait upon the attention and decision of one man. The division of labor proposed distributing the administration of justice among several courts or judges, has been found necessary in all civilized communities. Jethro's counsel is now given—and it is most wise and faithful, founded on the very nature of things, and intended to approve itself to God as it is also conditioned upon His approval. *And God shall be with thee.* This is included in Jethro's plan, not that Moses should do without God by any method he might suggest, but that God's presence and favor must be reckoned upon. *Be thou for the people to God-ward—before God.* (1) Moses is to be the Mediator or Representative standing between the people and God, and in the interest of the people, *bringing their causes unto God*—laying them before God as advocate, mediating as a representative of both parties (Gal. 3: 20). (2) Moses is to be judge, teacher, and expounder of the ordinances and laws, showing the people *the way to go and the work to do.* So he is to give judicial charges and decisions in the leading cases, explaining and enforcing the law. But for his relief in the details, he is to have subordinate judges to decide minor causes on trial. *Teach them, give them light*—instruct them in dark points. "There are here four points, (a) the *ordinances,* or specific enactments, (b) the *laws,* or general regulations, (c) the *way*—the general course of duty,—(d) the *work*—each specific act." *Sp. Com.*

21. Jethro here suggests most important advice as to the character and quality of his assistants. There are four leading qualifications here set forth, that may be held requisite for all civil officers, and especially for judges, who administer the laws and mete out justice among men. They must be men of *ability,* men of *piety,* men of *truthfulness,* men of *unselfishness. Thou shalt provide.* It would seem from Deut. 1: 13 that Moses left the selection of these captains or judges to the people. But he seems there rather to propose to them Jethro's plan for their approval, and then he proceeds to make the officers. "So I took the chiefs of your tribes and made them heads over you" (v. 15). *Able men*—lit., *men of might,* men of moral strength (1 Kings 1: 52). Such would be the men of real force of character. The same phrase is rendered men of activity (Gen. 47: 6), and in 1 Chron. 26: 6, 'mighty men of valor.' These were to be military captains, as well as civil judges. They were to be men of *ability,* not weak, facile, inefficient, unqualified men, but *able* men. *Such as fear God.* Pious men. A vital requisite. The fear of Jehovah is the beginning of wisdom. Men who have no fear of God before their eyes cannot properly administer justice, and are not fit to

CHAPTER XVIII.

and place *such* over them, *to be* rulers of thousands, *and* rulers of hundreds, rulers of fifties, and rulers of tens:

22 And let them judge the people at all seasons: and it shall be, *that* every great matter they shall bring unto thee; but every small matter they shall judge: so shall it be easier for thyself, and they shall bear *the burden* º with thee.

---

o Nu. 11: 17.

---

be trusted with the destinies of individuals, much less of the State. A man who robs God cannot be trusted with deciding upon the rights of a neighbor. The unjust judge was one who boldly confessed (to himself) that he feared not God nor regarded man. And the two things go together, as love of God and love of man go together. Hence also, a belief in a future state of Divine rewards and punishments is counted requisite to qualify a man for ordinary office in the state. much more for being a judge. *Men of truth.* Men of truth alone can be true men. Falsity, double-dealing, disregard of what is right and true, are vital disqualifications for administering justice. A liar on the bench may well be the terror of the good. A man who regards not his own word, how can he hold others to the truth? One who is himself a defrauder, how can he decide against the fraud of another? "Thou that sayest a man should not steal, dost thou steal?" Corrupt judges are the sorest curse of any community. And hence the election of judges by the people opens the way for corruption to instal itself in power where the people themselves have lost a proper sense of virtue and rectitude. *Hating covetousness.* What a stroke at the crying sin of the times! In every age, even in the wilderness, such a quality was to be insisted upon for the conservation of society. *Gain-hating.* Corrupt judges may have the temptation of making their office subservient to gain. And he that is accessible to bribes, may subvert justice for filthy lucre. *Rulers of thousands*, etc. This, it will be seen, is to be distinguished from the office of *Elders* in Numb. 11: 16, who were only seventy, and these captains, or chiefs, as judges, have been reckoned as numbering 78,600. But these officers were not to supersede the original patriarchal rule by which the father of a family was the governor of his household and clan, during life. It has been reckoned that "taking twenty to be the reasonable average of a grandfather's family, ten such families would amount to 200 individuals, and ten such heads are the smallest number allowed by the Talmudists to constitute a synagogue. In a people of at least 1,600,000 there would thus be 8,000 rulers of tens, 1600 rulers of fifties, 800 rulers of hundreds, and 80 rulers of thousands —making 10,480 rulers in all."—*Murphy.* *Keil* says, "These family groups, larger or smaller, were not every one to have a judge of its own, for the judges were to be chosen out of these heads, and must have been fewer, in all amounting to not many hundreds."

22. *At all seasons.* These judges were to sit at all times as occasion might require. And this subdivision of labor would very much lighten the burden of Moses. *Every great matter* was to be brought before him, as the highest tribunal, while minor cases could be disposed of by the inferior judges. Where the case was one of most grave import, involving the most serious questions, and most intricate and difficult of solution, it was to be referred to Moses. Cases might even be appealed to him from the lower tribunals. *And they shall bear.* "This constitution of the tribes with the subordinate degrees of sheikhs,

23 If thou shalt do this thing, and God command p thee *so*, then thou shalt be able to endure, and all this people shall also go to q their place in peace.

24 So Moses hearkened to the voice of his father-in-law, and did all that he had said.

25 And Moses chose able men out of all Israel, and made them heads over the people, rulers of thousands, rulers of hundreds, rulers of fifties, and rulers of tens.

26 And they judged the people at all seasons: the hard causes they brought unto Moses, but every small matter they judged themselves.

27 And Moses let his father-in-law depart; and r he went his way into his own land.

---

p 1Sa. 8: 7.   q Ge. 30: 25.   r Nu. 10: 29-30.

---

recommended to Moses by Jethro is the very same which still exists amongst those who are possibly his lineal descendants, the gentle race of the Towara."—*Stanley.*

23. If Moses should follow this course and God so *command* him —that is supposing always that this plan should have the Divine approval, then Moses shall be able to endure. Jethro here will have it understood that his counsel is first to be submitted to the Divine direction. The *Gr.* reads "If thou wilt do this, God will strengthen thee and thou shalt be able to stand." *Luther*—" If, then, thou canst judge as God bids thee." *Vulg*—" Thou shalt fulfil the government of God, and His precepts thou shalt be able to sustain." But the English version is required by the terms, *Go to their place in peace.* Satisfied, without complainings, and without the disturbances which else would be liable to break out. This may mean shall go to their tents in peace, after the decisions, or shall go to their place or land of Canaan, in peace and satisfaction.

24. *Moses hearkened—*gave respectful attention to his father-in-law, and followed his advice, and when he had received for it the Divine approval, which was part of the advice, he put the measure into operation. It was a most suitable organization for judicial processes, during the wilderness estate—to be surpassed by a more advanced arrangement when they should arrive in the Holy Land. Deut. 16: 18. Such exemplary deference did Moses pay to his relative, though himself so superior in rank, only that Jethro was a priest of God, and Moses was meek.

25. *Moses chose.* The people nominated and Moses chose from such. The appointment was with Moses.

27. *And Moses let his father-in-law depart,* lit., *dismissed his father-in-law. And he went his way into his own land* of Midian. The usual formalities and courtesies of sending away a distinguished guest, were doubtless observed—the escort —the partings, etc., suitable to the person and the relations. We learn very little of the two sons of Moses. He seems not to have put them in high official positions, as many another—if commanding such immense patronage—would have done.

LESSONS. (1) How blessed is it where all the branches of the household, not only blood relatives but marriage kin, are godly. The counsel of such may serve one in most trying times. (2) A true servant of God may give valuable counsel to one most exalted in secular and civil rank. (3) Overtasking one's self, even in religious duties, is a cutting short of one's days, and should be religiously avoided. (4) Division of labor best serves the cause of justice and charity. (5) Judges of the people ought to be able, pious, truthful and unselfish. (6) Government is a Divine ordinance—and good law is the basis of true liberty. (7) God's approval should be the qualifying conditions of all our counsel to others and of all our action for ourselves. (8) Courtesies in the family are most fitting and beautiful. How charming to see the most exalted in station pay respect to their obscure kindred, and defer to their pious advice, where it is approved of God.

This historical narrative, including Book I and Book II, brings us to Sinai, and introduces us to the legal transactions here put on record. The grand Redemptive fact now so signally accomplished is to stand as the Preface to the Law which the people are now to receive at the hand of Jehovah. The connection is strictly evangelical. The Gospel proclaims the Redemption by Christ Jesus as the highest motive to obedience. " I am the Lord (Jehovah) *thy* (covenant) *God, which have brought thee out of the land of Egypt, out of the house of bondage. Thou shalt have no other gods before me* (in my presence)—Chap. 20: 2, 3. So the finished work of Jesus Christ for man's Redemption is the preface to the Gospel obligations: and gratitude for what has already been done for us is the grand gospel motive to new obedience. The Law cannot be properly understood in any of its commandments except in the light of the Gospel. Morality, that is not Gospel morality on Christian principles of loving return for Redeeming Love, cannot be a pure morality. It may have the form, but it lacks the spirit, and leaves Christ and His salvation out of view. Jesus has cleft the sea for us, and has spoiled our enemies who are His enemies also, and now the song of victory may be already on our lips, and as the Redeemed people of God we are to receive the law from His mouth, and to have no other gods in His presence, and to march under His escort through all this wilderness, to the heavenly Canaan.

APPENDIX.

APPENDIX A.

HISTORICAL ILLUSTRATIONS OF THE OLD TESTAMENT.

By Rev. G. C. Rawlinson, M. A.,
Camden Professor of Ancient History, Oxford.

The narrative contained in the four books—Exodus, Leviticus, Numbers, and Deuteronomy—covers a space of probably less than two centuries; and the scene is chiefly laid in countries of which profane history tells us little or nothing at this early period. Illustration of the narrative from profane sources must, therefore, be almost entirely confined to that portion of it which precedes the departure from Egypt, or, in other words, to the time during which the descendants of Abraham remained in close contact with a civilized nation, whose records and monuments have come down to us. The same kind of agreement between the details of the Biblical narrative and the usages known to have prevailed in ancient Egypt, which has been pointed out with respect to the latter part of Genesis, may be traced likewise here; and further, the Exodus itself, or withdrawal from Egypt of an oppressed portion of the population, and their settlement in southern Syria or Palestine, may be shown to have left traces in Egyptian literature, traces which quite unmistakably point to some such series of transactions as those recorded in the sacred volume.

In proof of this latter point, to which precedence may be assigned on account of its exceeding interest, an exact translation will, in the first place, be given of two passages, one from the early Egyptian writer, Manetho, and the other from a later author of the same nation, Chæremon, both of whom were priests and learned in the antiquities of their country.

Manetho (as reported by the Jewish historian Josephus *) said:

"A king, named Amenophis, desired to behold the gods, like Horus, one of his predecessors, and imparted his desire to his namesake, Amenophis, son of Paapis, who on account of his wisdom and acquaintance with futurity was thought to be a partaker of the divine nature. His name-

---

* *Contr. Apion.* i. 26, 27.

sake told him that he would be able to see the gods, if he cleansed the whole country of lepers and the other polluted persons in it. The king was pleased, and collecting together all that had any bodily defect throughout Egypt, to the number of 80,000, he cast them into the stone-quarries which lie east of the Nile, in order that they might work there together with the other Egyptians employed similarly. Among them were some of the learned priests who were afflicted with leprosy. But Amenophis, the sage and prophet, grew alarmed, fearing the wrath of the gods against himself as well as against the king, if the forced labor of the men were observed, and he proceeded to foretell that there would come persons to the assistance of the unclean, who would be masters of Egypt for thirteen years. But as he did not dare to say this to the king, he put it all in writing, and leaving the document behind him, killed himself. Hereupon the king was greatly dejected; and when the workers in the stone-quarries had suffered for a considerable time, the king, at their request, set apart the city of Avaris, which was empty, having been deserted by the shepherds. Now this place, according to the mythology, was of old a Typhonian town. So when the people had entered the city, and had thus a stronghold on which to rest, they appointed as their leader a priest of Heliopolis, by name Osarsiph, and swore to obey him in all things. And he, first of all, gave them a law, that they should worship no gods, and should abstain from none of the animals accounted most holy in Egypt, but sacrifice and consume all alike; and further, that they should associate with none but their fellow-conspirators. Having established these and many other laws completely opposed to the customs of Egypt, he commanded the bulk of them to build up the town wall, and to make themselves ready for a war with Amenophis, the king. After this, having consulted with some of the other priests and polluted persons, he sent ambassadors to the shepherds, who had been driven out of Egypt by Tethmosis, to the city which is called Jerusalem, and after informing them about himself and his fellow-sufferers, invited them to join with him in an attack upon Egypt. He would bring them, he said, in the first place, to Avaris, the city of their forefathers, and would provide them amply with all that was necessary for their host; he would fight on their behalf, when occasion offered, and easily make the country subject to them. They, on their part, were exceedingly rejoiced, and promptly set out in full force, to the number of 200,000 men, and soon reached Avaris. Now when Amenophis, the Egyptian king, heard of their invasion, he was not a little disquieted, since he remembered what Amenophis, the son of Paapis, had prophesied; and though he had previously collected together a vast host of Egyptians, and had taken counsel with their leaders, yet soon he gave orders that the sacred animals held in the most repute in the various temples should be conveyed to him, and that the priests of each temple should hide away the images of the gods as securely as possible.

Moreover he placed his son, Sethos—called also Ramesses, after Rampses, his (i. e. Amenophis') father—who was a boy of five years old, in the hands of one of his friends. He then himself crossed the river with the other Egyptians, 300,000 in number, all excellent soldiers; but when the enemy advanced to meet him, he declined to engage, since he thought that it would be fighting against the gods, and returned hastily to Memphis. Then, carrying with him the Apis and the other sacred animals which had been brought to him, he proceeded at once with the whole Egyptian army to Ethiopia. Now the king of Ethiopia lay under obligations to him; he therefore received him, supplied his host with all the necessaries that his country afforded, assigned them cities and villages sufficient for the fated thirteen years' suspension of their sovereignty, and even placed an Ethiopian force on the Egyptian frontier for the protection of the army of Amenophis. Thus stood matters in Ethiopia. But the Solymites who had returned from exile, and the unclean Egyptians, treated the people of the country so shamefully, that their government appeared, to those who witnessed their impieties, to be the worst Egypt had known. For not only did they burn cities and hamlets, nor were they content with plundering temples and ill-treating the images, but they continued to use the venerated sacred animals as food, and compelled the priests and prophets to be their slayers and butchers, and then sent them away naked. And it is said that the priest who framed their constitution and their laws, who was a native of Heliopolis, named Osarsiph, after the Heliopolitan god Osiris, after he joined this set of people, changed his name, and was called Moses. . . . . . Afterwards, Amenophis returned from Ethiopia with a great force, as did his son Rampses, who was likewise accompanied by a force, and together they engaged the shepherds and the unclean, and defeated them, slaying many and pursuing the remainder to the borders of Syria."

The statement of Chæremon is as follows: *

"Isis having appeared to Amenophis in his sleep, and reproached him because her temple had been destroyed in the (shepherd) war, Phritiphantes, the sacred scribe, informed him that if he would purge the land of Egypt of all those who had any pollution he would be subject to no more such alarms. So he collected 250,000 defiled persons, and expelled them from the country. Two scribes, called Moses and Joseph, led them forth; the latter of whom was, like Phritiphantes, a sacred scribe; and both of these men had Egyptian names, the name of Moses being Tisithen, and that of Joseph Peteseph. They proceeded to Pelusium, and there fell in with 380,000 persons, who had been left behind by Amenophis, because he did not like to bring them into Egypt. So they made an alliance with these men and invaded Egypt; whereupon Amenophis, without waiting for them to attack him, fled away into Ethiopia, leaving his wife, who

* Ap. Joseph. *c. Apion.*, § 32.

was pregnant, behind him. And she, having hid herself in some caves gave birth there to a son, who was called Messenes, who, when he came to man's estate, drove the Jews into Syria, their number being about 200,000, and received back his father Amenophis out of Ethiopia."

From these passages it appears (1) that the Egyptians had a tradition of an Exodus from their country of persons whom they regarded as unclean, persons who rejected their customs, refused to worship their gods, and killed for food the animals which they held as sacred ; (2) that they connected this Exodus with the names of Joseph * and Moses; (3) that made southern Syria the country into which the unclean persons withdrew ; and (4) that they placed the event in the reign of a certain Amenophis, son of Rameses or Rampses, and father of Sethos, who was made to reign toward the close of the eighteenth dynasty, or about B. C. 1400–1300. † The circumstances by which the Exodus was preceded are represented differently in the Egyptian and in the Hebrew narrative, either because the memory of some other event is confused with that of the Jewish Exodus, or because the Egyptian writers, being determined to represent the withdrawal of the Jews from Egypt as an expulsion, were driven to invent a cause for the expulsion in a precedent war, and a temporary dominion of the polluted persons over their country. Among little points common to the two narratives, and tending to identify them are the following :—(1) the name of *Avaris*, given to the town made over to the polluted persons, which stands in etymological connection with the word "Hebrew ;" (2) the character of the pollution ascribed to them, leprosy, which may be accounted for, first, by the fact that one of the signs by which Moses was to prove his Divine mission consisted in the exhibition of a leprous hand (Ex. iv. 6), and, secondly, by the existence of this malady to a considerable extent among the Hebrew people at the time (Lev. xiii. and xiv.) ; (3) the mention of Heliopolis as the city to which the leader belonged, and the assignment to him of priestly rank, which arises naturally out of the confusion between Moses and Joseph (Gen. xli. 45); (4) the employment of the polluted persons for a time in forced labor ; (5) the conviction of Amenophis that in resisting the polluted he was "fighting against the gods;" (6) his fear for the safety of his young son, which recalls to our thoughts the last and most awful of the plagues ; (7) the sending away of the priests " naked," which seems an exaggeration of the

---

* It must be remembered that the Israelites did carry with them out of Egypt the body of Joseph (Exod. xiii. 19), and that there was, thus, some foundation for the Egyptian notion, that Moses *and Joseph* led them out.

† Egyptian chronology and the date of the Exodus are, both of them, still unsettled. M. Lenormant places the accession of the nineteenth dynasty in B. C. 1462 (*Manuel d'Histoire*, tom. i. p. 321) ; Sir G. Wilkinson in B. C. 1324 (Rawlinson's *Herodotus*, vol. ii. p. 308, 2d ed.) ; Mr Stuart Poole about B. C. 1340 (*Biblical Dictionary*, vol. i. p. 511). The date of the Exodus is variously given, as B. C. 1648 (Hales), 1652 (Poole), 1491 (Usher, Kalisch), and 1320 (Lepsius).

"spoiling of the Egyptians;" and (8) the occurrence of the word "Rameses" in the Egyptian royal house, which harmonizes with its employment at the time as a local designation (Ex. i. 11; xii. 37).

Another curious account of the Exodus was given by Hecatæus, a Greek of Abdera, who flourished in the time of Alexander, and was familiar with Ptolemy Lagi, the first Greek king of Egypt. This writer, as reported by Diodorus, * said:—

"Once when a plague broke out in Egypt, the people generally ascribed the affliction to the anger of the gods; for as many strangers of different races were dwelling in Egypt at the time, who practised various strange customs in their worship and their sacrifices, it had come to pass that the old religious observances of the country had fallen into disuse. The natives, therefore, believing that unless they expelled the foreigners there would be no end to their sufferings, rose against them, and drove them out. Now the noblest and most enterprising joined together, and went (as some say) to Greece and elsewhere, under leaders of good repute; the most remarkable of whom were Danāus and Cadmus. But the bulk of them withdrew to the country which is now called Judæa, situated at no great distance from Egypt, and at that time without inhabitants. The leader of this colony was the man called Moses, who was distinguished above his fellows by his wisdom and his courage. Having taken possession of the country, he built there a number of towns, and among them the city which is called Jerusalem, and which is now so celebrated. He likewise built the temple which they hold in so much respect, and instituted their religious rites and ceremonies; besides which he gave them laws and arranged their form of government. He divided the people into twelve tribes, because he regarded 12 as the most perfect number, agreeing, as it does, with the number of months that complete the year. But he would not set up any kind of image of the deity, because he did not believe that God had a human form, but regarded the firmament which surrounds the earth as the only God and Lord of all. And he made their sacrifices and their habits of life quite different from those of other nations, introducing a misanthropic and inhospitable style of living, on account of the expulsion which he had himself suffered."

With this may be compared the remarkable account in Tacitus, † which combines certain features which are Egyptian with others that have clearly come from the sacred narrative.

"Most writers agree," says Tacitus, "that when a plague which disfigured men's bodies, had broken out in Egypt, Bocchoris, the king, desirous of a remedy, sent and consulted the oracle of Ammon, which commanded him to purge his kingdom, by removing to foreign lands the afflicted persons, who were a race hateful to the gods. Search was there-

---

* Diod. Sic. xl. 3. (The passage is preserved to us by Photius, *Bibliothec.*, p. 1152.)
† *Hist.* v. 3. Compare the account of Lysimachus (*Fr. Hist. Gr.* vol. iii. p. 334).

fore made, and a vast multitude being collected together, was led forth and left in a desert. Then Moses, one of their number, seeing the rest stupefied with grief, advised them, as they were deserted both by gods and men not to expect help from either, but to confide in him, the heavenly leader, to whose assistance they would no sooner trust than they would be free from their troubles. His words won their assent, and in utter ignorance they marched whither chance led them. Their greatest trial was the want of water. Death seemed drawing near, as they lay prostrate on the plains, when, lo! a herd of wild asses was seen to quit its pasture and retreat to a piece of rocky ground whereon a number of trees grew. Moses followed upon their track, and finding a patch of soil covered with grass, conjectured the presence of water, and succeeded in uncovering some copious springs. Thus refreshed, they pursued their journey for six days, and on the seventh reached a cultivated tract, whereof they took possession, after driving out the inhabitants. Here they built their town and consecrated their temple."

From the diverse manner in which the story is told by different authors, we may conclude that the Egyptians in their formal histories took no notice of the occurrence, which sorely hurt their national vanity; but that a remembrance of it continued in the minds of the people, who possessed (it must be borne in mind) a copious contemporary literature,* and that this remembrance gradually took various shapes, all of them, however, more or less flattering to the Egyptians themselves, and unfair to their adversaries. The Hebrews were almost uniformly represented as unclean persons, afflicted with some disease or other, and their Exodus was declared to be an expulsion. Generally they were spoken of as Egyptians, which was not unnatural, considering their long sojourn in the country; † but sometimes it was allowed that they were foreigners. ‡ The miraculous events by which their departure was preceded were ignored partially or wholly; but there was a pretty general consent as to the name of their leader, as to the character of the laws which he gave them, and as to the quarter in which they obtained new settlements. The Egyptians never forgot, any more than the Hebrews, that there had been a time, when the two races had dwelt together; they looked on the Hebrews as a sort of Egyptian colony; and while from time to time they claimed, on that account, a dominion over their country, they were ready generally to extend to it that protection which colonies, according to the

---

* The hieratic Papyri of Egypt go back to a time anterior to the eighteenth dynasty. They comprise romances, epistolary correspondence, poems, etc.

† Compare Ex. ii. 19, where Reuel's daughters mistake Moses for "an Egyptian."

‡ See the account of Hecatæus (supra p. 62), and compare Tacit. Hist. v. 2: "Some writers tell us that they (i. e. the Jews) were a band of *Assyrians*, who being in want of territory, first took possession of a portion of Egypt, and soon afterwards became the inhabitants of the parts of Syria which lie near to Egypt."

ideas of the ancient world, were entitled to require from the fatherland. The relations between Egypt and Palestine were, for the most part, friendly from the time of the Exodus to the conquest of Egypt by the Romans.

In none of the profane accounts hitherto quoted has the remarkable event of the passage of the Red Sea by the Hebrews, in their flight, obtained any mention. There is, however, reason to believe, that this important feature of the history retained a place in the recollections of the Egyptian people, and even formed a subject of discussion and controversy among them. Artapanus, a Jewish historian, quoted by Alexander Polyhistor, * the contemporary of Sulla and Marius, wrote as follows :—

"*The Memphites say*, that Moses being well acquainted with the district, watched the ebb of the tide, and so led the people across the dry bed of the sea ; but *they of Heliopolis affirm*, that the king at the head of a vast force, and having the sacred animals also with him, pursued after the Jews, because they were carrying away with them the riches, which they had borrowed of the Egyptians. Then, they say, the voice of God commanded Moses to smite the sea with his rod, and divide it ; and Moses, when he heard it, touched the water with it, and so the sea parted asunder, and the host marched through on dry ground."

From these direct testimonies to the historical truth of the Exodus, we may now turn to the less striking, but perhaps even more convincing, indirect evidence, which is furnished by the minute agreement of the sacred narrative with the known usages of ancient Egypt.

The narrative of Exodus tells us, in the first place, that shortly after the death of Joseph an oppression of the Israelites began. A new king—perhaps the founder of a new dynasty—claimed the whole race as his slaves, and proceeded to engage them in servile labors, placing task-masters over them, whose business it was to "make their lives bitter with hard bondage" (Ex. i. 14). The work assigned to them consisted of brick-making, building, and severe field-labor. They worked under the rod, the laborers being liable to be " smitten " by the Egyptian taskmasters as they labored (ii. 11), and the native officers being punished by flogging if the tasks of the men under them were not fulfilled (v. 14). On the brick-makers a certain "tale of bricks" was imposed (v. 8), which had to be completed daily. Straw was a material in the bricks ; and this was at first furnished to the laborers, but afterwards they were required to procure straw for themselves, on which they spread themselves over the land and gathered stubble (v. 12). Details are wanting with respect to their other employments ; but in one place (Deut. xi. 10) we find it implied that one of the main hardships of the field-work was the toil of irrigation.

Almost every point of this narrative is capable of illustration from the Egyptian monuments. Notwithstanding the great abundance of stone in

* *Fragm. Hist. Gr.* vol. iii. pp. 223, 224.

Egypt, and the fact that most of the grander buildings were constructed of this material, yet there was also an extensive employment of brick in the country. Pyramids,* houses, tombs, the walls of towns, fortresses, and the sacred enclosures of temples, were commonly, or at any rate, frequently, built of brick by the Egyptians. † A large portion of the brickfields belonged to the monarch, for whose edifices bricks were made in them, stamped with his name. ‡ Chopped straw was an ordinary material in the bricks, § being employed as hair by modern plasterers, to bind them together, and make them more firm and durable. Captives and foreigners commonly did the work in the royal brickfields; and Egyptian taskmasters, with rods in their hands, watched their labors, and punished the idle with blows at their discretion. ‖ The bastinado was a recognized punishment for minor offences. ¶ "Stubble and straw" both existed in ancient Egypt, wheat being occasionally cut with a portion of the stalk; while the remainder, or more commonly, the entire stalk, was left standing in the fields.** And both stubble and straw have been found in the bricks.†† Finally, though agricultural labor is in some respects light in Egypt,‡‡ yet practically, from the continued succession of crops, from the intense heat of the climate, and from the exertions needed for irrigation, the lot of the cultivator has always been, and still continues to be a hard one.§§

Among the other Egyptian usages introduced to our notice in Exodus, the most remarkable are the following:—The employment of chariots, on a large scale, in war (xiv. 6, 7); the practice of the king to go out to battle in person (ib. 8); the hearing of complaints and transaction of business by the king in person (v. 15); the possession, by most Egyptians, of articles in gold and silver (xii. 35); the cultivation, in spring, of the following crops *chiefly*—wheat, barley, flax, and rye, or spelt (ix. 32); the keeping of cattle, partly in the fields, partly in stables (ix. 3. 19); the storing of water in vessels of wood and stone (vii. 19); the employment of midwives (i. 15-21); the use of the papyrus for boats (ii. 3), of furnaces (ix. 8), ovens (viii. 3), kneading-troughs (ib.), walking-sticks (vii.

---

* Herod. ii. 136.

† Wilkinson in Rawlinson's *Herodotus*, vol. ii. p. 183, 2d ed.

‡ Rosellini, *Monumenti*, vol. ii. p. 252; Wilkinson, *Ancient Egyptians*, vol. ii. p. 97.

§ Wilkinson; vol. i. p. 50; Rosellini, vol. ii. pp. 252, 259, etc.

‖ Wilkinson, vol. ii. p. 42; Rosellini, vol. ii. p. 249.

¶ Wilkinson, vol ii. p. 241.

** Wilkinson, vol. iv. pp. 85-93, !

†† Ibid. vol. i. p. 50.

‡‡ "The Egyptians," says Herodotus, "obtain the fruits of the field with less trouble than any other people in the world. They have no need to use either the plough or the hoe; the swine tread in their corn, and also thrash it." ii. 14. Compare Wilkinson's note in Rawlinson's *Herod.* vol. ii. p. 15, 2d. ed.

§§ See Kalisch, *Comment. on Exod*, p. 10; and compare Wilkinson, vol. iv. pp. 41-101.

10, 12), hand-mills (xi. 5), bitumen (ii. 3), and pitch (ib.). To these the following may be added from the later books of the Pentateuch—the necessary employment of irrigation in agriculture (Deut. xi. 10); the use, as common articles of food, of fish, cucumbers, melons, onions, garlic, and leeks (Num. xi. 5); and the practice of the kings to keep large studs of horses (Deut. xvii. 16).

Now here again, as in the later chapters of Genesis, almost every custom recorded can be confirmed either from the ancient accounts of Egyptian manners which have come down to us, or from the monuments, or from both. The only exception, of any importance, is the employment of midwives, which was probably rare, as it is in the East generally, and was also of a nature that would have been felt to render it unfit for representation. Even here, however, where ancient illustration fails, a strong confirmation of the narrative has been obtained by modern inquiry, the curious expression, "when ye see them upon the stools," being in remarkable accordance with the modern Egyptian practice, as stated by Mr. Lane.* "Two or three days," he says, "before the expected time of delivery, the *layah* (midwife) conveys to the house the *kursee elwilâdeh*, a chair of a peculiar form, upon which the patient is to be seated during the birth."

The monuments show that in ancient Egypt by far the most important arm of the military service was the chariot force. The king, the princes, and all the chiefs of importance fought from chariots.† Diodorus made the number of them in the army of Sesostris, 27,000,‡ and though this is a gross exaggeration, it shows the feeling of the Greeks as to the very extensive employment of chariots by the earlier monarchs. Cavalry were employed to a very small extent, if at all;§ and though this, at first sight, may seem at variance with the Mosaic narrative (Ex. xiv. 9. 17, 18. 23, etc.; xv. 1), yet a careful examination of the original text will lead to the conclusion that the force which pursued the Israelites was composed of chariots and infantry only.‖ The practice of the king to lead out his army in person, is abundantly evident,¶ and will scarcely be doubted by any. It was indeed a practice universal at the

---

* *Modern Egyptians*, vol iii. p. 142.
† Wilkinson, vol. i. pp. 335-341; Rosellini, vol. ii. p. 240.
‡ Diod. Sic. i. 54.
§ Rosellini inclines to the belief that the ancient Egyptians had no cavalry (vol. ii. pp. 232-259). Sir G. Wilkinson thinks they may have had a cavalry force, but that it was scanty (vol. i. pp. 289, 290). Both agree that no cavalry are represented on the monuments. Herodotus *once* speaks of an Egyptian commander as on horseback (ii. 162). Diodorus, on the other hand, gives Sesostris a numerous cavalry (i. 54).
‖ See the arguments of Hengstenberg (pp. 127-129), and Kalisch (*Comment. on Exodus*, pp. 182-184). The term translated "horsemen" in our version, refers probably to the riders in the chariots.
¶ Herod. ii. 102; Wilkinson, i. pp. 63, 65, 83, etc.

time among all Oriental sovereigns. The hearing of complaints and pronouncing of judgments by the king in person, was also very usual throughout the East; and the existence of the custom in Egypt is illustrated by many passages in ancient authors.*

The representations with respect to Egyptian agriculture, feeding of cattle, food, dress, and domestic habits are similarly borne out both by the ancient remains and the ancient authorities. The cultivation depicted on the monuments is especially that of wheat, flax, barley, and another grain, which is believed to correspond with the *cussemeth*, "rye," or "spelt," of the Hebrews.† Fish and vegetables formed the chief food of the lower classes; and among the vegetables especially affected, gourds, cucumbers, onions, and garlic are distinctly apparent.‡ According to Herodotus, some tribes of the Egyptians lived entirely on fish, which abounded in the Nile, the canals, and the lakes, especially in the Birket-el-Keroun, or Lake Mœris.§ The monuments represent the catching, salting, and eating of this viand.‖ We also see on the monuments that cattle were kept, both in the field, where they were liable to be overtaken by the inundation,¶ and also in stalls or sheds.** The wide-spread possession, by the Egyptians, of articles in gold and silver, vases, goblets, necklaces, armlets, bracelets, ear-rings, and finger-rings, is among the facts most copiously attested by the extant remains,†† and is also illustrated by the ancient writers, who even speak of so strange an article as "a golden foot-pan."‡‡ The employment of furnaces, ovens, and kneading-troughs, the common practice of carrying staves or walking-sticks, and the use of hand-mills for grinding corn, are likewise certified either by representations or by remains found in the country.§§

The storing of water in vessels of wood and stone, which is implied in Ex. vii. 19, is a peculiarly Egyptian custom, scarcely known elsewhere. The abundance of water in the Nile, and its wide diffusion by means of canals, render reservoirs, in the ordinary sense of the word, unnecessary

---

* See Herod. ii. 115; 121, § 3; 129, 173.
† Wilkinson, vol. ii. p. 398; vol. iv. pp. 85-99.
‡ Ibid. vol. ii. pp. 370-374; and compare vol. i. 277, and Herod. ii. 125.
§ Herod. ii. 92, 93, 149; iii. 91.
‖ Wilkinson, vol. iii. pp. 53, 56; ii. p. 401.
¶ Ibid. vol. iv. pp. 101, 102.
** Ibid. vol. ii. p. 134. Compare *Cambridge Essays* for 1858, p. 249.
†† "The ornaments of gold found in Egypt," says Sir G. Wilkinson, "consist of rings, bracelets, armlets, necklaces, ear-rings, and numerous trinkets belonging to the toilet" (vol. iii. p. 225). And again, "Gold and silver vases, statues, and other objects of gold and silver, of silver inlaid with gold, and of bronze inlaid with the precious metals, were also common at the same time" (ibid). Compare pp. 370-377.
‡‡ Herod. ii. 172.
§§ On the employment of furnaces, see Wilkinson, vol. iii. p. 164; of ovens and kneading-troughs, vol. v. p. 385; of walking-sticks, vol. iii. pp. 386, 387; and of handmills, vol. ii. p. 118.

in Egypt; and water would never be stored, if it were not for the necessity of purifying in certain seasons the turbid fluid furnished by the Nile, in order to render it a palatable beverage. For this purpose it has always been, and is still, usual to keep the Nile water in jars, stone troughs, or tubs, until the sediment is deposited, and the fluid rendered fit for drinking.*

The practice of making boats out of the papyrus, recorded in Ex. ii. 3,† is also specially Egyptian, and was not in vogue elsewhere. It is distinctly mentioned by Herodotus, Plutarch, and many other ancient writers,‡ and is thought to be traceable on the monuments.§ The caulking of these boats with pitch and bitumen, a practice not mentioned anywhere but in Exodus, is highly probable in itself; and is so far in accordance with the remains, that both pitch and bitumen are found to have been used by the Egyptians.‖ Bitumen, which is not an Egyptian product, appears to have been imported from abroad, and was even sometimes taken as tribute from the Mesopotamian tribes,¶ with whom the ancient Egyptians had frequent contests.

In illustration of the extensive possession of horses by the early kings of Egypt, it will be sufficient to adduce a passage from Diodorus, who says that "the monarchs before Sesostris maintained, along the banks of the Nile between Memphis and Thebes, two hundred stables, in each of which were kept a hundred horses."** Herodotus also notices that, prior to the reign of Sesostris, horses and carriages were very abundant in Egypt, but that subsequently they became comparatively uncommon, since the intersection of the whole country by canals rendered it unsuitable for their employment.†† They were still, no doubt, bred and employed, and even exported (1 Kings x. 29), to a certain extent; but from about the time of the nineteenth dynasty, Egypt ceased to be a great horse-breeding country.

Further, it may be observed that the state of the arts among the Hebrews when they quitted Egypt, which has sometimes been objected to as unduly advanced, is in entire accordance with the condition of art in Egypt at the period. The Egyptian civilization of the eighteenth and nineteenth dynasties embraces all the various arts and manufactures necessary for the construction of the Tabernacle and its appurtenances,

---

* Wilkinson, vol. iv. p. 100; Pococke, *Travels*, vol. i. p. 312.

† The word rendered "bulrushes" in our revision (*gomeh*) is generally admitted to signify some kind of papyrus—probably not that from which paper was made, but a coarser kind.

‡ Herod. ii. 96; Plut. *De Isid. et Os.* § 18; Theophrast. *De Plantis*, iv. 9; Plin. *H. N.* xiii. 11, etc.

§ Wilkinson, v. ii. pp. 60, 185.

‖ Ibid. vol. iii. p. 186; Rosellini, vol. i. p. 249.

¶ Wilkinson, in Rawlinson's *Herodotus*, vol. i. p. 254.

** Diod. Sic. i. †† Herod. ii. 108.

for the elaborate dress of the priests, and for the entire ceremonial described in the later books of the Pentateuch. The employment of writing, the arts of cutting and setting gems, the power of working in metals —and especially in gold, in silver, and in bronze—skill in carving wood, the tanning and dyeing of leather, the manufacture of fine linen, the knowledge of embroidery, the dyeing of textile fabrics, the employment of gold thread, the preparation and use of highly-scented unguents, are parts of the early civilization of Egypt, and were probably at their highest perfection about the time that the Exodus took place.* Although the Hebrews, while in Egypt, were, for the most part, mere laborers and peasants, still it was natural that some of them, and, even more, that some of the Egyptians who accompanied them (Ex. xiii. 38), should have been acquainted with the various branches of trade and manufacture established in Egypt at the time. Hence there is nothing improbable in the description given in the Pentateuch of the Ark and its surroundings, since the Egyptian art of the time was quite equal to their production.

The sojourn of the Israelites in the wilderness for forty years removed them so entirely during that space, from contact with any historic people, that we cannot expect to find, in the profane records that have come down to us, anything to confirm or illustrate the sacred narrative. That narrative must rest, first, on the profound conviction of its truthfulness which remained forever impressed upon the consciousness of the people; secondly, on its geographic accuracy, and on the perfect accordance with fact of what may be called its local coloring;† and thirdly, on the *quasi*-certainty that it is the production of an eye-witness. It may be added, that the circumstances recorded are too little creditable to the Hebrew people for any national historiographer to have invented them.

Recent criticism has attacked chiefly the numbers in the narrative.‡ There is certainly a difficulty in understanding how a population exceeding two millions could have supported itself, together with its flocks and herds, in a tract which, at the present day, barely suffices to sustain some tribes of Bedouins, numbering perhaps six thousand souls.§ Had the narrative made no mention of miraculous maintenance, this difficulty would have been almost insurmountable. As, however, the writer expressly declares that a miraculous supply of food was furnished daily during the whole period of the sojourn to the entire people, the main objection disappears. We have only to suppose that, although the tract, compared with Egypt, and even with Palestine, was a desert, yet that it was considerably better supplied with water, and so with pasturage, than it is at the present day. There are many indications that this was the

---

* See Hengstenberg, *Œgypten und Mose*, ch. v. pp. 133-143, E. F.
† See Stanley, *Sinai and Palestine*, Part i. pp. 1-57.
‡ Colenso, *The Pentateuch and the Book of Joshua Critically Examined*, pp. 31-138.
§ Stanley, p. 22.

case.* The Israelites apparently needed a miraculous supply of water twice only. If so, wells must have been numerous and abundant, water being to be found in most places at a little distance from the surface. But wherever in the desert this is the case, there will occur oases, and a sufficient vegetation for flocks and herds of a considerable size. The Israelites, no doubt, spread themselves widely over the peninsula during the forty years; and as the area of the desert is at least 1500 square miles, the numerous flocks and herds wherewith they entered the country may have maintained themselves, though, it is to be remarked, we are not told whether their numbers diminished or no.

In any case, a difficulty which is merely numerical is of no great account. Numbers, which, in early times, so far as we have any evidence on the subject,† were always expressed, in some abbreviated form, by conventional signs, are far more liable to corruption than any other parts of ancient manuscripts. The great fact recorded, which stands out as historically true, and which no petty criticism can shake, is the exit from Egypt of a considerable tribe, the progenitors of the later Hebrew nation, and their settlement in Palestine, after a sojourn of some duration in the wilderness. Of this fact the Hebrews and Egyptians were equally well convinced; and as both nations enjoyed a contemporary literature, and had thus the evidence on the point of witnesses living at the time, only an irrational scepticism can entertain a doubt respecting it.

APPENDIX B.

THE RESULTS OF THE SINAI EXPEDITION.

[From the Sinai Survey, "*Desert of the Exodus.*"]

By E. H. PALMER, M. A.

Bearings upon the History of the Exodus.—Authority for Identifying the Country Surveyed with the Sinai of the Bible.—Route of the Israelites from Egypt and Sinai.—Résumé of Arguments.—Conclusion.

VIEWED merely as a contribution to geographical science, the accurate investigation of a country so little known as Sinai is undoubtedly a valuable work. But the chief interest of the Peninsula must always lie

---

* Stanley, pp. 23-27; Highton, in *Biblical Dictionary*, vol. iii. pp. 1752-1754. The testimony of the recent explorers, Mr. Holland and Mr. Tristram, is to the same effect.

† On the numerical signs used in Ancient Egypt, see Wilkinson in Rawlinson's *Herodotus*, vol. ii. p. 51, and compare *Ancient Egyptians*, vol. iv. pp. 130, 131. On the signs used by the early Babylonians, see Rawlinson's *Ancient Monarchies*, vol. i. pp. 129-131.

in its connection with the Bible Narrative; and it is only in so far as they elucidate or illustrate Holy Scripture that we can judge of, or appreciate, the results obtained by the Sinai Expedition. I have endeavored, by portraying the country as it is, to enable the reader to form his own opinions upon this subject, but it may not be inappropriate here to mention briefly the conclusions at which we have ourselves arrived, and to point out how the various facts which we have brought to light bear upon the history of the Exodus.

The matter resolves itself into this: A circumstantial account is given in the Bible of an event so important that upon our acceptance or rejection of it as an historical fact depends the whole question of our religious belief,—of the truth or falsehood of the Old Testament. Such a position could not long remain unassailed, and we are accordingly met with numberless objections, which nothing but actual knowledge of the country can enable us to discuss, much less to answer.

I shall deal with the question as purely one of evidence, taking the plain unvarnished statements of the history, and comparing them one by one with the present topographical facts.

It may well be asked, what authority have we for assuming that the Peninsula now known by the name of Sinai is that in which the Mountain of the Law is situated; or that the Passage of the Red Sea took place at the head of the Gulf of Suez, rather than at the Gulf of Akabah?

The itinerary in Numbers xxxiii. supplies us with a conclusive answer. The Children of Israel reached the seacoast in three days after leaving Rameses, and no possible theory of the position of that town could bring it within three days' journey of the Gulf of Akabah. The Gulf of Suez is, however, distant exactly three days' journey from the site of Memphis, in which neighborhood at least the ancient capital of Egypt must have stood, and it is therefore certain that the Gulf of Suez is the Red Sea referred to in the history. The same authority tells us that the Children of Israel did not take the northern road to Palestine by way of Gaza, so that there is absolutely no other course which they could have taken, after crossing to the Asiatic coast, than the road which lies between the steep wall-like escarpment of Jebel er Ráhah and the Red Sea.

This would conduct them towards the mountainous district in the centre of the Peninsula, and it is consequently evident that we are so far right in looking for Mount Sinai in that region. Having satisfied ourselves that we are upon the track of the Israelites, we have next to determine the route which they must have taken. In many countries it would be impossible to pitch upon one road to the exclusion of all the rest, but, thanks to the peculiar nature of the country under consideration, we are enabled, by an exhaustive process, if not to prove, at least to arrive at a more than plausible conjecture upon, this point.

APPENDIX.

The Israelites were travelling in heavy marching order, taking with them their wives, children, household effects, and indeed all their worldly possessions. We learn that they even had wagons with them during their journey, for we are told, in Numbers vii. 3, that "the Princes of Israel brought their offering before the Lord, six covered wagons and twelve oxen."

Under these circumstances, difficult or intricate passes and defiles are out of the question, and our attention is confined to those roads which are passable for a large caravan with heavily laden beasts of burden.

It may be objected that, as the Israelite host was miraculously guided "by the Pillar of Cloud by day, and the Pillar of Fire by night," we need not, or ought not, to argue from the probabilities suggested by the physical features of the country. To this I would answer that we are expressly told that "God went before them by day in a pillar of cloud *to lead them the way,*" not to make for them a road, but to guide them in the best and easiest path, and we are therefore the more bound to take into consideration everything which could give one road preference over another.

The difficulty of providing water for the cattle by which they were accompanied has proved a great stumbling-block to many, but this Mr. Holland has considerably lessened by a novel and ingenious suggestion. He believes that, instead of being an encumbrance to the movements of the host, they were used as beasts of burden, and that, in addition to the camp-furniture, each carried its own supply of water, sufficient for several days, in water-skins slung at its sides, precisely as Sir Samuel Baker found them doing at the present day in Abyssinia.*

The spot bearing the name of Ayún Músa, Moses' Wells, is no doubt traditionally connected with the Exodus, and was very probably the first camping-place of the Israelites after crossing the Red Sea. From this point the road is unmistakable for the first three days, since it lies over a flat strip of desert, across which they would naturally choose the straightest and most direct path. The Bible dismisses this part of their journey in a few words; "they went out into the wilderness of Shur; and they went three days in the wilderness, and found no water." (Exodus xv. 22); but I doubt if a more suggestive description could possibly be given of this monotonous waterless waste, the only impressive feature of which is the long *shur*, or "wall," which forms its northern limit.

The next verse proceeds, "and when they came to Marah, they could not drink of the waters of Marah, for they were bitter." Now the soil throughout this part of the country, being strongly impregnated with *natrûn*, produces none but bitter or brackish water; and it is worth

---

* Paper read before the Church Congress, 1869.

observing, that the first of these springs with which we meet, Ain Hawwárah, is reached on the third day of our desert journey to Sinai.

They next "came to Elim, where were twelve wells of water, and threescore and ten palm-trees." Here again, our own experience accords with that of the Israelites, for our next station is in Wády Gharandel, which contains a considerable amount of vegetation, palm-trees in great numbers among the rest, and a perennial stream. It would be of course idle to contend that this is the identical oasis mentioned in Exodus, but I would remind the reader that a supply of water larger than usual, and a consequently larger proportion of vegetation, depends upon the geological configuration of the country, and that, although individual springs may disappear, and break forth again at other places in the vicinity, a few thousand years are not likely to make any very radical change in this respect. Whole districts may be, and often are, rendered barren and dry by the diminution of the rainfall, consequent upon neglect and the destruction of vegetation; but, where a spot like Gharandel still exists, in spite of the deteriorating influences which have been at work in Sinai, we may fairly assume that its fertility dates from a very remote period of antiquity.

"And they removed from Elim, and encamped by the Red Sea," (Num. xxxiii. 10). To reach the sea, two roads were open to them,—either to follow Wády Gharandel itself to its mouth, or to turn down the next practicable valley, Wády Taiyebeh. The first is extremely unlikely, as the cliffs and rough rocks which come down to the water's edge past this point would have impeded their further progress, and compelled them to retrace their steps; whereas from Wády Taiyebeh the coast is open and passable, and moreover the mouth of the valley affords a fine clear space for their encampment by the sea. There are two roads to Sinai, the upper one by Sarábít el Khádim, and the lower one by the coast; and the modern traveller who chooses the latter still turns off by Wády Taiyebeh, and reaches the sea-shore in a fair day's journey from Gharandel. There are several reasons which would have led to the selection of this route by the Israelite hosts; the rugged passes and narrow valleys on the upper road would have presented insuperable difficulties to a large caravan encumbered by heavy baggage and they would have passed through a district actually held by a large military force of the very enemies from whom they were fleeing. The Bible, however, speaks of no collision between the Egyptians and Israelites, during the whole of their wanderings, after the passage of the Red Sea. Between Wády Gharandel and Wády Taiyebeh, two valleys, Wády Useit and Wády Ethál, descend to the sea; but the first of these is precluded as a route to Sinai, for the same reason that leads us to reject Wády Gharandel, viz. that the cliffs of Jebel Hammám Far'ún, a short way south of its mouth, cut off progress along shore; and the second becomes impassable, even for pedestrians, towards its mouth: so that we are forced to the conclusion that Wády Taiyebeh was the only road down which the Children of Israel could have marched.

On the supposition that they did so, the wilderness of Sin will be the narrow strip of desert which fringes the coast south of Wády Taiyebeh; and although it is impossible to define with exactness the next two stations, Dophkah and Alush, we may fairly presume that they lay within the next two days' journey, which would bring the Israelites well into Wády Feirán. Travellers by this route in the present day do not follow Wády Feirán, but turn off by Wády Shellál, and make for Wády Mukatteb by the Nagb Buderah, but the road over that pass was unquestionably constructed at a date posterior to the Exodus, and, had it even existed at that time, would have been less practicable than Wády Feirán, and would not only have led the Israelites into collision with the Egyptians at Maghárah, but have presented a further difficulty in the pass of Jebel Mukatteb. Beyond Wády Feirán there is no practicable valley: Wády Hebrán, the most open of them all, being far too difficult and rugged to have admitted of their passing through it. I have already discussed the reasons, both legendary and geographical, for placing Rephidim at Hesy el Khattátín in Wády Feirán, and if we read the verse, Exodus xix. 12, "and they departed from Rephidim, and pitched in the wilderness of Sinai," as implying a break in the march between Rephidim and the Mount of the Law (as was suggested on page 161), we shall find that the natural route from Egypt to Sinai accords exactly with the simple and concise account given in the Bible of the Exodus of the Chosen People.

In these conclusions all the members of the Expedition are agreed. Mr. Holland, it is true, dissents upon one point, the position of Rephidim, which he would place at El Watíyeh, believing that the whole host of the Israelites turned off from Wády Feirán up Wády es Sheikh, and that the battle with the Amalekites took place long after Feirán had been passed. In the main facts of the route, however, and in the identification of Jebel Músa with Mount Sinai, our investigations have led us to form one unanimous opinion.

We are thus able not only to trace out a route by which the Children of Israel could have journeyed, but also to show its identity with that so concisely but graphically laid down in the Pentateuch. We have seen, moreover, that it leads to a mountain answering in every respect to the description of the Mountain of the Law; the chain of topographical evidence is complete, and the maps and sections may henceforth be confidently left to tell their own tale.

The arguments against objections founded on the supposed incapability of the Peninsula to have supported so large a host, I need not recapitulate here; in the evidence adduced of the greater fertility which once existed in Sinai, and in the actual measurements of its areas, the reader has all the data for himself to decide upon these points.

We cannot perhaps assign much importance to Arab traditions relating to the Exodus as an argument for or against the truth of the story, but it is at least interesting to know that such traditions are found, and it is satisfactory to have them in a collected and accessible form. Such legends, as we might expect, are chiefly attached to particular localities; they do not follow the Children of Israel by any single or consistent route through the Peninsula, but any spot possessing peculiar features, wherever it may be situated, is connected by the simple Arab with the grand, mysterious figure of the Hebrew prophet, whose memory still lingers in the wild traditions of Sinai.

Such spots are, (1) Moses' wells at 'Ayún Músa near Suez, and 'Ain Músa on Jebel Músa. (2) Moses' seats: at Abu Zenímeh, on the seashore near Hammám Far'ún, is shown the place where Moses watched the drowning of the Egyptians, and in the pass of El Watiyeh the chair-shaped rock, now called Magád en Nebí, is supposed to have received its peculiar shape from the impress of the prophet's form. Similar rocks are found in the valley (Wády ed Deir) in which the convent of St. Katharine is situated, and upon the summit of Jebel Músa itself. (3) Rocks struck by Moses; that in Wády Berráh supposed to have been cleft in twain by Moses' sword; the Hajjar el Magarin in the path along Wády Lejá, and Hesy el Khattátín in Wády Feirán. The Hajjar Músa in the vicinity of the convent, which is pointed out to pilgrims as the true rock in Horeb, is a palpable fiction of the monks, and is virtually disregarded by the Arabs. (4) Moses' Baths; as the Hammám Syedná Músa at Tor. The Bedawí version of the passage of the Red Sea, and the legend of the building of stone huts (*nawámis*) by the Children of Israel to keep off the plague of mosquitoes, I have already given. Enough has been said to prove that the inhabitants of the country are themselves thoroughly imbued with the idea that their own desolate and rocky land was once the scene of a great and wonderful manifestation of God to man.

The Mohammedan tradition, as elsewhere current also, evidently points to Jebel Músa as the true Mount Sinai. The description given by the commentators on the Corán of the "Holy wády of Towa," where Moses halted amidst the snow and mist, could scarcely apply to any other spot, while the distance, according to the same authority, of Midian from Egypt, exactly tallies with the position of Feirán. Whether, therefore, we look at the results obtained in physical geography alone, or take into consideration the mass of facts which the traditions and nomenclature disclose, we are bound to admit that the investigations of the Sinai Expedition do materially confirm and elucidate the history of the Exodus.

APPENDIX C.

THE ROCK SMITTEN IN HOREB.

Mr. Hurter, of the Syria Mission of the American Board, in the following letter, written to one of the professors at Andover, expresses much confidence that he has discovered the "identical rock from whence flowed the stream which quenched the thirst of the thousands of Israel;" and says, "future travellers will probably confirm this opinion:"—

"BEIRUT, Syria, *May* 23, 1863.

"Having recently returned from a visit to Mount Sinai, I thought you would be interested in the discovery of a spring of water under the east side of Mount Horeb, which I cannot learn has been noticed by any traveller who has written on Sinai, but which is so striking, that had it been seen, it would certainly have been mentioned. Travellers generally go to the Convent, and lodge there during their sojourn at Sinai; and those who prefer to remain outside the Convent, pitch their tents on the usual camping ground at the entrance of Wady Shu'eib, near the east side of the Wady, and under or close by a little hill, where we also encamped. Travellers almost always take a dragoman with them, and never attend to the supply of water for the prosecution of their journey. Not having a dragoman with us, we had to attend to the filling of the barrels ourselves. In coming towards Mount Horeb, we took the road followed by Dr. Robinson, by Wady er Rahah. On page 89 of the first volume of his Researches, he says: "On the left of Horeb, a deep and narrow valley runs up south-southeast, between lofty walls of rock, as if in continuation of the southeast corner of the Plain. In this valley, at a distance of nearly a mile from the Plain, stands the Convent." On the east side of this valley, and at its entrance, is a small hill, separated from the mountain by a road about one hundred feet across, which travellers follow in going to the Convent from Wady es Sheikh, while those who go to the Convent by Wady er Rahah pass on the west side of the hill. On the south side of this hill is the camping ground, and in getting to it we made a short circuit of five minutes' ride to avoid a precipitous bank.

"On arriving at our camping ground, we requested our cameleers, before dispersing to their homes, to fill our barrels with water. They said they would take two of them to a spring where there was a reservoir, into which they would place them. They pointed out to us the direction, on the west side of the valley, under Horeb, and we perceived a few trees at that place. Towards evening I told my party that I would go and see whether they had filled and sunk the barrels in the pool. The direction of the spring was straight across the valley from the camping-ground. After leaving the tents, in about two minutes I ascended the ground where we made the circuit, then passed down a slight declivity, after which the ground gradually rose until I reached the spring, in about ten minutes, by a rugged path over large boulders of Sinaite granite. Here I was surprised to find a spring of pure water issuing from a rent in the rock. The rent was in an oblique direction, the highest part of it on the left, and sloping down towards the right. The lowest part of the fissure was as high as a man's head from the ground. The surrounding rock is the solid red granite of Sinai, smooth on its face, and unbroken by fissure or seam. The fissure is about six feet long, four inches wide, five inches deep at the bottom, and twelve at the top, and runs down into the rock parallel with the perpendicular side of the mountain. The water seems to issue about two feet above the bottom of the rent, flowing over the lowest part of it in a stream about the thickness of a man's finger. The reservoir is about twelve feet long by five feet in width, and four feet deep, and was nearly full when I reached the place. When full, the water is let off to irrigate some twenty or more fruit trees. As I was the first (as far as I am aware) to observe this singular "rent" in the "Rock of Horeb," and am unable to find any allusion to it in the books of Burckhardt, Robinson, Stanley, or other travellers, I have thought it my duty to inform the public of the fact, in order that future travellers may not fail to see it. Could we suppose that Moses had a rod about six feet long, and that, raising the lower end of it as high as his head, he struck it obliquely against the granite cliff, and that a wedge-shaped cavity was thus miraculously formed, this rent would meet the conditions exactly.

"I would simply state that I made the above discovery on the 26th of February."

THE END.

BY EMILY SARAH HOLT.

The Well in the Desert,	1 25
An old Legend of the House of Arundel.	
Robin Tremayne. 12mo,	1 50
A Tale of the Marian Persecution.	
Isoult Barry of Wynscote,	1 50
A Tale of Tudor Times.	

BY THE AUTHOR OF "THE WIDE, WIDE WORLD."

A Story of Small Beginnings,	5 00

COMPRISING

What She Could, House in Town,
Opportunities, Trading.

Four volumes in a box.

Life of Christ. By Rev. WILLIAM HANNA, D.D. 3 vols. 12mo,	4 50
Kitto's Bible Illustrations. New edition. The 8 volumes in 4,	7 00
Ryle's Notes on Matthew,	1 50
Ryle's Notes on Mark,	1 50
Ryle's Notes on Luke. 2 vols.,	3 00
Ryle's Notes on John. Vols. 1 and 2, each,	1 50
*****Henry's Commentary on Bible.** Quarto. 5 vols.,	25 00
*****Pool's Annotations on the Bible.** 3 vols.,	15 00
The Word Series. By the Misses WARNER.	
Walks from Eden. (First half of Genesis)	1 50
House of Israel. (Second half of Genesis)	1 50
Star Out of Jacob. (On the Gospels)	1 50
*****Horne's Introduction to Study of Bible,**	5 00
Drummond on the Parables,	1 75
Blunt's Coincidences in the Old and New Testaments,	1 50
The Book and its Story,	1 50
Fresh Leaves from the Book, and its Story,	2 00
The Footsteps of St. Paul. By Dr. MACDUFF,	1 50
Dr. Newton's Jewel Case. 6 vols.,	7 50
Bonar's Bible Thoughts and Themes. 5 vols., uniform:	
Old Testament,	2 00
Gospels,	2 00
Acts,	2 00
Lesser Epistles,	2 00
Revelation,	2 00

Tales of Christian Life. By the author of the "Schönberg-Cotta Family." 5 vols. In a Box, - - - - - - - - - - 5 00

      Cripple of Antioch,   Two Vocations,
      Martyrs of Spain,   Tales and Sketches,
      Wanderings over Bible Lands.

The Wars of the Huguenots. By the Rev. Dr. HANNA. 16mo, - - 1 25

Dr. Chalmers' Sermons. *Cheap Edition.* 2 volumes in 1. 1105 double column pages. Price reduced to - - - - - - - - - 3 00

Charnock on the Attributes. *New and Cheap Edition.* 2 volumes in 1; containing 1149 large 8vo. pages. Price reduced to - - - - 3 00

McCheyne's Works. *Cheap and Neat Edition.* Comprising his Life, Letters, Lectures, and Sermons. 2 volumes in 1. 1074 pages. 8vo. Price reduced to - - - - - - - - - - - - - - - 3 00

D'Aubigne's History of the Reformation. 5 vols., - - - 6 00

D'Aubigne's History of the Reformation in the time of Calvin. 5 vols., - - - - - - - - - - - - 10 00

D'Aubigne's Life of Cromwell, - - - - - - - - 1 25

*****Jonathan Edwards' Works.** 4 vols. 8vo, - - - - - 12 00

Hill's Divinity. 8vo, - - - - - - - - - - - 3 50

Hodge on Ephesians, - - - - - - - - - - - 1 75

Hodge on Corinthians, 2 vols. - - - - - - - - 3 50

McCosh on the Divine Government, - - - - - 2 50

McCosh on Typical Forms, - - - - - - - - 2 50

McCosh on Intuitions of the Mind, - - - - 3 00

McCosh on the Defence of Truth, - - - - - - 3 00

McCosh on Logic, - - - - - - - - - - - 1 50

McCosh on Positivism and Christianity, - - - - 1 75

Guthrie's Works.   (For particulars, see our Catalogue,) - - -

Hamilton's Works,   " " " " - - -

Macduff's Works,   " " " " - - -

*****Murdoch's Mosheim's Ecclesiastical History.** 3 vols, - - 5 00

Reid's Voices of the Soul Answered in God, - - - 1 75

Young's Christ of History, - - - - - - - - 1 25

www.ingramcontent.com/pod-product-compliance
Lightning Source LLC
Chambersburg PA
CBHW020244170426
43202CB00008B/217